COLLECTION LATOMUS
VOL. 337

STUDIES IN THE *HISTORIA AVGVSTA*

LATOMUS
REVUE D'ÉTUDES LATINES
Rue du Palais St-Jacques 6, B-7500 Tournai
Adresse électronique/ info@latomus.be

La revue **Latomus**, fondée en 1937 par M.-A. Kugener, L. Herrmann et M. Renard est dirigée actuellement par M. David ENGELS, Directeur général et rédacteur en chef, et Mme Jacqueline DUMORTIER-BIBAUW, Directeur administratif (Directeur général honoraire : M. Carl DEROUX). Elle publie des articles, des notes de lecture, des comptes rendus, des notices bibliographiques, des informations pédagogiques ayant trait à tous les domaines de la latinité : textes, littérature, histoire, institutions, archéologie, épigraphie, paléographie, humanisme latin, etc.

Les quelque **1200 pages** qu'elle comporte annuellement contiennent une riche documentation, souvent **inédite** et abondamment **illustrée**.

Montant de l'abonnement au tome 71, 2012 :

Prix pour la Belgique :	85 €, port et TVA en sus.
Prix pour l'étranger :	102 €, port et TVA en sus.

Prix des tomes publiés avant l'année en cours :

pour la Belgique :	102 €, port et TVA en sus,
pour l'étranger :	117 €, port et TVA en sus.

Les quatre fascicules d'un tome ne sont pas vendus séparément.

C.C.P. **000-0752646-23** de la **Société d'Études Latines de Bruxelles.**

Une réduction de 20% est accordée aux professeurs de l'enseignement secondaire et de l'enseignement supérieur, aux chercheurs qui font partie d'organismes comme le F.N.R.S., aux étudiants.

Pour l'achat des tomes I à XXI, s'adresser à la Schmidt Periodicals GmbH, Dettendorf, D-83075 Bad Feilnbach 2 (Allemagne).
schmidt@periodicals.com www.periodicals.com

Correspondants :

IMPRIMERIE UNIVERSA, B-9230 WETTEREN (BELGIQUE)

COLLECTION LATOMUS
Fondée par M. Renard en 1939
Continuée par C. Deroux et J. Dumortier-Bibauw
VOLUME 337

Mark THOMSON

Studies in the *Historia Augusta*

ÉDITIONS LATOMUS
BRUXELLES
2012

To Ann Moffatt

ISBN 9782-87031-2780
D/2012/0415/4

INTRODUCTION

Structure, Sources and Theories

The *Historia Augusta* (hereafter the *HA*) is one of the most difficult and intriguing works to survive from the ancient world [1]. In the form in which it has come down to us, the *HA* is a corpus of thirty books concerning the lives of emperors and usurpers from the birth of Hadrian to the death of Carinus (76-285), but apparently ignoring the period from the accession of Philip to the capture of Valerian (244-260) [2]. Some of these thirty books deal with individual

(1) Modern editions are based upon the Codex Palatinus latinus 899 (P), supplemented in places by some Carolingian excerpts and a class of humanistic manuscripts (Σ) : Pecere 1995 ; Marshall 1983 ; Ballou 1914 ; Idem 1908 ; Dessau 1894 ; Mommsen 1890. The full title of the collection appears in P (in the *index uitarum* and also in the final colophon) : *Vitae Diuersorum Principum et Tyrannorum a Diuo Hadriano usque ad Numerianum*. The phraseology of the preface to the *Opilius Macrinus* seems to echo this title (OM 1, 1) : *Vitae ... principum siue tyrannorum siue Caesarum*. The short title *de Vita Principum* also appears in the text : A 1, 2 ; Pr. 2, 7. The revised Teubner edition is cited throughout this study : Hohl et al. 1971 [first ed. 1927]. This remains the only critical edition of the entire corpus based upon an accurate understanding of the manuscript stemma. Editions and translations of many lives have appeared in the Budé series : Callu et al. 1992 (*de Vita Hadriani*, *Aelius* and *Antoninus Pius*) ; Turcan 1993 (*Opilius Macrinus*, *Diadumenus Antoninus* and *Antoninus Heliogabalus*) ; Desbordes and Ratti 2000 (*Valeriani Duo* and *Gallieni Duo*) ; Paschoud 1996 (*Diuus Aurelianus* and *Tacitus*) ; Idem 2001 (*Probus, Quadrigae Tyrannnorum* and *Carus et Carinus et Numerianus*). The Budé editors report the readings of many newly collated manuscripts, and offer ample exegetical material. Chastagnol produced a version of the text with a French translation and copious historical notes : Chastagnol 1994. Although invaluable to the historian, this work lacks a critical apparatus, while Chastagnol himself acknowledged the limitations of his Latin text. The Loeb translation, based upon a somewhat eccentric Latin version, is at times inaccurate : Magie 2006 [first ed. 1921-1932]. Also noteworthy is a seventeenth-century variorum edition, which reproduces the comments of Casaubon (1559-1614) and Salmasius (1588-1653) : Casaubon et al. 1671. There is a concordance, which sometimes reports defective readings : Lessing 1964 [first ed. 1901-1906].

(2) All dates are AD, unless otherwise noted. A lacuna consumes the reigns of several emperors : Philip the Arab (244-249), Decius (249-251), Hostilian (251), Trebonianus Gallus (251-253), Volusianus (251-253) and Aemilianus (253). The preface to the *Diuus Aurelianus* claims that Pollio wrote lives from the two Philips up to the divine Claudius : A 2, 1. The *Valeriani Duo* mentions a letter sent by Sapor, king of the Persians, which does not appear in the received text : Val. 4, 1. Nevertheless, many critics have argued that the lacuna covering the period from the death of Gordian III until the capture of Valerian is a fraudulent device : A. Birley 1976 ; Idem 1967 : 115-116 ; 125-126. Others have accepted this claim : Desbordes and Ratti 2000 : 68 ; 200 ; Callu 1992 : xlviii-xlix ; den

rulers, while others discuss several members of an imperial dynasty or those usurpers who assumed the purple during a particular era ([3]). These biographies are variously attributed to six authors, none of whom is attested elsewhere in the historical record : Aelius Spartianus, Iulius Capitolinus, Vulcacius Gallicanus (v.c), Aelius Lampridius, Trebellius Pollio and Flavius Vopiscus Syracusius ([4]). These authors dedicate their works to Diocletian (284-305), Constantine (306-337) and private individuals under Constantius I (293-306) ([5]). The attributions

Hengst 1981 : 70-72. Birley drew attention to several passages in the lives that seem to allude to this arrangement in an oblique manner : A 42, 4 ; 6. It is astonishing that the *Gallieni Duo* also begins with the capture of Gallienus' father Valerian, omitting the customary inventions concerning childhood, youth, private career and omens. The author flaunts this arrangement (Gall. 1, 1) : *enimuero unde incipienda est Gallieni uita, nisi ab eo praecipue malo, quo eius uita depressa est ?*

(3) The lives of usurpers (Avidius Cassius, Pescennius Niger and Clodius Albinus) and minor rulers (Aelius, Geta and Diadumenus) appear independently until the middle of the collection. Lives of several emperors, generally members of family groups, appear together in the *Maximini Duo* (Maximinus Thrax and his son), *Gordiani Tres* (Gordian I, Gordian II and Gordian III), *Maximus et Balbinus* (the co-rulers Maximus and Balbinus), *Valeriani Duo* (Valerian and his son), *Gallieni Duo* (Gallienus and his son Saloninus), *Diuus Claudius* (Claudius II and a brief entry on Quintillus), *Tacitus* (Tacitus and Florianus) and *Carus et Carinus et Numerianus* (Carus, Carinus and Numerian). Further lives of usurpers are gathered in two compendia : the *Tyranni Triginta* and the *Quadrigae Tyrannorum* (Firmus, Saturninus, Proculus and Bonosus). The *Tyranni Triginta* contains brief entries on thirty-two persons described as usurpers : Cyriades, Postumus, Postumus Iunior, Lollianus, Victorinus, Victorinus Iunior, Marius, Ingenuus, Regilianus (Regalianus), Aureolus, Macrianus, Macrianus Iunior, Quietus, Odenathus, Herodes, Maeonius, Ballista, Valens, Valens Superior, Piso (!), Aemilianus, Saturninus (!), Tetricus Senior, Tetricus Iunior, Trebellianus (!), Herennianus, Timolaus, Celsus (!), Zenobia, Victoria, Titus and Censorinus (!). Of these, Celsus and Censorinus are wholly spurious ; Trebellianus, also an invention, may take his name from a passage in Eutropius (Eutr. *Breu.* IX, 8, 1). Piso (Gall. 2, 2-4) and Saturninus (Gall. 9, 1 ; Q 11, 1) appear in the *Gallieni Duo*, but are not elsewhere attested. Although dubious, these two cannot be dismissed outright. "Domitianus" (Gall. 2, 6 ; T 12, 14) may be an obscure usurper of the reign of Aurelian (Zos. I, 49, 2), who has left two small coins (one on display in the Ashmolean).

(4) The attributions appear as follows. Aelius Spartianus : *de Vita Hadriani*, *Aelius*, *Didius Iulianus*, *Seuerus*, *Pescennius Niger*, *Antoninus Caracallus* and *Antoninus Geta*. Iulius Capitolinus : *Antoninus Pius*, *Vita Marci Antonini Philosophi*, *Verus*, *Pertinax*, *Vita Clodii Albini*, *Opilius Macrinus*, *Maximini Duo*, *Gordiani Tres* and *Maximus et Balbinus*. Vulcacius Gallicanus (v.c.) : *Auidius Cassius*. Aelius Lampridius : *Commodus Antoninus*, *Diadumenus Antoninus*, *Antoninus Heliogabalus* and *Alexander Seuerus*. Trebellius Pollio : *Valeriani Duo*, *Gallieni Duo*, *Tyranni Triginta* and *Diuus Claudius*. Flavius Vopiscus Syracusius : *Diuus Aurelianus*, *Tacitus*, *Probus*, *Quadrigae Tyrannorum* and *Carus et Carinus et Numerianus*.

(5) The dedications appear in various places. Diocletian : Ael. 1, 1 ; 2, 2 (Galerius and Constantius are Caesars) ; MA 19, 12 ; V 11, 4 ; AC 3, 3 ; S 20, 4 ; PN 9, 1 ; OM 15, 4. Constantine : Cl. A 4, 2 ; G 1, 1 ; Hel. 34, 1 ; AS 65, 1 ; Max. 1, 1 ; Gd. 1, 1 ; 34, 6. The

and dedications found throughout the corpus, woven together in a complex and apparently arbitrary manner, have confused and perplexed many generations of historians.

It was Dessau who first exposed the basic spuriousness of the *HA*, in two articles that are rightly considered classic examples of nineteenth-century German scholarship (6). Modern authorities generally agree that the *HA* was the work of one author, an anonymous scholar writing between about 395 and about 400 (7). This learned impostor was wholly responsible for some distinctive features of the corpus : its attributions and dedications, its prefaces, epilogues and rhetorical digressions, as well as its spurious documentation (which includes letters, speeches, harangues, acclamations, omens, verses and citations from dubious authorities, not to mention references to inscriptions, artefacts and buildings). This devious author also fabricated plausible information on the backgrounds, private careers and reigns of emperors and usurpers who were otherwise obscure. He has set innumerable traps for unwary readers, ensnaring countless students of Roman history.

Although prepared to invent, our impostor drew upon authentic sources wherever they were available, sometimes employing works that are no longer extant. He slavishly incorporated materials derived from previous writers, following the normal practice of his day (8). Because the *HA* preserves both genuine and spu-

author refers to Constantius I as Caesar : Gall. 7, 1 ; 14, 3 ; Cl. 1, 1 ; 3, 1 ; 9, 9 ; 10, 7 ; 13, 2. Constantius later appears as emperor (*imperator*) : A 44, 5. The private individuals apostrophised by Pollio remain anonymous : Val. 7, 1 ; 8, 5 ; T 11, 7 ; 22, 12 (a descendant or descendants of Herennius Celsus) ; 31, 8-10 (an amateur scholar, asked to emend his manuscript) ; 33, 7-8 ; Cl. 3, 1 ; 5, 5 (a patron of games). These apostrophes move from second person plural forms (Val. 7, 1 ; 8, 5 ; T 11, 7 ; 22, 12) to a combination of second person singular forms and third person honorific formulae (T 31, 8-10 ; 33, 7-8 ; Cl. 3, 1 ; 5, 5). Vopiscus dedicates his works to the urban prefect Iunius Tiberianus (A 1, 1), a person possibly called Pinianus (A 1, 9 ; 43, 1 ; 43, 5), a Celsinus (Pr. 1, 3) and a Bassus (Q 2, 1 and perhaps also Car. 21, 2-3). Hohl printed "Pinianus" at A 1, 9 ; other conjectures include "Pianus," "Ulpianus" and "Tiberianus."

(6) Dessau 1892 ; Idem 1889.

(7) Much of the scholarship is collected in two series of conference proceedings. The *Bonner Historia-Augusta-Colloquia* (*BHAC*) were held from 1963 until 1989. The *Historiae Augustae Colloquia* (*HAC*) began in 1991 and have continued until the present. The first conference held on the subject appears separately : Sartori 1963. There are many excellent surveys of the scholarship : A. Birley 2003 ; Idem 1967 ; Chastagnol 1994 : xiii-xxxiv ; Idem 1970a ; Idem 1964 : 43-71 ; Zecchini 1993 : 39-49. There is also a comprehensive bibliography : Merten 1985-1987. Syme's work on the subject remains fundamental : Syme 1978 ; Idem 1976 ; Idem 1971a ; Idem 1971b ; Idem 1968a ; Idem 1966. On earlier criticism, see also Béranger 1980.

(8) "In the main line of the *Vitae* (down to Caracalla), the author is a compiler, crude and hasty, seldom caring or requiring to invent." Syme 1968a : 26. Here one thinks of the anonymous redactors of the *Origo Gentis Romanae* and the *Epitome de Caesaribus*, the epitomators Aurelius Victor and Eutropius, Donatus in his role as the redactor of the

rious material, it poses especially difficult historical problems. For the period from Hadrian (born 76, reigned 117-138) to Elagabalus (reigned 218-222) our impostor relied upon a series of imperial biographies, generally associated with the name of Marius Maximus (urban prefect 217-218, consul for the second time in 223) ([9]). This lost work most likely incorporated lives of Nerva, Trajan, Hadrian, Antoninus Pius, Marcus Aurelius, Verus, Commodus, Pertinax, Didius Iulianus, Severus, Caracalla and Elagabalus (although probably not Macrinus, perhaps considered a usurper) ([10]). Marius Maximus seems to have influenced the hypothetical common source of the epitomators Aurelius Victor and Eutropius (a work known as the "Kaisergeschichte"), as well as the anonymous redactor of the *Epitome de Caesaribus*, the scholiast on Juvenal and even the poet Ausonius. Ammianus bemoaned his influence ([11]). Cassius Dio may have drawn upon Marius Maximus for information about the emperors immediately before his own times ([12]). This admittedly tentative hypothesis may explain the numerous parallels between the *de Vita Hadriani* and the remnants of the equivalent section of Cassius Dio's history ([13]). These two versions, both crude para-

Suetonian life of Virgil (the so-called *Vita Donati*), not to mention Jerome and Servius and their frequently tralatitious commentaries on sacred and secular texts. Note also Macrobius' frank admission that he had reproduced the wording of his sources : Macr., *Sat.* praef. 4.

(9) Marius Maximus (*PIR* M 308 L. Marius Maximus Perpetuus Aurelianus) : A. Birley 1997 ; Peter 1967 [second ed. 1914 ; first ed. 1870-1906] : II, 121-129. The biographer is cited on numerous occasions in the relevant lives : H 2, 10 ; 12, 4 ; 20, 3 ; 25, 4 ; Ael. 3, 9 ; 5, 5 ; AP 11, 3 ; MA 1, 6 ; 25, 10 ; AC 6, 6-7 ; 9, 5 ; 9 ; C 13, 2 ; 15, 4 ; 18, 2 (a lengthy document follows) ; P 2, 8 ; 15, 8 ; S 15, 6 ; Cl. A 3, 4 ; 9, 2 ; 5 ; 12, 14 ; G 2, 1 ; Hel. 11, 6. His name appears in other contexts throughout the corpus : AS 5, 4 (a reference to his life of Severus) ; 21, 4 ; 30, 6 (a reference to his life of Hadrian) ; 48, 6 ; 65, 4 (references to his life of Trajan) ; Pr. 2, 7 ; Q 1, 1-2. Barnes and Syme (among others) have argued that there were in fact two biographical sources : an unknown biographer from Hadrian to Caracalla, as well as Marius Maximus from Hadrian to Elagabalus. See : Benario 1980 : 1-13 ; Syme 1972a ; Idem 1971a : 9-15 ; Idem 1971b : 113-145 ; Idem 1968a : 89-93 ; Idem 1968b ; Barnes 1978 ; Barbieri 1954. Many scholars reject this view : Molinier 1998 ; A. Birley 1995 ; Schlumberger 1976a ; Idem 1974 : 124-133 ; Cameron 1971.

(10) A citation of Marius Maximus in the scholia on Juvenal clearly relates to the reign of Nerva : *Schol. Iuu.* IV, 53(2). Our impostor twice referred to a lost life of Trajan : AS 48, 6 ; 65, 4. Marius Maximus apparently wrote two books on Marcus Aurelius, the second concerning his reign after the death of Verus : AC 9, 5.

(11) Amm. XXVIII, 4, 14.

(12) Millar denied the possibility in his celebrated study of Cassius Dio : Millar 1964 : 61. Nevertheless, two recent critics have hinted that Cassius Dio may have drawn on the biographies of Marius Maximus in his accounts of the reigns of Nerva, Trajan and Hadrian : Chausson 2005 : 120 ; Meckler 2005 : 230-231.

(13) The abridgement of the eleventh-century scholar Johannes Xiphilinus preserves aspects of the relevant portions of Cassius Dio.

phrases, agree in many apparently trivial details ([14]) ; their characterisations of Hadrian are closely similar ([15]) ; meanwhile the same individuals surface in each account ([16]) ; while both texts apparently drew upon similar sources, quite possibly at second hand ([17]).

Once the copious tradition of imperial biography was exhausted, our impostor turned to narrative histories written in Greek, which provided much less detailed information. The influence of Herodian (early 3rd cent.) has been detected chiefly in the *Vita Clodii Albini*, *Alexander Seuerus*, *Maximini Duo*, *Gordiani Tres* and *Maximus et Balbinus* ([18]). Dexippus (ca. 210-273) was a supplementary source in the period from Alexander Severus to Gordian III, and the main source on the reigns from Valerian to Claudius II ([19]). An unnamed Greek historian, sometimes identified as Eunapius (ca. 345-ca. 414), provided some information on military campaigns discussed in the *Diuus Aurelianus* and *Probus* ([20]). The

(14) Travelling throughout the world, Hadrian never covered his head, regardless of the weather : Cass. Dio LXIX, 9, 4 ; H 23, 1. Hadrian favoured the Hellenistic poet Antimachus over Homer (Cass. Dio LXIX, 4, 6) and wrote works imitating him (H 16, 2).

(15) Hadrian was interested in many arts and disciplines, contending with grammarians, architects, poets and philosophers : Cass. Dio LXIX, 3, 1-4, 6 ; H 14, 8-11 ; 15, 10-13. Hadrian fought no major wars : Cass. Dio LXIX, 25, 1 ; H 21, 8. He managed great military reforms : Cass. Dio LXIX, 5, 2 ; 9, 1-6 ; H 10, 2-11, 1. There was opposition to Hadrian's deification, due to his purges of the Senate : Cass. Dio LXIX, 2, 5 ; H 27, 1-2.

(16) Some minor figures include the sophist Favorinus (Cass. Dio LXIX, 3, 4 ; H 15, 12-13 ; 16, 10) and the architect Apollodorus (Cass. Dio LXIX, 4, 1-3 ; H 19, 13), as well as the freedman Heliodorus (Cass. Dio LXIX, 3, 5 ; H 15, 5 ; 16, 10). Four men of consular rank (Nigrinus, Palma, Celsus and Lucius) were executed at the beginning of Hadrian's reign (Cass. Dio LXIX, 2, 5 ; H 7, 2 ; 9, 3) ; towards the end the nonagenarian Servianus was compelled to take his own life and Fuscus too fell from favour (Cass. Dio LXIX, 2, 5 ; 17, 1 ; H 23, 2-3 ; 8). Antinous' death provoked speculation about infernal rites : Cass. Dio LXIX, 11, 2 ; H 14, 5. Hadrian's father was Aelius Hadrianus Afer (H 1, 2) or Hadrianus Afer (Cass. Dio LXIX, 3, 1), although Attianus acted as his guardian (Cass. Dio LXIX, 1, 2 ; H 1, 4 ; 4, 2 ; 9, 3). Hadrian gave Marcus Aurelius the nickname Verissimus : Cass. Dio LXIX, 21, 2 ; MA 1, 10. Our author claims that Annius Verus, grandfather of Marcus Aurelius, was prefect of the city and twice consul : MA 1, 1. Cassius Dio correctly states that he was consul three times : Cass. Dio LXIX, 21, 1.

(17) Cassius Dio apparently cited the autobiography of Hadrian (Cass. Dio LXIX, 11, 2 ; H 1, 1 ; 7, 2 ; 16, 1), as well as some of his personal letters (LXIX, 17, 3).

(18) Chastagnol 1994 : lxi-lxiii ; Barnes 1978 : 82-89 ; Mommsen 1890 : 260-270. There are numerous citations : Cl. A 1, 2 ; 12, 14 ; Dd. 2, 5 ; AS 52, 2 ; 57, 3 ; Max. 13, 4 ; 33, 3 ; Gd. 2, 1 ; MB 1, 2 ; 15, 3 ; 16, 6 ; T 32, 1 (out of chronological sequence).

(19) Chastagnol 1994 : lxiv-lxvi ; Barnes 1978 : 57-59 ; 109-111 ; *contra*, Paschoud 1991. Note the citations : AS 49, 3 ; 5 ; Max. 32, 3-4 ; 33, 3 ; Gd. 2, 1 ; 9, 6 ; 19, 9 ; 23, 1 ; MB 1, 2 ; 15, 5 ; 16, 3-6 ; Gall. 13, 8 (as an historical actor) ; T 32, 1 (out of chronological sequence) ; Cl. 12, 6. It is not clear whether this material is derived from Dexippus' history (from mythical times until 269/270) or from his account of the "Scythian" wars.

(20) Chastagnol 1994 : xxiii ; lxii-lxiii ; Barnes 1978 : 112-123. The preface to the *Diuus Aurelianus* (A 1, 6) describes the relevant material using the phrase *bella charactere historico digesta.*

HA also includes short extracts from the Latin epitomators Aurelius Victor and Eutropius, both of whom wrote many decades after the reign of Constantine. Other lost sources of the same genre (notably the so-called "Kaisergeschichte") seem also to have influenced our author ([21]). The same basic material was assiduously reworked within a conservative scholarly milieu, which lacked fresh sources of evidence on the events of the second and third centuries ([22]).

When authentic sources failed him, our author resorted to outright fabrication. It is by no means clear what might have prompted this descent into fraud ([23]). Some critics have characterised our impostor as a polemicist, propagandist or apologist, who produced a deliberately tendentious work. According to this line of interpretation, the spurious attributions found throughout the lives intentionally concealed the author's identity, freeing him to express controversial views on religious and political subjects ([24]). Moreover, the author could intervene authoritatively in contemporaneous debates by producing apposite documents purportedly from the distant past. His account of the second and third centuries might even be read as a coded commentary on the events of his own times. Seeck, Baynes, Hartke, Stern and Straub advanced arguments based upon considerations such as these, although they disagreed among themselves on exactly when and why the impostor wrote ([25]). Hartke championed perhaps the most influential version of this theory. He claimed that our author wrote soon after the battle of the river Frigidus (5 September 394), in order to express the views of pagan aristocrats implicated in the failed usurpation of Eugenius (392-394) ([26]).

(21) Chastagnol 1994 : lxvi-lxxi ; Barnes 1978 : 90-97 ; Dessau 1892 : 562-563 ; Idem 1889 : 361-374.

(22) Some scholars would disagree with aspects of this synopsis. Zecchini argued that the impostor drew upon a range of lost Greek sources on the period from Aurelian to Numerian : Zecchini 1999 ; Idem 1995. Barnes subsequently expressed some doubts about his earlier identification of the anonymous Greek historian : Barnes 1995 : 13-17. Paschoud claimed that the author drew upon the lost (Latin !) history of Virius Nicomachus Flavianus : Paschoud 1996 : xxxix-xliii.

(23) Mommsen asked who might benefit (*cui bono*) from such a crime : Mommsen 1890 : 229.

(24) Nonetheless, in the same period Eunapius openly criticised the Christianisation of the empire, commenting directly on the destruction of pagan temples.

(25) Seeck argued that the lives had been written during the reign of the Gallic usurper Constantine III (407-411), explaining their references to the dynasty of Constantine in this way : Seeck 1912. Baynes claimed that the corpus was written during the reign of Julian the Apostate (360-363), in order to promote the controversial religious policies of that ephemeral ruler : Baynes 1928 ; Idem 1926 ; Idem 1924. Stern suggested that the lives were composed under Constantius II (337-361), in an attempt to reconcile the emperor with the senatorial aristocracy of Rome : Stern 1953 (but note the remarks of Courcelle 1954).

(26) Hartke 1951 ; Idem 1940.

Hartke even sought to identify the author with Nicomachus Flavianus the Younger, allegedly writing in disgrace after the death of his father Virius Nicomachus Flavianus ([27]). According to Hartke, themes developed throughout the *HA* (notably its criticism of the imperial government, glorification of the Senate and apology for pagan religious practices) reflected the ideology of cadres affiliated with the Nicomachi. Placing the text later in the reign of Honorius (395-423), Straub saw the *HA* as a covert polemic against the Christianisation of the empire, written in response to the apologetic works of Orosius and Augustine ([28]).

Syme reacted against interpretations of this kind, denying that the author had any strong political or religious motivations ([29]). Syme described the *HA* as "a work of erudite imposture imbued with literary fantasy" and "a congenial masterpiece of erudition and fraud" ([30]). In discussing the corpus, Syme advocated "an approach leading by way of sources, structure and composition towards authorship," focussing upon the "language and style, habits, devices and

(27) Recently Festy attempted to revive this hypothesis : Festy 2007. He noted a parallel between an epilogue to the *Antoninus Heliogabalus* and the famous inscription rehabilitating the memory of Virius Nicomachus Flavianus (possibly drafted by his son) : *CIL* VI, 1783 (set up in 431) ; Virius Nicomachus Flavianus 15, *PLRE* I, 347-349. Both texts allude to the "jealously of evil-minded men" (*liuor inproborum*), apparently a rare collocation, although hardly an original idea. Demougeot argued that Virius Nicomachus Flavianus himself was the author, yet again situating our impostor within the upper reaches of the pagan establishment of the city of Rome : Demougeot 1953. Ratti reprised the argument : Ratti 2007. But Flavianus, praised in stone for his attainments as a stylist, wrote an historical work known as the *Annales*, which he dedicated to the Emperor Theodosius. By contrast, the *HA* is a corpus of biographies, openly confessing their pedestrian style, dedicated to Diocletian, Constantius I and Constantine, ascribed to six spurious authors, and probably written after about 395. We cannot equate these two works, as Ratti sought to do.

(28) Straub 1963 ; Idem 1952 (but note also Chastagnol 1994 : cxxxiii-cxxxiv ; Syme 1968a : 73 ; Cameron 1965). Some passages in the lives clearly reflect the concerns of late antique pagans, including points of conflict or difference with Christianity : Geffcken 1920. Note for example references to the Sibylline books (Gd. 26, 2 ; Gall. 5, 5 ; A 18, 5-20, 8) and to Apollonius of Tyana (AS 29, 2 ; A 24, 3-9). Eunapius, quite possibly the source of the *Diuus Aurelianus*, may have influenced some of these passages. A spurious letter ascribed to Hadrian satirises the Samaritans, Jews and Christians of Alexandria, whose ethnic origins as well as their religious views exposed them to contempt : Q 8, 1-10 (noting also 7, 4). Our author probably contrasted the enlightened syncretism of Alexander Severus (AS 29, 2) with the intolerant monotheism of Elagabalus, perhaps a coded criticism of the Christianising policies of Constantine or even Theodosius : Turcan 1993. Nonetheless, Dio Cassius and Herodian (not to mention Marius Maximus) had already savagely attacked Elagabalus' religious innovations. Our author was more interested in elaborating topics concerning food and sex.

(29) Syme 1978.

(30) Syme 1971a : 112 ; 1971b : 280.

predilections revealed in the writing" ([31]). Syme also emphatically denied that there was any connection between our impostor and the Roman magnates of the age of Theodosius. He imagined that the author "may have had his habitation somewhere on the fringes of high society, a gambler and a racing man … and at the same time an irreverent fancier of curious learning." He was "a decayed aristocrat, writing a kind of *Satiricon*," "a retired schoolmaster, or a clerk in some government department," "a librarian or a copyist employed on classical texts," "somebody who in the leisure of an obscure existence saw a sudden chance of literary diversion and succumbed to the seductions of fraud and mystification" ([32]). He was "a classical scholar with the tastes of a *grammaticus*, and a collector of oddities, perverse and whimsical," "a scholar, scholiast and parodist," "a scholar or a librarian" ([33]).

None of the interpretations discussed above is entirely satisfactory, although all contain elements of truth. Ideological considerations certainly shaped aspects of the *HA*, although in more subtle ways than is generally realised. The *HA* seems to have been intended for a select readership : individuals associated with the senatorial order and above all the great families of the Roman aristocracy. The presence throughout the corpus of genealogies and documents apparently flattering to the Roman elite (discussed in Chapter Three) is especially significant from this perspective. Dubious scholarship of this kind promoted the accumulation of symbolic capital within privileged cultural networks established around traditional social hierarchies. Our author might have had good reasons to orientate his work in this direction. The great families had significant influence over cultural production, since they often controlled the reception, dissemination and perpetuation of literary works (as shown in Chapter Six). While the *HA* may in some respects have affirmed the identity of this elite group, there is no indication that it was destined for a broader audience. For this reason, terms such as 'polemical,' 'apologetic' and 'tendentious' seem inappropriate (and may be anachronistic).

Some aspects of the *HA* can best be understood through an intertextual reading. Our author clearly situated his work within existing traditions of writing about emperors and usurpers, responding to the demands of various literary modes. Arguably, the *HA* bridged the gap between the traditions of imperial biography and imperial panegyric (a theory discussed at greater length in Chapter One). The spurious documents found throughout the lives imitate the scrupulous research of Suetonius and Marius Maximus ; the latter author was

(31) Syme 1971a : 105. "The *HA* ought to have been studied as a whole, for its own sake : language and style, the structure, the literary genre (half-way between biography and romance)." Syme 1971b : 279.

(32) Syme 1968a : 197-198.

(33) Syme 1968a : 52 ; 1971a : 6.

popular among the Roman aristocracy towards the end of the fourth century. But corpora of panegyrics (for example the extant *Panegyrici Latini*) may have provided the model for the notorious apparatus of attributions and dedications. Several poorly attested works of the fourth century (discussed at length in Chapter Three) demonstrate an interest in the careers of usurpers, perhaps helping to explain the inclusion of these figures in our collection. The *HA* should also be seen in the context of developments in the sphere of life writing across the fourth century, most notably the rapid evolution of hagiography and the popularity of romance narratives.

An approach grounded in hermeneutics may refine our discussion of fraud and imposture in important ways. Such an approach should avoid careless and unhelpful generalisations about late antique mentalities ([34]). It must also take into account the ways in which modern preconceptions may obscure our reading of ancient discursive practices. Our impostor may not have shared some modern understandings of authenticity, which are themselves historically conditioned. Some of our author's fabrications may follow relatively widely accepted norms of late antique scholarship. We might even entertain the contestable notion that some of his devices reflected respectable methods of undertaking scholarly research in his period. Our author often suffers from comparison with Ammianus, who wrote within the conventions of classical historiography. But our impostor really belongs alongside scholiasts, antiquarians, rhetoricians, authors of technical treatises and compilers of administrative documents. When placed next to these minor writers, our author may appear less eccentric and marginal than is sometimes assumed. In any case, a re-evaluation of some basic assumptions underlying and surrounding the text may prove fruitful in the long run.

Despite more than a century of scholarship since Dessau, we cannot definitively say what prompted our impostor to perpetrate his enormous fraud. Explanations involving ideology, polemic, propaganda or tendency, not to mention fear of persecution, may continue to persuade some critics. I myself suspect that our author was motivated chiefly by a desire to produce a great work of scholarship, which would fill the gaps in the tradition. He had every reason to continue the works of Marius Maximus, since great patrons were apparently closely interested in this author. During the last decades of the fourth century, writers of the imperial era found new favour after a long period of neglect, reversing the archaising tendency prevalent in Latin literature since the Antonine period. Roman scholars were involved in copying, correcting, glossing and redacting previously obscure texts. Under these circumstances, the rediscovery of an otherwise unknown work would attract great prestige in elite society. Our

(34) Nonetheless, writing on medieval historiography may provide interesting points of comparison. See, for example, G. R. Evans 2007 : 1-7 (on questions of historical authenticity).

impostor may have imagined that he was creatively reinventing the past through the invention of appropriate evidence. We cannot be certain that he viewed his project as essentially fraudulent. Nor was his identity necessarily obscure to his first readers, since our author may conceivable have posed as the redactor or discoverer of an earlier work. There is even the possibility that he allowed certain privileged readers to see through his pretence of multiple authorship and early date. In any case, once our impostor had decided to write a new series of imperial biographies, many of the ideological, intertextual and hermeneutic constraints described above naturally conditioned the work he produced.

* *
*

The chapters that follow examine some basic issues surrounding the *HA* : its authorship, date, context, redaction and reception. Chapter One discusses the attributions of authorship to Aelius Spartianus, Iulius Capitolinus, Vulcacius Gallicanus (v.c.), Aelius Lampridius, Trebellius Pollio and Flavius Vopiscus Syracusius. It argues that one writer was responsible for all thirty books ascribed to these six supposititious authors. The evidence for this claim (which emerges from various sources) is quite overwhelming. The attributions of authorship are incoherent, in that they cannot be reconciled with any sensible theory of the composition of the lives. Many of the spurious authors lack a coherent range of dates or canon of works. Comments made throughout the lives appear to contradict the attributions themselves. Some idiosyncratic features are found throughout the lives, regardless of their attributions to the various supposititious authors. The six authors perpetrate the same frauds, apparently without compunction : a clear indication of their common spuriousness. All six introduce bogus names, spurious documents, fabricated authorities and suspicious omens. For these reasons, one should reject the attributions to Spartianus, Capitolinus, Gallicanus, Lampridius, Pollio and Vopiscus as manifestly false, concluding instead that one individual was responsible for all thirty biographies.

The imposture of collective authorship may bear some relation to the circulation of genuine corpora of panegyrics, which combined the work of various orators accumulated within a school context. An extant collection (the *Panegyrici Latini*), probably compiled in the last decade of the fourth century, included numerous speeches from the reigns of Diocletian and Constantine. Since panegyric and biography were hardly distinct genres in the Late Antiquity, collections of speeches may have provided our author with a viable model. Moreover, late antique readers might have divined hidden meanings in the pseudonyms themselves : connections with imperial dynasties (Aelius, Iulius and Flavius), ingenious etymologies (Spartianus, Capitolinus, Lampridius and Trebellius) and other verbal associations (Gallicanus and Syracusius), even connections with persons known from literature (Pollio and Vopiscus) or scholarship (Vulcacius). These pedantic connections, discerned through admittedly dubious exegetical procedures, place the *HA* in the ambience of the schools.

Chapter Two examines the date at which our scholarly impostor wrote. The dedications to Diocletian, Constantine and private individuals of the reign of Constantius I found throughout the corpus cannot be genuine. They are an elaborate fraud. Historically inaccurate and internally contradictory, they even apostrophise the wrong emperors. Indeed, some of the dedications are so inapposite in their flattery or impudent in their criticism that they could not have been addressed to any reigning emperor. Since we cannot rely on the dedications, we must instead look within the text for other indications of date. The administrative terminology of the lives is especially suspect, since it reflects the institutional framework of the Roman state around the turn of the fifth century. Some of the lives appear to allude to political events of the last decades of the fourth century, most notably the usurpation of Eugenius (392-394), a development of considerable importance to the Western elite. On this basis, we can argue that the lives were written after about 395, probably close to the year 400. One could claim with reasonable certainty (although perhaps at the risk of vagueness) that the corpus appeared early in the reign of the Western Emperor Honorius (395-423).

While ascertaining the date of the *HA* remains important, we can say much more about this work by closely examining its cultural context. Perhaps the best place to begin is with a discussion of the intended audience of the corpus. Chapter Three argues that the author sought out readers among the great families of the Roman aristocracy, among the senatorial order more generally, and among the networks associated with these groups. Many scholars have noted that bogus names reported in the *HA* reflect the nomenclature of aristocrats prominent in the reign of Theodosius. Our author adorned the pedigrees of the great Roman houses with spurious ancestors, adopting a mode of flattery that was common among writers of his period. Some of the forged documents found throughout the lives seem to bolster the pretensions of the senatorial class as a whole, providing precedents and models for senatorial intervention in the government of the empire. Moreover, networks of cultural production centred on the Roman aristocracy provide a meaningful literary context for our author's interest in imperial biography. Two works in particular (the scholia on Juvenal and the cookery book attributed to Apicius) help reveal the immediate context of the impostor. Meanwhile, the poet and patron Ausonius seems to have shared his curiosity about usurpers.

At this point our discussion takes a strange turn, *sed curiositas nihil recusat.* Chapter Four reveals some apparent connections between Flavius Vopiscus Syracusius and an antiquarian and poetaster called Iunius or Iulius Naucellius, who was active in the last years of the fourth century. Like Vopiscus, Naucellius claimed to be a Syracusan : an intriguing coincidence. Moreover, our sources suggest that Naucellius was born in the first decade of the fourth century, quite possibly around 304, the year of the urban prefecture of Iunius Tiberianus, in whose state carriage the suppositious Vopiscus first appears. Naucellius' antiquarian interests and aristocratic connections suggest some affinities with our author, although circumstantial considerations of this kind may associate without identifying the two figures. The appearance of an imposture, or perhaps an impersonation (the *Sulpiciae conquestio*), in a collection of poems connected with Naucellius (the *Epigrammata Bobiensia*) invites further comment. This spurious diatribe, which elaborates upon material drawn from Suetonius and the exegetical tradition on Juvenal, clearly belongs within the same milieu as the *HA*. Nonetheless, the material presented in Chapter Four does not amount to an identification of the author of the *HA*.

Chapter Five discusses the process of redaction by which the *HA* attained its present form. A reassessment of the available evidence suggests that the peculiar arrangement of the lives within the earliest manuscripts (notably the Codex Palatinus latinus 899 and some Carolingian excerpts) may reflect the activities of the author himself. Indeed, the lives can be divided into three groups on the basis of their sources, citations, attributions and dedications. Furthermore, the borders of these three groups seem to coincide with apparent discontinuities in the corpus, including the lacuna covering the period from the death of Gordian III until the capture of Valerian. The author seems to have worked by adulterating any materials he derived from genuine sources with spurious digressions and marginal accretions. Where necessary, we should return to the evidence of the tradition, leaving aside the rationalising emendations of modern editors.

Evidence on the reception and transmission of the *HA* in the centuries before our earliest manuscripts is sadly wanting, and so no definitive statements can be made on these subjects. Nevertheless, Chapter Six presents what little information we have. It seems that the late Roman aristocracy played a role in preserving the corpus until the sixth century. Material from the *Maximini Duo* appears in a fragment of a lost historical work of Q. Aurelius Memmius Symmachus, probably the great-grandson of Symmachus, the senatorial magnate of the second half of the fourth century. The available evidence (although extremely limited) indicates that an association between the *HA* and the great families of the Roman aristocracy persisted for many generations after the author himself wrote. Palaeographical considerations (as well as the analogous fate of many related manuscripts) may suggest that an ancient manuscript of the *HA* survived the seventh and eighth centuries somewhere in North Italy (and the monastery of St. Columban at Bobbio has been mentioned in this context). Some traditions associated with this centre (notably the *Epigrammata Bobiensia* and Arusianus Messius' *Exempla elocutionum*) may provide helpful analogies. A previously unrecognised allusion to the *de Vita Hadriani* in Einhard's *Vita Karoli Magni* is perhaps the earliest echo of the *HA* in medieval literature. The work of the ancient historian may cease at the beginning of the ninth century, when the manuscript tradition of the *HA* was established on a secure basis.

Figure One : Basic Information on the *Historia Augusta*

	Titles	Abbreviations	Attributions	Dedications
I	*de Vita Hadriani* (1)	H (*Hadr.*) (2)	Aelius Spartianus	None
II	*Heluius* *(Aelius)*	Ael. (*Ael.*)	Aelius Spartianus	Diocletian : Ael. 1, 1 ; 2, 2. Galerius and Con - stantius are Caesars (293-305) : Ael. 2, 2.
III	*Antoninus Pius*	AP (*Ant. Pius*)	Iulius Capitolinus	None
IV	*Vita Marci Antonini Philosophi*	MA (*Marc.*)	Iulius Capitolinus	Diocletian : MA 19, 12.
V	*Verus*	V (*Ver.*)	Iulius Capitolinus	Diocletian : V 11, 4.
VI	*Auidius Cassius*	AC (*Au. Cass.*)	Vulcacius Gallicanus (v.c.)	Diocletian : AC 3, 3.
VII	*Commodus Antoninus*	C (*Comm.*)	Aelius Lampridius	None
VIII	*Heluius Pertinax*	P (*Pert.*)	Iulius Capitolinus	None
IX	*Didius Iulianus*	DI (*Did. Jul.*)	Aelius Spartianus	None
X	*Seuerus*	S (*Sev.*)	Aelius Spartianus	Diocletian : S 20, 4.
XI	*Pescennius Niger*	PN (*Pesc. Nig.*)	Aelius Spartianus	Diocletian : PN 9, 1.
XII	*Vita Clodii Albini*	Cl. A (*Clod. Alb.*)	Iulius Capitolinus	Constantine : Cl. A 4, 2.
XIII	*Antoninus Caracallus*	Cc. (*Carac.*)	Aelius Spartianus	None
XIV	*Antoninus Geta*	G (*Get.*)	Aelius Spartianus	Constantine : G 1, 1.
XV	*Opilius Macrinus*	OM (*Macr.*)	Iulius Capitolinus	Diocletian : OM 15, 4.
XVI	*Diadumenus Antoninus*	Dd. (*Diad.*)	Aelius Lampridius	None
XVII	*Varius Antoninus Heliogabalus (Antoninus Heliogabalus)*	Hel. (*Elag.*)	Aelius Lampridius	Constantine : Hel. 34, 1.

(1) The colophons of P preserve most of the original titles of the individual lives. This study generally refers to the individual lives by their ancient titles (a few trivial exceptions are noted).

(2) While Hohl's abbreviations for the lives are used throughout this study, an alternative system (in parentheses) is also widely accepted.

	Titles	Abbreviations	Attributions	Dedications
XVIII	*Alexander Seuerus*	AS (*Alex. Seu.*)	Aelius Lampridius	Constantine : AS 65, 1.
XIX	*Maximini Duo*	Max. (*Maxim.*)	Iulius Capitolinus	Constantine : Max. 1, 1.
XX	*Gordiani Tres (Gordiani Tres)* (3)	Gd. (*Gord.*)	Iulius Capitolinus	Constantine : Gd. 1, 1 ; 34, 6.
XXI	*Maximus siue Puppienus et Balbinus* (*Maximus et Balbinus*)	MB (*Max. et Balb.*)	Iulius Capitolinus	None
XXII	*Valeriani Duo*	Val. (*Val.*)	Trebellius Pollio	An anonymous dedicatee : Val. 7, 1 ; 8, 5.
XXIII	*Gallieni Duo*	Gall. (*Gall.*)	Trebellius Pollio	Constantius I (Caesar) : Gall. 7, 1 ; 14, 3.
XXIV	*Tyranni Triginta*	*T* (*Tr. tyr.*)	Trebellius Pollio	An anonymous descendant of Herennius Celsus (!) : T 11, 7 ; 22, 12. An anonymous scholar (asked to emend his manuscript) : T 31, 8-10 ; 33, 7-8.
XXV	*Diuus Claudius*	Cl. (*Claud.*)	Trebellius Pollio	Constantius I (Caesar) : Cl. 1, 1 ; 3, 1 ; 9, 9 ; 10, 7 ; 13, 2. Diocletian and Maximian are Augusti, while Galerius is a Caesar (293-305) : Cl. 10, 7. Anonymous patron of games : Cl. 3, 1 ; 5, 5.
XXVI	*Diuus Aurelianus*	A (*Aur.*)	Flavius Vopiscus Syracusius	Iunius Tiberianus (urban prefect 12 September 303- 4 January 304) : A 1, 1. Pinianus (?) : A 1, 9 ; 43, 1 ; 5. Constantius I (Augustus) : A 44, 5.
XXVII	*Tacitus*	Tac. (*Tac.*)	Flavius Vopiscus Syracusius	None

(3) The title *Gordiani tres* appears in the preface to the life (Gd. 1, 4) and also in the *index uitarum* of P.

	Titles	Abbreviations	Attributions	Dedications
XXVIII	*Probus*	Pr. (*Prob.*)	Flavius Vopiscus Syracusius	Celsinus : Pr. 1, 3.
XXIX	*Firmus, Saturninus, Proculus et Bonos[us]* (*Quadrigae Tyrannorum*) (4)	Q (*Quadr. tyr.*)	Flavius Vopiscus Syracusius	Bassus : Q 2, 1.
XXX	*Carus et Carinus et Numerianus*	Car. (*Car.*)	Flavius Vopiscus Syracusius	A friend : Car. 21, 2-3.

Figure Two : Sources of the *Historia Augusta*

Marius Maximus	Marius Maximus wrote a lost continuation of Suetonius, probably during the reign of Alexander Severus. His works were the chief source of the *de Vita Hadriani*, *Antoninus Pius*, *Vita Marci Antonini Philosophi*, *Verus*, *Commodus Antoninus*, *Heluius Pertinax*, *Didius Iulianus*, *Seuerus*, *Antoninus Caracallus* and *Antoninus Heliogabalus* (known as the primary lives). His account of the reigns of Hadrian, Marcus Aurelius and Severus informed the *Aelius*, *Auidius Cassius*, *Pescennius Niger*, *Vita Clodii Albini* and *Antoninus Geta* (known as the secondary lives).
Herodian	Herodian's extant history was a basic source of the *Opilius Macrinus*, *Diadumenus Antoninus*, *Alexander Seuerus*, *Maximini Duo*, *Gordiani Tres* and *Maximus et Balbinus*.
Dexippus	Dexippus' lost history provided crucial information in the period from the accession of Gordian III to the death of Claudius II. He was frequently cited in the lives from the *Alexander Seuerus* to the *Maximus et Balbinus*, where he was a subsidiary source.
Eunapius (?)	An unnamed Greek historian (possibly Eunapius) provided information about the military campaigns of Aurelian and Probus, together with some miscellaneous information on Tacitus and other emperors.
Epitomators	Short extracts from the epitomators Aurelius Victor and Eutropius appear throughout the *HA*. Other works within the same tradition (notably the so-called "Kaiser-geschichte") seem also to have influenced the corpus.

The above table essentially summarises Chastagnol's account of the sources of the HA, which is itself based heavily upon Barnes' research. Barnes, however, argued that there were two biographical sources of the lives from Hadrian to Elagabalus.

(4) The manuscripts call the *Quadrigae Tyrannorum* by a much simpler title (*Firmus, Saturninus, Proculus et Bonos[us]*), although a passage towards the end of the *Probus* (Pr. 24, 8) supplies the relevant phrase. Moreover, Cassiodorus described as a *quadriga* a compendium of excerpts from four canonical authors : Cass., *Inst.* I, 15, 7.

CHAPTER ONE

Authorship

The Attributions of Authorship. The attributions of authorship found in the *HA* have long been problematic ([1]). Indeed, humanist scholars recognised many of the difficulties involved. Casaubon (1559-1614), for example, speculated that the *Pescennius Niger* (attributed to Spartianus) and the *Vita Clodii Albini* (attributed to Capitolinus) might actually have been written by the same author ([2]). He expressed the same opinion concerning the *Opilius Macrinus* (attributed to Capitolinus) and the *Diadumenus Antoninus* (attributed to Lampridius) ([3]). More radical than Casaubon, Salmasius (1588-1653) ascribed everything from the *de Vita Hadriani* to the *Alexander Seuerus* to Spartianus, entirely eliminating in the process all the attributions of authorship to Lampridius and Gallicanus ([4]). Salmasius was motivated in part by considerations of style : *eadem uero in multis prope uerba, ut si diuersi sint auctores censendi, uno ueluti ore locuti uideri debeant* ([5]). Nonetheless, the true basis of his argument may have been an erroneous attribution of authorship found in a collection of extracts made in the Carolingian period ([6]). The tireless Fabricius (1668-1736) devised an even more elaborate theory, suggesting that there were perhaps only four authors : Capitolinus, "Aelius Lampridius Spartianus," Pollio and Vopiscus ([7]). Gibbon naturally disdained an apparently sterile and pedantic question.

(1) For some discussions of the problem of authorship, see : den Hengst 2002 ; Zecchini 1993 ; Barnes 1978 : 13-18 ; White 1967 ; Hohl 1912.

(2) Casaubon comm. ad PN 1, 1 [1671 : I, 642] ; Cl. A 1.1 [683] ; Salmasius comm. ad Cl. A 1, 1 [683].

(3) Casaubon comm. ad Dd. 1, 1 [1671 : I, 771] ; Salmasius comm. ad Dd. 1, 1 [771-772].

(4) Salmasius comm. ad Ael. 1, 1 [1671 : I, 3].

(5) Salmasius comm. ad AC 1, 1 [1671 : I, 439].

(6) Note, for example, the ninth-century manuscript that Callu identified as Π (Vaticanus Palatinus latinus 886) in his introduction to the Budé edition : Callu 1992 : xcviii. This manuscript contains excerpts from the first nineteen lives, under the misleading title *ex libro Spartiani de uita Caesarum*. Sadly, the content of these otherwise valuable excerpts has little or no bearing upon the question of authorship.

(7) Fabricius 1773-1774 [first ed. 1697] : III, 3, 6 [93]. Fabricius merged Aelius Spartianus and Aelius Lampridius, merely dismissing Vulcacius Gallicanus (v.c.).

While the attributions of authorship were long considered dubious, Dessau was the first to reject them outright. He demonstrated that the attributions preserved in the manuscripts were hopelessly contradictory. Spartianus and Capitolinus dedicate some of their works to Diocletian (284-305) and some to Constantine, sole emperor after his defeat of Licinius (324), leaving an unexplained pause of twenty years in both of their literary careers ([8]). At the same time, it is almost impossible to ascribe a coherent series of biographies to Spartianus, Capitolinus, Gallicanus or Lampridius, because the attributions of authorship in the lives from Hadrian to Elagabalus appear in a seemingly random order. There are also cross-references between the lives attributed to the suppositious authors, which are not always compatible with the stated chronology of the works involved ([9]). Comments made in the prefaces and epilogues to individual lives seem to refer to the whole corpus, or to large sections of the corpus ([10]). These observations render the attributions of authorship dubious, and it is difficult to see how one might resolve the contradictions within the corpus.

There is no overt indication that the six suppositious authors worked in collaboration (although Vopiscus does mention Pollio, Capitolinus and Lampridius) ([11]). Furthermore, the tortuous chronology implied by the dedications presents a formidable barrier to any theories of mutual influence. Nevertheless, Dessau noted that the spurious authors shared some allegedly distinctive characteristics : citations of the biographer Marius Maximus ([12]) ; catalogues of physi-

(8) Dessau 1889 : 337-338. A similar problem afflicts the hapless Lampridius. His *Antoninus Heliogabalus* and *Alexander Severus* are dedicated to Constantine, while his *Commodus Antoninus* and *Diadumenus Antoninus* bear no overt dedications. Nonetheless, he is named as a biographer in a life allegedly written in the reign of Constantius I : Pr. 2, 7. Moreover, the *Vita Marci Antonini Philosophi*, attributed to Capitolinus and dedicated to Diocletian, refers to the *Commodus Antoninus* : MA 19, 5-6. Thus, Lampridius' 'career' also spans the reigns of Diocletian, Constantius I and Constantine.

(9) Dessau 1889 : 378-379. The *Pescennius Niger*, attributed to Spartianus and dedicated to Diocletian, alludes to the *Vita Clodii Albini*, attributed to Capitolinus and dedicated to Constantine : PN 9, 3. Capitolinus, the alleged author of the *Vita Clodii Albini*, cites (Cl. A 1, 4) a passage from his own (!) *Pescennius Niger* (PN 8, 1), a work actually ascribed to Spartianus. Lampridius suggests that he considered incorporating his account of the reign of Diadumenus into his (!) life of Macrinus (Dd. 6, 1). The *Opilius Macrinus* is actually ascribed to Capitolinus. The *Tyranni Triginta*, attributed to Pollio, alludes to the *Quadrigae Tyrannorum*, attributed to Vopiscus (allegedly writing somewhat later) : T 31, 8. Supposedly writing under Constantius, Vopiscus cites Capitolinus (Pr. 2, 7), who dedicates some works to Constantine. Further cross-references complicate the situation yet further : Ael. 2, 9-10 ; MA 19, 5-6 ; Dd. 6, 1 ; Hel. 19, 1 ; AS 35, 1.

(10) Ael. 1, 1 ; 7, 5 ; AC 3, 3 ; Hel. 35, 2-6 ; AS 64, 1-2.

(11) A 2, 1 ; Pr. 2, 7. Capitolinus and Lampridius are mentioned in a catalogue of spurious authorities.

(12) Dessau 1889 : 379-385. Although many writers drew upon his works, only Ammianus (Amm. XXVIII, 4, 14) and the scholiast on Juvenal (*Schol. Iuu.* IV, 53(2)) mentioned Marius Maximus by name.

cal or moral characteristics ([13]) ; bogus verses, often concocted from lines of Virgil, sometimes allegedly translated from the Greek ([14]) ; as well as word play on the names of the emperors ([15]). Spartianus, Capitolinus, Gallicanus, Pollio and Vopiscus include among their works lives of usurpers, something nowhere else attempted in ancient literature ([16]). Spartianus, Capitolinus, Pollio and Vopiscus discuss minor figures, generally the intended successors of the ruling house. Once again, these biographies are unprecedented in ancient scholarship.

One could add many items to this catalogue of eccentric features. The aberrant nomenclature of two female relatives of Elagabalus, found across three lives, may represent a point of affinity between Capitolinus and Lampridius ([17]). There is apparently no evidence for the existence of either the Commodian gardens or the Varian gardens, and so Spartianus and Vopiscus are apprehended in the same fraud ([18]). The *Antoninianae puellae* and *Mammaeanae puellae* were spurious alimentary orders, modelled upon a genuine order discussed in the lives of Antoninus Pius and Marcus Aurelius (the *Faustinianae puellae*) ([19]). Both

(13) Ael. 5, 1-2 ; PN 6, 5 ; Cl. A 13, 1-2 ; G 4, 1 ; Dd. 3, 2 ; AS 44, 1 ; Max. 2, 2 ; Gd. 18, 1 ; 31, 4 ; MB 7, 4 ; Val. 8, 1 ; Cl. 13, 5 ; Dessau 1889 : 381. Such passages were perhaps more common than Dessau imagined : E. C. Evans 1935.

(14) H 2, 8 ; PN 12, 5-6 ; OM 11, 3-7 ; 12, 9 ; Dd. 8, 7 ; AS 4, 6 ; 14, 5 ; Max. 27, 4 ; T 11, 5-7 ; Cl. 10, 4-7 ; Velaza 1996 ; Chastagnol 1994 : xvii ; lxxix-lxxxi ; Clover 1991 ; Dessau 1892 : 582-583.

(15) White 1967 : 117 ; Dessau 1889 : 384-385. Arguably, word games of this kind were more common in late antique literature than Dessau suspected. There are puns on names throughout Ausonius' works, for example. Acindynus : Aus., *Epig.* 41-42. Auxilius : *Epig.* 81. Bonus : *Epig.* 116-121. Chrestus : *Epig.* 41-42. Hilaria : *Parent.* 6, 3-6. Iucundus : *Prof.* 9. Lascivus : *Prof.* 7, 5-8. Maura : *Parent.* 5, 3-6. Meroë : *Epig.* 21. Pastor : *Parent.* 11, 5-10. Probus : *Epist.* 9(b), 35-52.

(16) Dessau 1889 : 380.

(17) Symiamira (Iulia Soemias Bassiana, the mother of Elagabalus) : OM 9, 2 ; Hel. 2, 1 ; 4, 4 ; 14, 4 ; 18, 2 ; Turcan 1993 : 133-134. The form "Symiasera" is found in Eutropius : Eutr., *Breu.* VIII, 22. Note also Varia (spurious grandmother of Elagabalus) : OM 9, 1 ; 4 ; Hel. 10, 1 ; 12, 3 ; 31, 4 ; AS 1, 2.

(18) PN 6, 8 ; A 1, 2. According to Spartianus, a mosaic "in the Commodian gardens" (*in Commodianis hortis*) depicted Pescennius Niger's participation in the rites of Isis : PN 6, 8. The whole story is probably based upon a passage in the *Commodus Antoninus* : C 9, 4. The "Varian gardens," nowhere else recorded, probably allude to the Emperor Elagabalus. The sense is completed in the *Antoninus Heliogabalus*. That emperor, fearing a mutiny, retreated to the Gardens of Spes Vetus (*ad hortos Spei Veteris*) : Hel. 13, 5. The life in question includes allusions to "the gardens in which Varius was" (*in hortos, in quibus erat Varius*) and "the gardens, where Varius was found" (*in hortos, ubi Varius inuenitur*) : Hel. 14, 2 ; 5. Iunius Tiberianus' promenade from the Palatine to the Varian gardens (in the preface to the *Diuus Aurelianus*) may represent the tradition of imperial biography up to Elagabalus.

(19) Dd. 2, 10 ; AS 57, 7. Compare AP 8, 1 ; MA 26, 6. Our author innovated, also devising orders of boys.

Pollio and Vopiscus mention a spectacle known as a *Cyclopea*, a word apparently unknown elsewhere ([20]). These two purported authors also draw upon the testimony of suppositious grandfathers, allegedly active in the reign of Diocletian ([21]). The oracular utterances of Gallic druidesses embellish the works of Lampridius and Vopiscus ([22]).

The language of the corpus provides further evidence of unitary authorship ([23]). Dessau noted some otherwise extremely rare words and phrases found throughout lives, despite the boundaries established by the various attributions of authorship ([24]). There have been significant advances in lexicography since

(20) Gall. 8, 3 ; Car. 19, 3 ; Desbordes and Ratti 2000 : 132-133 ; *TLLO*, II, col. 784, 6.

(21) T 25, 3 ; Q 9, 4 ; 15, 4 ; Car. 13, 3 ; 14, 1 ; 15, 1 ; Chastagnol 1994 : cxxx-cxxxi. The model is surely Suetonius : Suet., *Cal.* 19, 3. There is also a spurious father at A 43, 2. Here the model is probably Suet., *Oth.* 10, 1.

(22) AS 60, 6 ; A 44, 4-5 ; Car. 14, 2.

(23) Generalisations about usage made throughout this work are based upon the consultation of various printed dictionaries (Glare 1968-1982, Souter 1996 [first printed 1949] and Lewis and Short 1955 [first printed 1879], among others), as well as the *Thesaurus Linguae Latinae* (*TLL*), where it is available, and the electronic databases of the *Bibliotheca Teubneriana Latina* (*BTL*) [1999] and the *Library of Latin Texts* (*CLCLT*) [2002]. I have also referred to works on the language of the *HA* itself : Paschoud 1989 ; Moes 1980 ; Paucker 1870. Please note that my comments represent soundings taken for historical purposes, not independent contributions to lexicography.

(24) *In litteras mittere*, to commit to writing : AC 3, 3 ; PN 1, 1 ; Hel. 1, 1 ; 18, 4 ; AS 3, 2 ; 5 ; 48, 6 ; Gd. 21, 5 ; Val. 8, 3 ; Gall. 18, 6 ; 19, 1 ; 21, 5 ; A 1, 8 ; 24, 9 ; Tac. 11, 7 ; *TLL* VII, 2, col. 1516, 49 ; *BTL* ; *CLCLT* ; den Hengst 1981 : 25-26 ; Dessau 1889 : 388. Not otherwise attested in the extant corpus of Latin literature. *Participatus*, the division of power between two emperors : V 3, 8 ; AC 7, 4 ; DI 8, 3 ; S 8, 14 ; PN 5, 6 ; OM 5, 1 ; Max. 8, 1 ; T 6, 1 ; *TLL* X, 1, col. 500, 4 ; *BTL* ; *CLCLT* ; Dessau 1889 : 389. Tiberius Claudius Donatus and Petrus Chrysologus (as reported in *CLCLT*) employed the word with more general reference to the government of an empire or kingdom. *Rebellio* (masculine gender, generally used in the plural), a rebel : MA 29, 4 ; AC 9, 11 ; Gall. 19, 6 ; *BTL* ; *CLCLT* ; Souter 1996 : 341 ; Dessau 1889 : 389-390. (Note also Pr. 9, 1, which probably refers to rebellions.) Found otherwise only in the pseudo-Hegesippus and in Benedict of Nursia. We can add to this list. Capitolinus and Gallicanus are apparently the only authors to use the word *excaldatio* (AC 5, 11 ; Cl. A 5, 7), which refers to the heating of water, although the verb form *excaldare* (AC 5, 5) occurs in a range of medical writers : *TLL* V, 2, col. 1198, 30 ; 37 ; *BTL* ; *CLCLT*. Vopiscus appears to have coined the noun *epigrammatarius*, while Spartianus may have invented the adjective *epigrammaticus*. *Epigrammatarius*, an author of epigrams : Tac. 16, 3 ; Q 7, 4 ; *TLL* V, 2, col. 667, 12 ; *BTL* ; *CLCLT* ; Moes 1980 : 174. *Epigrammaticus*, concerning epigrams : Ael. 5, 9 ; *TLL* V, 2, col. 667, 17 ; *BTL* ; *CLCLT* ; Moes 1980 : 174. Neither word is found outside the *HA*. Even more distinctive is the noun *mythistoria*, used exclusively by Capitolinus, and the adjective *mythistoricus*, known only from the works of Vopiscus. *Mythistoria*, fabulation : OM 1, 5 ; *TLL* VIII, col. 1762, 5 ; *BTL* ; *CLCLT* ; Moes 1980 : 178. *Mythistoricus*, concerning fabulation : Q 1, 2 ; *TLL* VIII, col. 1762, 9 ; *BTL* ; *CLCLT* ; Moes 1980 : 178.

Dessau, and these have in many cases confirmed his intuitions about the occurrence of particular words or phrases ([25]). Nevertheless, Adams dismissed evidence of this kind as "interesting but inconclusive," suggesting that these oddities could be "clichés in use in literary varieties of Latin or borrowed by one Scriptor from another" ([26]). Seeking more compelling proofs, Adams demonstrated that all six authors differentiated in similar ways pairs of otherwise close synonyms ([27]). He argued that these distinctions were "idiolectical rather than general in the language" ([28]). Adams also noted peculiarities in the formation of the periphrastic tenses of the passive voice, found throughout the six authors ([29]). All these philological arguments seem to point towards unitary authorship. By contrast, computer studies have proved inconclusive ([30]). There is as yet no precedent for using statistical measures to determine how many otherwise unknown authors wrote a particular book ([31]). Moreover, the uneven distribution of authentic and inauthentic material throughout the corpus may vitiate the use of crude quantitative methods ([32]).

The presence of spurious material throughout the corpus further undermines the attributions of authorship : a common thread of fabrication and imposture runs through the works of the six suppositious authors, while "the whole compilation is permeated with fraudulence" ([33]). There are several hundred bogus names in the *HA*, apparently fictitious historical authorities, office holders, senators and generals, not to mention the apocryphal ancestors, relatives and descendants of many emperors. The author invented documentary and material

(25) In some cases, Dessau's views have been qualified. For example, the idiom *conflictum habere* (in place of *proelium committere*) occurs in the pseudo-Hegesippus, Vegetius, Augustine and the *Gallic Chronicle* of 452 (*Chron. Gall.* 384 [9]) : Cl. A 9, 1 ; OM 8, 2 ; Gall. 4, 2 ; T 9, 3 ; 11, 4 ; Cl. 5, 1 ; Car. 10, 1 ; *TLL* IV, col. 237, 31 ; *BTL* ; *CLCLT* ; Adams 1977 : 93 ; Dessau 1889 : 387.

(26) Adams 1977 : 93.

(27) Adams 1977 ; Idem 1972 ; Idem 1971.

(28) Adams 1977 : 93.

(29) Adams 1977 : 95.

(30) As often happens, the computers appear to disagree among themselves. Marriott argued for unitary authorship, while Gurney and Gurney and Meissner argued for plural authorship : Gurney and Gurney 1998a ; Idem 1998b ; Idem 1998c ; Meissner 1992 ; Marriott 1979. Meanwhile, Rudman criticised Gurney and Gurney on methodological grounds, while Gurney and Gurney criticised Meissner and Sansone criticised Marriott : Rudman 1998 ; Sansone 1990.

(31) Usually one assesses whether a dubious work belongs to the canon of a known author (canonicity). Even here there is room for doubt. An epigonous pseudepigraphon might be more characteristic of the master than an authentic work.

(32) Similar objections could be raised to studies of authorship based upon prose rhythm : Béranger 1983. Note also Zernial 1956.

(33) Syme 1968a : 1.

evidence, including letters, speeches and harangues, decrees and acclamations of the Senate, verses and omens, coins, inscriptions, art objects, heirlooms and palaces : an astonishingly elaborate authenticating apparatus ([34]). There are even references to spurious legions. Often enough these fabrications closely imitate the work of earlier writers in the genre of imperial biography ([35]). For example, genuine names recorded in either Suetonius or Marius Maximus subsequently reappear, attached to dubious figures of a later period ([36]).

The arguments originally presented by Dessau and amplified by subsequent generations of scholars are quite sufficient to demonstrate the spuriousness of Aelius Spartianus, Iulius Capitolinus, Vulcacius Gallicanus (v.c.), Aelius Lampridius, Trebellius Pollio and Flavius Vopiscus Syracusius ; these writers have been exposed as figments. We are confronted by six otherwise unknown authors (each a minor impostor in his own right), all displaying the same apparently aberrant characteristics. It seems most likely that one writer is responsible for all these symptoms of fabrication, fraud and invention. Under these circumstances, it would be most unwise to grant any credence to the attributions of authorship.

A Model for Collective Authorship. It is a relatively easy matter to expose our impostor, but the really difficult thing is to explain his devices. There is no precedent for a spurious corpus of imperial biographies attributed to six different authors, allegedly accumulated over the reigns of Diocletian, Constantius I and Constantine. Fortunately for us, an authentic compilation from the end of the fourth century furnishes a useful analogy. The collection known as the *Panegyrici Latini* includes speeches of praise addressed to Trajan, Theodosius, Julian, Constantine, Constantius I, Maximian and a provincial governor, with a pronounced bias towards texts from the turn of the fourth century. Although some speeches remain anonymous, six orators are acknowledged : Pliny, Pacatus, Claudius Mamertinus, Nazarius, Eumenius and another and more dubious Mamertinus. The extant corpus forms a coherent series of panegyrics, docu-

(34) Dessau 1892 : 577-578 ; 591. “The author of the *HA* picks up the literary markers of historical writing – citation of texts, agglomeration of detail, authorial intrusion into the narrative – and manipulates those markers to excess to provide his work with a sort of hyperauthenticity.” Meckler 1996 : 374.

(35) These parallels with Suetonius have been studied in depth : Chastagnol 1972 : 109-123.

(36) Syme noted many examples : Syme 1976 ; Idem 1966. Palfurius Sura, known to Marius Maximus as a delator of the reign of Domitian (Suet., *Dom.* 13, 1 ; Iuv. IV, 53 ; Cass. Dio, *Epit.* LXVII, 1, 2 ; *Schol. Iuu.* IV, 53(1) ; *PIR* P 68, M. Palfurius Sura), reappears some centuries later as an authority on the reign of Gallienus (Gall. 18, 6). The spurious praetorian prefect Baebius Macer, mentioned in the *Diuus Aurelianus* (A 13, 1), took his name from an urban prefect of the reign of Hadrian (H 5, 5). Lollius Urbicus, a governor of Britain during the reign of Antoninus Pius (AP 5, 4), was born again as a suppositious authority on the reign of Diadumenus (Dd. 9, 2).

menting the most significant emperors from Maximian to Theodosius in more or less reverse chronological order. Pliny's speech in praise of Trajan (the *Panegyricus*), a celebrated literary archetype, appears alongside these lesser works.

The *Panegyrici Latini* emerged over a period of about a century ([37]). At the core of the collection are five panegyrics associated with the city of Autun and delivered between 298 and 311 (V-IX). Two panegyrics (X and XI) delivered at Trier seem to have become associated with the Autun group at a somewhat later stage. The three speeches ascribed to Pacatus, Claudius Mamertinus and Nazarius (II-IV) were then added to this group of seven (V-XI). This proposed reconstruction finds strong support in the manuscript tradition. Most significant is the apparently inaccurate colophon to panegyric five : INCIPIVNT PANEGYRICI DIVERSORVM VII. The last of the panegyrics (XII) was probably added after the rest of the collection took shape, since it appears out of all chronological sequence. Moreover, the colophon to panegyric five was likely written before panegyric twelve made its appearance. It would be difficult to say when Pliny's speech in praise of Trajan (I) became associated with the extant corpus of speeches, given the popularity of this text in the fifth century ([38]).

The existence of works such as the *Panegyrici Latini* might help to explain the otherwise incomprehensible arrangement of the *HA*. Our impostor may have imitated key aspects of such a corpus : notably its organic development, collective authorship, (predominantly) tetrarchic date and imperial subject matter. The fact that many of the extant panegyrics address emperors of the turn of the fourth century is of course interesting, since the dedications in the *HA* apostrophise rulers of this period. There was, of course, no need for our impostor to address these emperors at all, and his approach may owe something to the panegyrics themselves. Nonetheless, the corpus of speeches known to us (with its distinctly Gallic provenance) may not have been the only such collection that circulated in

(37) Nixon and Saylor Rodgers 1994 : 3-8. Note in particular the following paragraph (at p. 5) : "To ignore the vexed question of the relative dates of VIII and IX, speeches V-IX appear in reverse chronological order ; X and XI, delivered at Trier perhaps by the same orator, apparently from Trier, seem to have been appended together in chronological order to form a collection of seven. Later someone prefaced this collection with the speeches of Pacatus, Claudius Mamertinus and Nazarius, preserving the reverse chronological order, and either he, or someone else, set Pliny's *Panegyricus* at the beginning. *Panegyric* XII, however, is isolated, for the heading *panegyrici diuersorum VII* takes no account of it, nor has it been placed immediately before the first of these ; evidently it was a later addition."

(38) Passages from Pliny's *Panegyricus* appear together with fragments of the speeches of Symmachus in a palimpsest manuscript originally copied in the sixth century (*CLA* I, 29). This arrangement may have been devised at an earlier date. Macrobius (Macr., *Sat.* V, 1, 7) had claimed that Pliny and Symmachus were pre-eminent in the luxuriant and ornate style.

Late Antiquity. Every rhetorical school would have an interest in glorifying its most distinguished masters ; every aspiring official would seek out approved models of eloquence or verbosity. Perhaps our impostor modelled his creation on some such collection, and expected his readers to understand his invention in those terms. Moreover, collections of panegyrics may have shaped late antique interpretations of the *HA*, providing some sort of precedent for its apparently eccentric pretence of multiple authorship.

The *Panegyrici Latini* provides another sort of model. The great bulk of the speeches are authentic documents from the reigns of Diocletian, Constantius I and Constantine, which may well have been rediscovered towards the end of the fourth century. The latest orator included in the corpus is Pacatus, who delivered a delicate panegyric of Theodosius (389) and was elevated to various imperial offices in the years that followed ([39]). One might speculate that Pacatus introduced the extant collection to the Roman aristocracy soon after he delivered his speech : "It is tempting to argue that Pacatus, the author of the latest panegyric in the collection, was its editor. While nearly all the panegyricists are in debt to their predecessors in the corpus, Pacatus' debts are perhaps the heaviest and most diverse" ([40]). Pacatus, one of Ausonius' protégés, was also a correspondent of the great orator Symmachus. One could easily imagine that our impostor emerged from a similar milieu. The appearance of a corpus of panegyrics may have helped to stimulate the production of a series of biographies from around the turn of the fourth century. This genuine discovery, or a related development, may perhaps have inspired our impostor to fabricate his dedications and to adopt his tiresome pseudonyms.

Several scholars have drawn attention to parallels between the panegyrics and the *HA* ([41]). Given that panegyrics are generic and derivative almost by definition, it would be unwise to place too much emphasis on these similarities. Nevertheless, there is some evidence that our author consciously orientated his work with reference to the pre-existing rhetorical tradition. Sections of the *Diuus Claudius*, *Diuus Aurelianus* and *Probus* are written in a frankly panegyrical mode. There is also an obscure reference towards the end of the *Antoninus Heliogabalus*, perhaps to a collection of speeches, although not exactly matching the composition of any known collection ([42]). It is noticeable that the *HA* fits

(39) *PLRE* I, 272, Latinius Pacatus Drepanius.

(40) Nixon and Saylor Rodgers 1994 : 6.

(41) Desbordes and Ratti 2000 : 69 ; 162-163 ; 175 ; Paschoud 1996 : 32, n. 42 ; 33, n. 43 ; Chastagnol 1994 : xc-xci ; Syme 1968a : 113-115.

(42) The author announced his intention to write lives of Elagabalus' successors, including Alexander Severus and the short-lived rulers that followed him. He hoped also to celebrate Claudius and Aurelian : Hel. 35, 2. He went on to suggest that Diocletian, Maximian and Constantine ought to be joined to these emperors : Hel. 35, 4. Our impostor claimed

Figure One : The *Panegyrici Latini*

MS Order	Chron. Order	Author	Addressee	
I	(I)	Pliny	Trajan	
II	(XII)	Pacatus	Theodosius	Three panegyrics by named orators of the fourth century.
III	(XI)	Claudius (?) Mamertinus	Julian	These speeches appear in reverse chronological order.
IV	(X)	Nazarius	Constantine	
V	(VIII)	-	Constantine	◀ INCIPIVNT PANEGYRICI DIVERSORVM VII
VI	(VII)	-	Constantine	
VII	(VI)	-	Maximian and Constantine	Seven panegyrics ascribed to "various orators," some named.
VIII	(V)	-	Constantius I (Caesar)	These speeches also appear essentially in reverse chronological order.
IX	(IV)	Eumenius	The prefect of the Gauls	
X	(II)	Mamertinus (?)	Maximian	
XI	(III)	The same teacher (?)	Maximian	
XII	(IX)	-	Constantine	Another panegyric, apparently not envisaged by the colophon at V(VIII), which appears out of chronological sequence.

rather neatly between the works of Suetonius (Caesar to Domitian) on the one hand and the *Panegyrici Latini* (including key emperors from Diocletian and Maximian to Theodosius) on the other ([43]). Considering its scope, the corpus forms a juncture between Suetonius' *de Vita Caesarum* and the collection of speeches associated with Pacatus. One could argue that our impostor was conscious of the traditions of imperial biography and imperial panegyric, seeking to accommodate his work to the demands of both forms. Moreover, one might argue that developments in life writing in the fourth century, notably the rapid evolution of hagiography, narrowed any perceived differences between biography and panegyric.

that others would devote more eloquent works to Constantine : Hel. 35, 5. Moreover, Licinius, Severus, Alexander (probably Domitius Alexander, who rose against Maxentius in Africa) and Maxentius would receive their fair measure of praise : Hel. 35, 6.

(43) An exhaustive and authoritative panegyric of Trajan appears in manuscripts of the *Panegyrici Latini* ; this fact might possibly explain the omission of lives of Nerva and Trajan from the *HA*.

Some Pseudonyms. Aelius Spartianus, Iulius Capitolinus, Vulcacius Gallicanus (v.c.), Aelius Lampridius, Trebellius Pollio and Flavius Vopiscus Syracusius are mere pseudonyms. One would struggle to find any trace of these writers in the tradition, and the form "Spartianus" is nowhere else attested ([44]). The names of the authors are clearly spurious, but they are not necessarily meaningless. Attempting to tease out hidden significance, modern scholars have advanced various interpretations of these sobriquets, in the process sometimes inadvertently mimicking the dubious exegetical practices of our learned impostor. Etymological fantasy, inveterate paronomasia, ingenious genealogies and typological comparisons were legitimate tools of late antique scholarship. Nevertheless, the modern disciplines of philology and history will not easily admit conjectures based upon these approaches. While it may be interesting enough to seek occult meanings in the names of the authors, we must avoid being dragged too far out into a sea of conjecture.

The pseudonyms have a genealogical dimension. The names Aelius, Iulius, Flavius are all associated with imperial dynasties, which included illustrious members of the *gens Aelia* (Hadrian and his successors), the *gens Iulia* (the Julio-Claudians) and the *gens Flauia* (the Flavians). It is rather striking that Aelius Spartianus should open the collection with a biography of the Emperor Hadrian (Publius Aelius Hadrianus) ([45]). The notion that Claudius II had somehow restored the Flavian dynasty may partly explain the subsequent invention of a Flavius Vopiscus Syracusius ([46]). One might also explore the pseudonyms through etymological analysis. Honoré argued that the names Spartianus, Capitolinus and Lampridius involved "puns based on a simple typology of imperial character" ([47]). Honoré supplied some relevant etymologies : "'Spartianus,' for example, could mean harsh or Spartan, 'Capitolinus' friendly with the Capitolium or senate, 'Lampridius' frivolous and fond of night-lights. Each emperor is then assigned the biographer most suited to his character" ([48]). Honoré

(44) Our impostor may have provided two of the authors with dubious forebears. Pollio cites the spurious authority "Cornelius Capitolinus" (shades of Tacitus !) : T 15, 8. Spartianus introduces "Lampridia," allegedly the mother of Pescennius Niger : PN 1, 3.

(45) Note Ael. 2, 6 : *in Aeliorum familia, hoc est in Hadriani*. Note also CLAUD., *de Cons. Hon. VI*, 420-421.

(46) Censorinus, a wholly spurious figure who appears at the end of a long catalogue of usurpers (the *Tyranni Triginta*), allegedly owned a very beautiful mansion adjacent to "the temple to the Flavian tribe" (the *gentes Flauiae*) : T 33, 6. The long preface to the *Diuus Claudius*, which immediately follows the entry on Censorinus, claims that that emperor perpetuated the Flavian dynasty (the *gentes Flauiae*) : Cl. 3, 6. On the Flavian connections of Claudius II, see BRUGGISSER 2007 : 91, n. 30.

(47) HONORÉ 1987 : 171.

(48) HONORÉ 1987 : 171. Capitolinus is connected with the Temple of Jupiter Optimus Maximus (also known as Jupiter Capitolinus), a meeting place of the Senate.

argued that Spartianus dealt with "strict emperors, unfriendly to the senate, hence Spartan," while Capitolinus dealt with "emperors on good terms with the senate" and Lampridius with "frivolous emperors such as Commodus and Elagabal" ([49]). One could draw parallels between the alleged etymological associations of the names Spartianus, Capitolinus and Lampridius and the word play on the names of emperors found widely throughout the lives themselves ([50]).

While Honoré's explanations of the names Spartianus and Capitolinus are convincing, his attempt to derive the name Lampridius from the word *lampas* (which he translated "night-lights") seems somewhat forced. Fortunately, there is a better alternative available, although it is perhaps excessively recondite. One might choose instead to associate the name Lampridius with the noun **lampreda*, which is the root of our word for "lamprey." Although the word *lampreda* is not attested in ancient literature, it seems probable that it was current in the late Roman period, and that it entered the Romance languages from this source ([51]).

(49) Honoré 1987 : 171.

(50) Honoré's "simple typology of imperial character" seems to hold for the period from Hadrian to Elagabalus. Although not a great conqueror, Hadrian can be described as a 'Spartan' emperor : as the successor of Trajan, or as the man suspected of executing four consulars (H 7, 1-4) and committing other cruel acts (15, 1-9 ; 20, 3 ; 25, 8 ; 27, 2). He was also a reformer of military discipline (H 10, 1-11, 2 ; 14, 10 ; 17, 2 ; 21, 9). It would be perfectly reasonable to describe Antoninus Pius and Marcus Aurelius as 'Capitoline,' given the extraordinary reputation of the Antonine emperors among the senatorial elite : AP 5, 3 ; 6, 3 ; 5 ; 8, 10 ; 10, 6-9 ; 12, 1-3 ; MA 1, 1 ; 8, 3 ; 10, 1-12 ; 12, 1-5 ; 18, 1-3. Commodus, depicted as cruel (C 10, 1-7 ; 11, 1-7), debauched (3, 6 ; 5, 4 ; 11 ; 10, 8-9) and incompetent (14, 1-15, 8), deserves to be branded 'Lampridian.' Pertinax might be considered a 'Capitoline' ruler because of his unwillingness to assume power (P 4, 10 ; 13, 1-4 ; 15, 8), his measures against delation (6, 8 ; 7, 1), his administrative reforms (6, 6-8, 11) or his deference towards the Senate (13, 2). Didius Iulianus, who came to power in a coup of the praetorians (DI 2, 7 - 3, 3) and menaced the Senate (6, 7) was perhaps a more 'Spartan' emperor. Severus and Caracalla, who executed great numbers of their political enemies, naturally belong in the 'Spartan' category : S 9, 8 ; 12, 1-6 ; 13, 1-9 ; 14, 1 ; 12-13 ; 15, 5-6 ; 18, 4. Elagabalus, whose luxurious banquets were described in fanciful detail, was manifestly 'Lampridian.' The *Aelius*, *Verus* and *Antoninus Geta* probably follow the attributions of the *de Vita Hadriani*, *Vita Marci Antonini Philosophi* and *Antoninus Caracallus* respectively ; the senatorial Clodius Albinus contrasts with the martial Pescennius Niger. The basic typologies submerged beneath the names Spartianus, Capitolinus and Lampridius played an important role in the elaboration of the corpus, even after these particular pseudonyms had been abandoned. Distinguished by military service and feats of arms, the Emperor Aurelian was salutary to the state, but formidable to the Senate, and built a reputation for cruelty. The elderly Tacitus, allegedly a devotee of humane letters, supposedly assumed the purple at the instigation of his senatorial colleagues, despite his advanced age. Carinus, the unworthy son of the Emperor Carus, indulged unnatural passions and profligate luxury in the manner of a Commodus or Elagabalus.

(51) Variants of this word are found in many modern Romance languages : *lamprèda* in Italian, *lamprea* in Spanish, *lamproie* in French, from which our word "lamprey" was

Moreover, the word *lampreda* seems to have been common enough in medieval Latin, since both Blatt and Niermeyer list examples beginning from early in the tenth century ([52]). There is another reading in an eighth-century glossary, which is variously reported in the works of reference ([53]). The derivation of Lampridius from **lampreda* makes obvious sense ; the dissolute emperor indulges himself in luxurious foods, especially the most exquisite kinds of seafood. Such puns are not unprecedented in the literature of the fourth century. One thinks immediately of the witnesses named in the satirical testament of the condemned piglet M. Grunnius Corocotta : Lardio, Ofellicus, Cyminatus, Lucanicus and Tergillus, among others, in the consulship of Clibanatus and Piperatus ([54]). The word "Lucanicus" also occurs as an apparently risible victory title in the *Antoninus Caracallus*, perhaps because of its association with a kind of sausage ([55]). Nor would the name Lampridius contain the only 'proto-Romance' pun in the *HA*. The "enormous size" of the pleasure-seeking Gordian II may be explained with reference to Spanish and Portuguese (*gordo*) ([56]).

The etymologies, typologies and commonplace material associated with the names Spartianus, Capitolinus and Lampridius might have been comprehensible to an audience among the Roman elite of the fourth century. In a speech delivered before the Senate in 389, Pacatus described the court of Theodosius as more austere than a Spartan gymnasium (using the adjective *Spartanus*) ([57]). Pacatus had already described the rigours that Theodosius endured while on campaign : days spent fighting and nights on watch, the extremes of climate, military rations, tents instead of the palace ([58]). Vegetius, in another work dedicated to

derived in the thirteenth century. According to Wartburg and Gamillscheg, the French word is attested as early as the twelfth century : Wartburg 1948-1983 [vols. I-V first ed. 1922-1950] : V, 146-147 ; Gamillscheg 1969 [first ed. 1928].

(52) Blatt 1957 ; Niermeyer 1984 [first ed. 1976].

(53) The *TLL* includes an entry on the noun *lampreda*, a cross-reference to another entry on the word *naupreda*, which has not yet appeared : *TLL* VII, 2, col. 912, 38. The word *lampreda* seems to have appeared in a glossary perhaps as early as the eighth century : Bloch and Wartburg 1975 [first ed. 1932] ; Hofmann 1938-1954 ; Dauzat 1938. Wartburg and Gamillscheg give similar information. The word *lampreda* may have been a variant of *naupreda*, which is attested in a list of animals in the fifth-century Gallic author Polemius Silvius : Pol. Silv., *Lat.* 3 [*MGH AA* IX 1, 544].

(54) Chastagnol 1994 : 434, n. 2 ; Champlin 1987.

(55) Cc. 5, 6. Chastagnol described this reference as *une plaisanterie certainement ajoutée par le rédacteur lui-même.* Chastagnol 1994 : 412, n. 1.

(56) Gd. 21, 2 : *erat corporis uasti*. The vulgar Latin *gurdus* took on the sense of "fat, well-fed" in Portuguese, Spanish and Provençal.

(57) *Pan. Lat.* II(XII) 13, 4 : *ad hoc aulam omnem Spartanis gymnasiis duriorem.*

(58) Many of these passages find parallels in the *HA*. *Pan. Lat.* II(XII) 8, 3 : *Et prius quidem quam ad illa uenio quae aeui maturus egisti, summatim tuum illud attingam cum patre diuino castrense collegium, actas sub pellibus hiemes, aestates inter bella sudatas,*

Theodosius, praised the Lacedaemonians as the first people to reduce war to an art (perhaps a dubious distinction) ([59]). Pacatus also contrasted Theodosius' virtues with the dissolute lifestyles of some previous emperors, who demanded fish from distant shores, birds from foreign lands or flowers out of season. The *HA* often ascribes similar characteristics to its more depraved rulers ([60]). Several of the *Panegyrici Latini* celebrate or anticipate the triumphant return of the emperor to Rome, culminating in his appearance on the Capitol ([61]). While none

dies noctesque proeliando aut uigilando consumptas, grauissimas pugnas terra marique pugnatas. Compare AC 6, 2 : *delicias omnes de castris summouit iussitque eos hiemem sub pellibus agere, nisi corrigerent suos mores*. Note *Pan. Lat.* II (XII) 13, 3 : *modico et castrensi cibo ieiunua longa solantem*. Compare H 10, 2 : *cibis etiam castrensibus in propatulo libenter utens*. PN 10, 3-4 : *idem iussit uinum in expeditione neminem bibere, sed aceto uniuersos esse contentos. idem pistores sequi expeditionem prohibuit, bucellato iubens milites et omnes contentos esse*. 11, 1 : *ante omnes militarem cibum sumpsit*. Note *Pan. Lat.* II(XII) 13, 2 : *a te uoluisti incipere censuram, et impendia palatina minuendo, nec solum abundantem reiciendo sumptum sed uix necessarium usurpando dimensum, quod natura difficillimum est, emendasti uolentes*. Compare AS 15, 2 : *purgauit et Palatium suum comitatumque omnem abiectis ex aulico ministerio cunctis obscenis et infamibus nec quemquam passus est esse in Palatinis non necessarium hominem*. It is interesting to note that a description of Pescennius Niger's stern military discipline ends with the claim that as emperor he refused to become the subject of panegyrics (perhaps hinting that such claims were commonplace in that genre) : PN 11, 5-6.

(59) Veg., *Epit.* III praef. : *Verum apud Athenienses non solum rei bellicae sed etiam diuersarum artium uiguit industria, Lacedaemoniis autem praecipua fuit cura bellorum.*

(60) His comments find many parallels in the outrageous conduct of the Emperor Elagabalus. Note *Pan. Lat.* II(XII) 13, 4 : *flagitare remotorum litorum piscem, peregrini aeris uolucrem, alieni temporis florem*. Compare Hel. 23, 7 : *marinae aquae colymbos exhibuit, in mediterraneis locis maxime*. 23, 8 : *ad mare piscem numquam comedit, in longissimis a mare locis omnia marina semper exhibuit*. Note *Pan. Lat.* II(XII) 14, 1 : *Nam delicati illi ac fluentes, et quales tulit saepe res publica, parum se lautos putabant nisi luxuria uertisset annum, nisi hibernae poculis rosae innatassent, nisi aestiuam in gemmis capacibus glaciem Falerna fregissent*. Compare Hel. 24, 1 : *momentarios de rosato et rosis piscinas exhibuit et lauit cum omnibus suis caldarias de nardo exhibens*. Note also Hel. 19, 5-7 ; 20, 1 ; 24, 3-5 ; 29, 1 ; 8. Note *Pan. Lat.* II(XII) 14, 3 : *Vt taceam infami saepe dilectu scriptos in prouinciis aucipes ductasque sub signis uenatorum cohortes militasse conuiuiis, nonne cognouimus cuiusdam retro principis non prandia saepe sed fercula sestertium milies aestimata patrimoniorum equestrium pretia traxisse* ? Compare Hel. 24, 3 : *idem numquam minus centum sestertiis cenauit, hoc est argenti libris triginta ; aliquando autem tribus milibus sestertium cenauit omnibus supputatis, quae inpendit.* Note also AP 7, 5 : *et mensa eius per proprios seruos, proprios aucupes, piscatores ac uenatores instrueretur*. Note Hel. 27, 3 ; 30, 1.

(61) *Pan. Lat.* VII(VI) 8, 7 : *Te primo ingressu tuo tanta laetitia, tanta frequentia populus Romanus excepit ut, cum te ad Capitolini Iouis gremium uel oculis ferre gestiret, stipatione sui uix ad portas Vrbis admitteret.* X(II) 13, 4 : *O quanto nunc, imperator, illa ciuitas esset augustior, quanto magis hunc natalem suum diem coleret, si uos stipatos uestro senatu in illa Capitolini Iouis arce conspiceret !* Compare Claud., *de Cons. Stilich.* III, 30-34.

of these parallels necessarily demonstrates literary influence, it is interesting to see how different texts elaborate upon the same themes and reflect common ideas about the imperial office.

The name Vulcacius Gallicanus may have suggested the honorific that accompanies it (v.c.). There may also be an element of association or allusion. The *Auidius Cassius*, ascribed to Gallicanus, occurs after the *Vita Marci Antonini Philosophi*, ascribed to Capitolinus. We should perhaps remember that the Gauls unsuccessfully besieged the Capitol late in the fourth century BC (the traditional date is 390 BC) (62). By the end of the fourth century AD, the Gauls were notoriously prone to revolution, as our author himself noted (63). They were also impressive talkers. Gallic orators were especially prized for their eloquence, at least among Symmachus and his associates (64). The sobriquet Gallicanus might apply to a whole class of people : the provincials, affiliated with Ausonius and the Gallic schools, who appear frequently enough in the correspondence of Symmachus (65). These newcomers might well advertise their provincial connections even after they arrived in Rome. By contrast, the name Vulcacius may have scholastic connotations (66). In one of his many controversial works, Jerome reminded Rufinus (a bitter adversary and sometime friend) of a commentator on Cicero called Vulcatius, whom they had read at school (67). Jerome casually invoked the same commentator in a letter to Magnus, a prominent Roman orator (68). We can easily imagine our impostor in some school or other, poring over commentaries on Cicero (69).

(62) An incident noted by countless writers, including of author the dubious *Sulpiciae conquestio* : *Epig. Bob.* 37, 41-44.

(63) T 3, 7 ; Q 7, 1.

(64) Symmachus sought a Gallic rhetorician to train his son : Symm., *Ep.* VI, 34. He himself had been trained by a Gallic rhetorician. Note Symm., *Ep.* IX, 88, 3 : *Gallicanae facundiae haustus requiro.*

(65) Matthews 1971. One thinks of course of Ausonius and Pacatus. The imperial official Protadius, who received sources for his history of Gaul from Symmachus, may provide another example : *PLRE* I, 751-752, Protadius 1. He was urban prefect in 400/401.

(66) The renderings Vulcacius, Vulcatius and Volcatius are alternative spellings of the same name (and are also palaeographically equivalent, since *o* and *u*, *c* and *t* are easily confused in minuscule hands).

(67) Hier., *contra Ruf.* I, 16 [*CCSL* LXXIX 15, 27].

(68) Hier., *Ep.* 70, 2 (using the spelling Volcatius). The letter is dated 396 or 397.

(69) Of course, other explanations are possible. An allusion to "Vulcatius Terentianus" in the *Gordiani Tres* suggests a connection with Volcatius Sedigitus (fl. 100 BC), a Republican scholar cited in relation to Terence and comedy in general : Gd. 21, 5 ; Syme 1968a : 121-122. Other individuals who bore this name are attested. There was the consul of 347 : *PLRE* I, 782-783, Vulcacius Rufinus 25. There was also Lucius Volcatius Tullus (consul in 66 BC) and his son of the same name (consul in 33 BC). Servius' commentary refers to a Vulcanius, sometimes amended to read Vulcatius : Serv., *Ecl.* IX, 46.

Once one starts punning, the habit can be hard to break. We might also advance an etymological explanation for the name Trebellius, based upon its obvious paranomastic possibilities. Trebellius Pollio catalogues the thirty usurpers who allegedly revolted during the reigns of Gallienus and Valerian : a derivation from *rebellis* and its cognates may be unavoidable in these circumstances. Pollio's works include an account of the career of an apocryphal usurper called Trebellianus, a figment apparently derived by deforming the name of the genuine usurper Regilianus ([70]). While it would be convenient to blame this corruption on our author, it seems that the variant Trebellianus had already made an appearance in the tradition of Eutropius before it occurred in the *Tyranni Triginta* ([71]).

Some scholars have sought to explain the pseudonyms as allusions to figures found in literature. Den Hengst suggested that the names Capitolinus and Pollio might be derived from a passage in Juvenal ([72]). He also argued that comments on the works of Pollio found in the prefaces ascribed to Vopiscus were derived from criticism that Suetonius had ascribed to the historian Asinius Pollio ([73]). Birley argued that the names Pollio and Vopiscus alluded to persons in Cicero's speeches and dialogues ([74]). Perhaps appropriately, one C. Iulius Caesar Strabo Vopiscus introduces a digression on humour in the *de Oratore* ([75]). Admittedly, the received text of the dialogue identifies this individual only by the name Caesar, although a glossator or commentator may have supplied the necessary information. Cicero's Vopiscus contends that Sicilians, Rhodians, Byzantines and Athenians excel in wit, perhaps casting some light on Vopiscus' alleged Syracusan origins ([76]).

The connection between the Ciceronian figure and the spurious author is especially appropriate, given the context in which the dubious Vopiscus first appears. Vopiscus makes his entrance on the Hilaria, a festival of wild rejoicing

(70) T 26, 1-7 ; Syme 1968a : 43-52. He was an emperor and even struck coins, we are assured.

(71) Eutr., *Breu.* IX, 8, 1. This issue is discussed further in Chapter Six.

(72) Den Hengst 1981 : 68-69. Note Iuv. VI, 385-388 : *quaedam de numero Lamiarum ac nominis Appi | et farre et uino Ianum Vestamque rogabat, | an Capitolinam deberat Pollio quercum | sperare et fidibus promittere.*

(73) A 2, 1 ; Q 1, 3 ; Suet., *Iul.* 56, 4 ; den Hengst 1981 : 106-107.

(74) A. Birley 2002. See also : Reekmans 2003 ; Idem 1997. Note also that the poet Statius dedicated some works to another Vopiscus, praised for his learning : Stat., *Silu.* I prol. ; I, 3.

(75) Cic., *de Orat.* II, 217-297.

(76) Cic., *de Orat.* II, 217 : *itaque cum quosdam Graecos inscriptos libros esse uidissem 'de ridiculis,' nonnullam in spem ueneram posse me ex iis aliquid discere. inueni autem ridicula et salsa multa Graecorum – nam et Siculi in eo genere et Rhodi et Byzantii et praeter ceteros Attici excellunt – ; sed qui eius rationem quondam conati sunt artemque tradere, sic insulsi extiterunt, ut nihil aliud eorum nisi ipsa insulsitas rideatur.*

during which social conventions were suspended. Herodian associated this festival with spectacle, licence, revelry and above all disguise, claiming that during this period it was difficult to tell true from false ([77]). Herodian's comments reveal the connotations of the festal setting of the preface to the *Diuus Aurelianus*. Apparently joking, the urban prefect Iunius Tiberianus instructs Vopiscus to write whatever he wants, safe in the knowledge that great historians such as Livy, Sallust, Tacitus and Pompeius Trogus themselves committed numerous errors ([78]). This suspect injunction may represent a deliberate hint on the part of the author that his collection of biographies was grounded in falsehood. As Syme observed, "a Prefect of the City in the carnival season encouraged the author to go forward on paths of mendacity" ([79]). We could read the preface to the *Diuus Aurelianus* as a coded revelation of the devious purposes of the author, a sort of confession of hoaxing : "And here and there the deceiver lifts the veil, gently. The exordium of the *Vita Aureliani* conveys the prime disclosure. It is urbane and elegant" ([80]). By situating this preface on the Hilaria, a festival of masquerade and social mixing, the author perhaps gave some indication of the spirit in which the rest of his work was to be read, alerting a knowing audience to his fabrications. But perhaps an alternative interpretation is available to us. We might claim that the preface to *Diuus Aurelianus* represents a ludic moment in an otherwise more serious text. The author deliberately shifted into a festal mode, marking this transition by invoking the Hilaria. In that setting, he felt free to make claims and even revelations that he would otherwise have avoided. That moment was not perhaps sufficient to destabilise the general economy of the text.

A pattern has emerged from our analysis of the six pseudonyms. We first observed that its imposture of collective authorship and early date, together with the imperial subject matter of the *HA*, brought to mind a collection such as the *Panegyrici Latini*. Next we found that the names Spartianus, Capitolinus and Lampridius disclosed typologies of character possibly related to commonplace material found in the panegyrics themselves. We wondered whether Vulcacius Gallicanus might not have taken his name from a lost commentator on Cicero, apparently popular in the Roman schools towards the end of the fourth century. It also transpired that Flavius Vopiscus Syracusius may have been modelled on a disputant in one of Cicero's dialogues on oratory, no doubt a text familiar to rhetoricians and their students. Trebellius Pollio may have taken his name from a figure discussed in the speeches. Finally, one might add that a Bordeaux rhetorician active late in the fifth century bore the name Lampridius, although

(77) Herod. I, 10, 5.
(78) A 2, 2.
(79) Syme 1978 : 187.
(80) Syme 1968a : 2.

this was probably a mere coincidence ([81]). Taken together, these observations suggest that the six figments known as Spartianus, Capitolinus, Gallicanus, Lampridius, Pollio and Vopiscus may have emerged from a scholastic context. Both grammar and rhetoric seem to have exercised their malign influence over our impostor, who may have belonged among the minor intellectuals reciting their speeches and correcting their manuscripts in the Forum of Trajan late in the fourth century.

Conclusion. The corpus of thirty books known as the *HA* was the work of one author, an impostor with scholarly proclivities. The evidence for single authorship is overwhelming, and it is for this reason that the modern consensus is built around this hypothesis. The attributions of authorship are themselves incoherent, so that the careers of several of the supposed authors (Spartianus and Capitolinus and perhaps also Lampridius) stretch over several decades. Otherwise eccentric features appear throughout the lives ascribed to all six suppositious authors, who lapse into similar errors and perpetrate the same frauds. Moreover, a number of linguistic quirks are replicated throughout the corpus, reflecting the curious usage of one writer. Bogus names, some derived from the nomenclature of genuine figures, are ubiquitous. Even the six pseudonyms themselves seem to contain various double meanings, suggesting that the whole apparatus of attributions was an elaborate imposture. Corpora of imperial panegyrics may have provided the model for this travesty of collective authorship.

Despite all the arguments advanced in this chapter, there can be no suggestion that the *HA* is an homogenous work. The incorporation of material from diverse sources (sometimes crudely paraphrased) has left its traces in the text. The figure we have described as an author was responsible for incorporating the work of many other writers into his compilation. At the same time, our impostor was much more than a redactor. His intentions, his interests, his genius for improvisation are heavily imprinted upon the collection. If we were to excise all the fabrications of our impostor a very different work would remain : a crude paraphrase of an earlier series of imperial biographies, as well as some fragments reflecting the traditions of abbreviated history in Latin and narrative history in Greek. These remnants would be most instructive to historians, but they would bear little resemblance to the text we possess. We can now turn to the question of the date and context of the *HA*, presenting a broad range of evidence that contradicts the dedications (to Diocletian, Constantine and private individuals allegedly active under Constantius I) found throughout the lives.

(81) The name Lampridius is first attested in an inscription of 428 : *CIL* III, 14239 (8) ; *PLRE* II, 656, Lampridius 1. A Gallic aristocrat of the age of Sidonius Apollinaris also went by that name : *PLRE* II, 656, Lampridius 2. He taught rhetoric at Bordeaux, and was killed by his slaves in 476. One might wonder whether the ancestors of this unfortunate orator were active in the same profession a century earlier, although we cannot base any conclusions on speculation of this kind.

CHAPTER TWO

Date

The Date of the Corpus. We have established that one author assumed the identities of Aelius Spartianus, Iulius Capitolinus, Vulcacius Gallicanus (v.c.), Aelius Lampridius, Trebellius Pollio and Flavius Vopiscus Syracusius. It is now time to discuss the date at which this scholarly impostor wrote, compiled and translated. The dedications to Diocletian, Constantine and private individuals under Constantius I found throughout the lives are clearly spurious. While it is easy enough to reject these apostrophes, determining the actual date of the corpus is much more challenging. There are indications that the *HA* was written between the death of Theodosius and the turn of the fifth century (i.e. between 395 and 400) ([1]). We can be reasonably certain that it was composed early in the reign of the Western Emperor Honorius (395-423). This chapter presents the sort of evidence that ancient historians look for when trying to establish the date of a problem text : administrative terminology and allusions to events. While such material is clearly valuable, it also raises very great methodological difficulties. Moreover, merely establishing the date of a text is not especially informative. The next chapter will attempt to place the *HA* within its context, focusing on networks of cultural production associated with the Roman aristocracy in the last decades of the fourth century.

The Dedications in the *HA*. Dessau demonstrated that those passages in the *HA* that name the Emperors Diocletian, Constantius I and Constantine could not have been written during their reigns. Lampridius would not have offered panegyrics of Diocletian, Maximian, Maxentius and Licinius to Constantine, who ruthlessly execrated these figures after their deaths ([2]). Pollio, who allegedly wrote at Rome before 305, would have addressed the Emperor Maximian, and not Constantius I (a Caesar in distant Gaul) ([3]). Capitolinus, Spartianus and Gallicanus would not have dedicated their works to Diocletian, when they too

(1) Syme suggested a date "in or about the year 395." Syme 1968a : 220. Chastagnol seems ultimately to have preferred the year 399, or even perhaps 400 : Chastagnol 1994 : xxxi-xxxii. Given the limits of the evidence, these positions are not easily distinguishable.

(2) Dessau 1889 : 338-339.

(3) Dessau 1892 : 564-568.

wrote at Rome ([4]). The various dedications found throughout the *HA* reflect the ascendancy of the house of Constantine, which was by no means established during the period in which Pollio and Vopiscus are meant to have written. It is especially suspicious that Pollio and Vopiscus (both allegedly writing before 306) should refer to a genealogical link between Constantius I and Claudius II, since this connection was first invented after the fall of Maximian (310), who provided the regime of Constantine with an element of dynastic legitimacy up until his death ([5]). These observations suggest that the dedications are an imposture, which obscures the actual date of the text.

It seems that the authenticity of the dedications can be doubted on historical grounds. Furthermore, some of the dedications in the *HA* could not have been addressed to any reigning emperor. The author, for example, gave some inapposite advice to the Emperor Constantine about the influence of eunuchs :

> I know, emperor, how dangerous it is to say these words to an emperor who has been in subjection to such people, but (now that you have learned for the good of the state how much evil these pests bring with them, and how they defraud emperors) you keep them in their proper place, prohibiting them from wearing the *chlamys*, but instead confining them to the necessary duties of your household ([6]).

This was not the sort of praise that Roman emperors were accustomed to receive. Nor would Constantine have welcomed the suggestion that he had expressly commissioned a life of the depraved Elagabalus, a farrago of gluttony and smut ([7]). The emperor addressed in these terms was almost certainly already dead, and it would have required considerable bravery to voice such sentiments during the reign of his immediate successor. What appear to be barely dissimulated criticisms of Constantine may have taken their cue from the *Caesares* of the Emperor Julian, who bitterly traduced his uncle. Nevertheless, the hostile tradition is well represented in other late antique sources.

The anachronistic character of the dedications suggests that they were written some time after the death of Constantine, since a close contemporary would have

(4) Dessau 1889 : 337.

(5) On the connection with Claudius II, see : Hel. 35, 2 ; Gall. 7, 1 ; 14, 3 ; T 31, 6 ; Cl. 1, 1 ; 3, 1 ; 10, 1-7 ; 13, 2-3 ; A 44, 4-5 ; Baldini 2002 ; den Hengst 1981 : 81-82 ; Syme 1974 ; Seeck 1912 : 594-595 ; Dessau 1892 : 579-582 ; Idem 1889 : 340-344. Lampridius, Pollio and Vopiscus corroborate the anachronistic pedigree.

(6) AS 67, 1 : *scio, imperator, quo periculo ista dicantur apud imperatorem, qui talibus seruiit, sed salua re publica posteaquam intellegisti, quid mali clades istae habeant et quemadmodum principes circumueniant, et tu eos eo loci habes, ut nec clamide uti iusseris, sed de necessitatibus domesticis delegaris.* Chastagnol described this as an *allégation invraisemblable dans un écrit adressé à l'empereur ainsi critiqué.* Chastagnol 1994 : 636, n. 1.

(7) Hel. 35, 1.

been less likely to make such errors. Sometimes even the language of the apostrophes reflects their late date ([8]). Once one accepts that the dedications are spurious, there is no good reason to place the lives in the reigns of Diocletian, Constantius I and Constantine. Since we cannot accept the evidence of the dedications at face value, we must instead look throughout the corpus for whatever indications of its date are available. The following pages discuss some administrative terminology and allusions to events found in the *HA*. This evidence strongly suggests that the author wrote at some point soon after about 395, although it cannot rule out an even later date.

Some Administrative Anachronisms. Arguments involving administrative anachronisms have played a considerable role in the long controversy over the date of the *HA* ([9]). Scholars have argued for more than a century that references to aspects of the Roman administration found throughout the lives reflect conditions much later than the reigns of Diocletian, Constantius I and Constantine. Nevertheless, arguments derived from institutional arrangements and official terminology are often problematic ([10]). Our knowledge of the evolution of the Roman state over the course of the fourth century is quite fragmentary. The first mention of an apparent innovation in inscriptions, legislation or literary sources is not necessarily a reliable indication of the date at which that change was made. It is very difficult to prove definitively that an institution or practice lacked obscure antecedents, and "official posts or titles can turn out to have existed well before their assumed earliest attestations" ([11]). Furthermore, the meanings of

(8) For example, when the author claimed that he wrote "out of consideration for the Caesar Constantius" (*intuitu Constanti Caesaris*), he may have used the form *intuitu* in an anachronistic manner : Max. 16, 2 ; T 5, 2 ; Cl. 1, 1 ; *TLL* VII, 2, col. 97, 46 ; *BTL* ; *CLCLT*. This usage appears very frequently in authors from the second half of the fourth century.

(9) Syme noted that : "Arguments based on laws and institutions, on civilian and military posts, have been a frequent exhibit." Syme 1978 : 176. I would like to thank Peter Brennan for his generous help with this section, although of course any errors remain my own.

(10) Syme argued that anachronisms "can hardly permit a close dating." Syme 1968a : 188.

(11) Syme 1978 : 177. Here the imperial victory titles provide a salutary example. The Emperor Probus is lauded as a conqueror of the Franks (*Francicus*) : Pr. 11, 9. Seeck argued that the victory title *Francicus* was first attested in the reigns of Valentinian, Valens and Gratian : Chastagnol 1994 : cxviii ; Seeck 1894 : 218. Barnes noted, however, that a new inscription bearing the title had come to light from the reign of Julian. Barnes also argued convincingly that the title could have been employed as early as the reign of Constantine, when the Caesar Crispus won victories over the Franks (in 319) : Barnes 1994. Here, as ever, the problem is one of documentation (at p. 14) : "[T]he epigraphical attestation of victory titles for all Roman emperors after Constantine is extremely sporadic."

terms may change over time ([12]). Nor can we always rely on the sources themselves. The enactment of laws was a repetitious affair, and the law codes display a bias towards more recent constitutions. The extant administrative documents are often the end product of a long process of quite unsystematic revision, creating almost impossible problems for modern readers ([13]). Given the difficulties in assigning dates to these key sources, a measure of caution is justified in dealing with the evidence of so-called administrative anachronisms.

Some features of the *HA* exacerbate our already considerable difficulties. The administrative terminology of the text does not belong to one period only. Earliest in putative date are some archaising references to Republican or pseudo-Republican institutions, the blighted harvest of dubious antiquarian research ([14]). Our impostor seriously believed that it was possible somehow to restore the original state of the empire, to return the government to its pristine condition ([15]). He enriched the efforts of his imagination with words and notions lifted from his sources. The lives of emperors from Hadrian to Elagabalus include abundant administrative terminology from the second century AD, carried across from a much earlier series of imperial biographies, which itself drew upon earlier documents and sources. This accurate and sometimes obsolete administrative vocabulary accompanies genuine information on the ancestry, nomenclature and private careers of the emperors in question. Other references to the administration probably reflect the language of the common source of the fourth-century epitomators, perhaps written as early as the reign of Constantine ([16]). We must also concede that the author himself had some direct experience of the Roman bureaucracy of his day, and it is possible that he exercised an administrative

(12) For example, we are told that the emperor Carinus made his *cancellarius* urban prefect : Car. 16, 3. This passage probably refers to a mere porter, rather than the high official recorded in the *Notitia Dignitatum*, an inscription of uncertain date (*CIL* VI, 9226, 10-11) and the works of Cassiodorus and Sidonius Apollinaris : *TLL* III, col. 226, 35 ; *BTL* ; *CLCLT*.

(13) Kulikowski 2000 : 360.

(14) These figments include the proconsular governor of Ciliciae (A 42, 2 ; Car. 4, 6), the otherwise unprecedented and manifestly spurious *senatus consultum tacitum* (Gd. 12, 1-4) and the notorious interregnum between the reigns of Aurelius and Tacitus, already established in the tradition by the error of Aurelius Victor. There is also a wildly anachronistic reference to the "minor priests," modelled on Livy : OM 7, 2 ; Liv. XXII, 57, 3. See : Paschoud 1996 : 197 ; Chastagnol 1994 : lxxxii ; cxv ; 458, n. 1 ; 716. n. 2 ; 1014, n. 2.

(15) AC 14, 6 ; Val. 4, 2 ; 6, 3 ; T 5, 1 ; Tac. 12, 1 ; 18, 4 ; 19, 1 ; 3 ; 6 ; Pr. 6, 1. Gallicanus, Pollio and Vopiscus express this commonplace idea.

(16) The claim that Diocletian commanded the *domestici* probably appeared in the common source of the *Carus et Carinus et Numerianus* (Car. 13, 1) and Aurelius Victor's *Caesares* (Aur. Vic., *Caes*. 39, 1). This common source, the so-called *Kaisergeschichte*, almost certainly reflected developments of the reign of Constantine.

function at some point in his career ([17]). We cannot assume, however, that our impostor presented a full and accurate account of the administrative arrangements of his own period, since that was never his purpose.

We must remember that our sensitivity to historical anachronisms is quite unusual. Adopting an essentially diachronic approach, stressing the causal relations between events, we comprehend the past as an irreversible succession of distinct periods. By contrast, some late antique texts demonstrate a synchronic understanding, according to which aspects of different eras persist simultaneously within a moralising rhetorical tradition of examples and comparisons ([18]). Vegetius, for instance, wrote his treatise on military affairs based upon on materials that described Roman armies of much earlier periods ([19]). The force he depicted seemed to span a period of several hundred years, and Vegetius had no real sense of how the Roman army might have evolved over this time. Vegetius, or the tradition on which he drew, constructed an idealised image of the Roman military as it used to be at some point in the ancestral past ([20]). His notion that a long period of peace led to the degeneration of military discipline was ultimately derived from Sallust ([21]). This claim seems almost wilfully blind to us, since Vegetius wrote after a century of almost incessant warfare, which culminated in the defeat at Adrianople (378). Even worse was to come in the reign of Honorius.

Administrative documents themselves demonstrate similar ways of thinking. Kulikowski noted that the description of the Western empire in the *Notitia Dignitatum* reflects "an unknown number of progressively overlaid changes" and "cannot be subjected to precise or unitary dating." He claimed that, "[T]here is no indication that any systematic effort was ever made to delete the record of obsolete offices or destroyed or disbanded units" ([22]). He described the extant version as "an essentially antiquarian work with a more or less purely ideological purpose" ([23]). While this intervention represents a helpful correction to false assumptions surrounding our Roman sources, the opposition between administrative documents and antiquarian treatises is almost certainly false. The rhetoric of late antique government was suffused with dubious appeals to antiquity, since

(17) Honoré 1998.

(18) These modes of thinking, represented in some antiquarian works, administrative documents and technical treatises, seem to have existed alongside the quite different norms exemplified in the historical works of Ammianus.

(19) Veg., *Epit.* I, praef. ; 8. There are some references to fourth-century developments : Veg., *Epit.* I, 17 (Herculean legions of Diocletian and Maximian) ; 20 (Goths, Alans and Huns) ; III, 26 (Huns and Alans).

(20) Veg., *Epit.* I, 10 (*ueteres*) ; 11 (*antiqui*) ; 13 (*maiores*). The ancients were almost divine in their wisdom : Veg., *Epit.* II, 20-21.

(21) Veg., *Epit.* I, 8 ; 28.

(22) Kulikowski 2000 : 375.

(23) Kulikowski 2000 : 359.

innovations often usurped the authority of ancient precedent. We can also draw potentially instructive parallels with other kinds of texts. The world depicted in the *Tabula Peutingeriana* includes the imperial capitals of Rome, Constantinople and Antioch alongside the town of Herculaneum (destroyed by a volcanic eruption in 79) and the independent kingdom of the Cottian Alps (suppressed by Nero), as well as marginal zones called Francia and Alemannia (leaving aside some rather dubious Biblical geography). The Arch of Constantine incorporates spolia from the reigns of Trajan, Hadrian and Marcus Aurelius, apparently insensitive to differences of style. A panel in its fourth-century frieze depicts Constantine delivering a speech from the Rostra. He is flanked by two good emperors (Marcus Aurelius and Hadrian) and surrounded by architectural symbols of previous reigns.

Because his mindset was so different from our own, our scholarly impostor may not have perceived his own anachronisms as such. These anomalies involve almost every aspect of the Roman government : the organisation of the army, the division of the provinces, the administration of Italy and the status of the urban prefecture. It is perhaps best to begin with the army, the largest and most elaborate part of the Roman state ([24]). Over the course of the fourth century, a distinction in status developed between the field army (*comitatenses*) and the frontier soldiers (*limitanei*, *riparii* or *ripenses*), much to the advantage of the former. The nature and timing of this change remains the subject of much controversy, and it would be unhelpful to enter that debate here ([25]). Nonetheless, a reference to the *limitanei* in the *Probus* (purportedly written in the reign of Constantius I) is probably anachronistic ([26]). Far more troubling, however, is the suggestion that Alexander Severus granted some frontier soldiers inalienable title to land, which their sons inherited along with the obligation to serve in the army ([27]). This measure, probably inconceivable in the reign of Alexander Severus, prefigures much later developments ([28]). An early reference to this form of title appears in a law

(24) For surveys of the development of the late Roman army, see : Nicasie 1998 ; Southern and Ramsey Dixon 1996 ; Jones 1973 [first ed. 1964] : I, 607-686.

(25) For a range of views, see : Nicasie 1998 : 18-22 ; Southern and Ramsey Dixon 1996 : 15-20. The earliest attestation of the distinction between *comitatenses* and *ripenses* occurs in a law of Constantine of 325 : *CTh* VII, 20, 4 ; Southern and Ramsey Dixon 1996 : 35-37.

(26) Pr. 14, 7 ; Chastagnol 1994 : clxix-clxx ; Syme 1968a : 46-47. The word *limitaneus* occurs in sources from the second half of the fourth century, although sometimes with reference to a much earlier period. *Limitaneus* (substantive), frontier soldier : PN 7, 7 ; *CTh* XI, 1, 21 (385) ; *CI* I, 27, 2, 8 ; 13 (534) ; *TLL* VII, 2, col. 1418, 11 ; *BTL* ; *CLCLT*. *Limitaneus* (adjective), concerning the frontier : AS 58, 4 ; Pr. 14, 7 ; *TLL* VII, 2, col. 1417, 83 ; *BTL* ; *CLCLT*.

(27) AS 58, 4.

(28) Schwartz claimed : *[C]ette phrase suppose des conquêtes territoriales non attestées sous cet empereur et il faut admettre que le rédacteur de l'Historia Augusta a*

of 409, although not in relation to the soldiers of the frontier ([29]). By contrast, Eastern laws of 423 and 443 seek to prevent the alienation of lands set aside for frontier soldiers ([30]). Jones argued convincingly that the *limitanei* were assigned fields at a late date, and he seems to have placed this development around the turn of the fifth century ([31]). On this basis, we might argue that the relevant passage in the *Alexander Severus* contains an administrative anachronism, which places the life somewhere in the reigns of Theodosius or Honorius. The author seems to have assumed that the army had always been arranged as it was in this later period.

Some military terminology found throughout the lives may provoke further comment. The word *lusoria* appears from the end of the fourth century to describe patrol boats used on the Rhine frontier, although the boats themselves may have been instituted much earlier ([32]). Ammianus discussed *lusoriae* in the context of Julian's campaigns in Gaul (356-359), while patrol boats may possibly have played a role in campaigns against the barbarians conducted in the reign of Constantius I ([33]). The word *draconarius*, applied to standard bearers, first occurs in Vegetius and Ammianus, although the Roman army used dragon standards from a much earlier date ([34]). The term *bucellatum* first appears in a law of 360, although again Roman soldiers must surely have eaten rations before then ([35]). The words *carrago* and *drungus*, applied to barbarian formations, do

antidaté cette institution de soldats-paysans qu'il voyait peut-être fonctionner de son temps. Schwartz 1970 : 237. Nonetheless, MacMullen was inclined to accept the authenticity of this passage : MacMullen 1963 : 12-18.

(29) *CTh* VII, 15, 1 (409) ; Syme 1968a : 46-47. Syme conceded that "The practice may have had a much earlier origin." The law in question refers to the practice as long-established, but few Roman legislators flaunted their novelties.

(30) *CTh* VII, 15, 2 (423) ; *Nou. Theod.* II, 24, 4 (443) ; Jones 1973 : I, 653 ; II, 1272, n. 108.

(31) Jones 1973 : I, 649-651. This view finds recent endorsement : Southern and Ramsey Dixon 1996 : 57.

(32) *Lusoria*, patrol boat (apparently used on the Rhine frontier) : Q 15, 1 ; Veg., *Epit.* II, 1 ; *CTh* VII, 17, 1 (412) ; *TLL* VII, 2, col. 1868, 50 ; *BTL* ; *CLCLT* ; Reddé 1986 : 130-133 ; Demougeot 1953 : 379-380. The phrase *lusoria nauis* occurs twice in Ammianus (Amm. XVII, 2, 3 ; XVIII, 2, 12). The word *lusoria* was applied to pleasure boats from a very early period.

(33) *Pan. Lat.* VII(VI) 4, 2-3.

(34) *Draconarius*, standard bearer : A 31, 7 ; Amm. XX, 4, 18 ; Veg., *Epit.* I, 20 ; II, 7 ; 13 ; *TLL* V, 1, col. 2065, 13 ; *BTL* ; *CLCLT* ; Desbordes and Ratti 2000 : 135-136 ; Moes 1980 : 247. Found otherwise in John of Lydus (transliterated into Greek), the law codes and some inscriptions. The Roman army used *dracones* from an earlier date. See Nem., *Cyn.* 85.

(35) *Bucellatum*, biscuit, rations : AC 5, 3 ; PN 10, 4 ; Pr. 4, 6 ; *TLL* II, col. 2228, 5 ; *BTL* ; *CLCLT* ; Syme 1968a : 112. Found otherwise in Ammianus (Amm. XVII, 8, 2), Paulinus of Nola, Plinius Valerianus, the law codes (from 360) and (transliterated into Greek) in Olympiodorus.

not appear in the literary language until the end of the fourth century, when they were grudgingly admitted to the classicising idiom ([36]). Considered together, these apparently anachronistic terms might provide an indication of date, although this line of argument could be opposed on various grounds.

The usage of writers of the second half of the fourth century is probably over-represented in the extant corpus of Latin literature, while comparatively little survives from the reigns of Diocletian and Constantine. For that reason, much of the terminology noted above may have been in circulation before the dates at which it is first attested in our works of reference. Commenting on the occurrence of the word *drungus*, Rance argued "its first appearance in *extant* texts in the late fourth century is due primarily to the absence of earlier authors prepared to use such Vulgar Latin terminology inconsistent with stylistic purity" ([37]). Only "a dearth of earlier extant texts either with sufficient technical content or without prejudice against 'barbarian' or vulgar vocabulary" prevented the word from appearing much earlier ([38]). Even where an author comments that a word is new, we cannot assume that it is a neologism, since it may be a new word only with reference to the literary norm ([39]). Nevertheless, these arguments need not entirely prevent us from using the evidence of vocabulary as an indication of date. The evolution of the literary language may itself provide information on date, based upon the point at which non-literary vocabulary broke into otherwise classicising texts. After all, our impostor shares several different items of technical vocabulary with writers such as Ammianus (*bucellatum*, *carrago*, *draconarius* and also *iudiciale carpentum*) and Vegetius (*draconarius*, *drungus* and *lusoria*) ([40]). The most likely explanation is that these authors wrote at around the same time ([41]).

Our author was constantly vigilant for abuses of the system of military requisitioning, and several spurious imperial letters impose restraints upon the exac-

(36) *Carrago*, wagon-train (a German loan word) : Gall. 13, 9 ; Cl. 6, 6 ; 8, 2 ; A 11, 6 ; *TLL* III, col. 497, 28 ; *BTL* ; *CLCLT* ; Desbordes and Ratti 2000 : 159-160 ; Paschoud 1996 : 88-89 ; Chastagnol 1994 : lxxxix ; 924-926 ; Syme 1968a : 112. Found otherwise only in Ammianus (Amm. XXXI, 7, 7). *Drungus*, war band (of barbarians) : Pr. 19, 2 ; *TLL* V, 1, col. 2071, 1 ; *BTL* ; *CLCLT* ; Rance 2004 ; Syme 1968a : 112. Found otherwise in Vegetius (Veg., *Epit.* III, 16 ; 19). The word appears in Greek from the fifth century onwards. Rance claimed (at p. 100) : "This is the only non-technical Latin work to contain the word *drungus*, though the author of the *Historia Augusta* appears to have been in some measure sensitive to contemporary military terminology."

(37) Rance 2004 : 104.

(38) Rance 2004 : 126.

(39) Note the following examples from Vegetius : Veg., *Epit.* II, 1 (*uexillatio*) ; 7 (*draco*) ; 19 (*supernumerarius*) ; III, 1 (*comes*).

(40) Vegetius and our author also use the verb *epitomare* : T 30, 22 ; Veg., *Epit.* I, 8 ; *TLL* V, 2, col. 692, 76 ; *BTL* ; *CLCLT* ; Moes 1980 : 133.

(41) Chastagnol has argued that our author imitated Vegetius : Chastagnol 1974.

tions of the soldiery ([42]). Here the impostor reflected the interests and values of the landed elite, who naturally desired to limit the impact of taxation on their estates and dependants. The author was an astute critic of practices stigmatised in the law codes. A spurious imperial grant in the *Diuus Claudius* forbids the commutation of rations into gold (*adaeratio*), considered as an abuse of the tax system ([43]). A law of 325 prohibited the practice of extracting money payments from the provincials in place of rations, although it did not use the word *adaeratio* ([44]). A law of 364 indicated that members of the imperial bodyguard might obtain the market price for their subsistence allowances, "in accordance with ancient custom" ([45]). Nonetheless, several laws promulgated late in the fourth century reiterated the prohibition against commutation ([46]). We might choose to connect the spurious grant found in the *Diuus Claudius* with this apparent program of legislation. In any case, commutation seems to have been regularised in the first decade of the fifth century ([47]). The same might be said about the practice of extorting perquisites from the rations of the troops (*stellatura*) ([48]). Pescennius Niger and Alexander Severus are shown punishing tribunes who obtain such payments ([49]). Once again, the author seems to have castigated a practice that was gaining respectability late in the fourth century, since a law of 406 regulates *stellatura* as an established right ([50]). One might argue that our impostor's conservative sensibilities prompted him to oppose abuses that were either widely accepted or in the process of being regularised in his own day. His generally fierce views on the enforcement of military discipline and his sometimes perceptive complaints about a range of other administrative practices support this suggestion ([51]).

(42) Goffart 1988 : 46, n. 16 ; 47, n. 18-19.

(43) Cl. 14, 14 ; Southern and Ramsey Dixon 1996 : 81 ; Chastagnol 1994 : clxvi-clxix ; Jones 1973 : I, 645-646.

(44) *CTh* VII, 4, 1 (325). The verb *adaerare*, meaning 'reduce to cash terms, value' first occurs towards the end of the fourth century : Cl. 14, 14 ; Amm. XXXI, 14, 2 ; *TLL* I, col. 562, 37 ; *BTL* ; *CLCLT*.

(45) *CTh* VII, 4, 10 (364) : *iuxta ueteris moris obseruantiam*.

(46) *CTh* VII, 4, 18 (393) ; 19 (393) ; 20 (393) ; 21 (396) ; 22 (396).

(47) *CTh* VII, 4, 26 (406) ; 29 (407) ; 30 (409) ; 31 (409) ; 32 (412) ; 34 (414) ; 35 (423) ; 36 (424) ; Goffart 1988 : 51-53.

(48) *Stellatura*, a portion of the rations paid to the military tribunes, a form of corruption : PN 3, 8 ; AS 15, 5 ; *BTL* ; *CLCLT* ; Souter 1996 : 387 ; Syme 1968a : 112. Found otherwise in the law codes from the end of the fourth century onwards.

(49) PN 3, 8 ; AS 15, 5.

(50) *CTh* VII, 4, 28, 1 (406) ; Southern and Ramsey Dixon 1996 : 81.

(51) Macrinus had hoped to abolish the legal force of the decisions of previous emperors, substituting in their place the general operation of the law, so that special favours did not give rise to general abuses : OM 13, 1 ; Turcan 1993 : 139-140. A spurious letter urges a fictitious prefect to draw rations from provinces in which goods are most plentiful : T 18, 7. The author claimed that Ballista avoided supernumerary or superfluous

The forms of provincial administration envisaged in the lives are often suspect or anachronistic (and sometimes quite ridiculous). A reference to the prefect of Illyricum and Gaul (*praefectus Illyrici et Galliarum*) is manifestly spurious, since this otherwise unknown prefecture combines two regions that were not even geographically contiguous ([52]). Barnes argued that "the two components of this fictitious and composite prefecture only acquired separate existence in 340 and 343" ([53]). Moreover, the whole system of regional prefectures had developed gradually from the reign of Constantine onwards ([54]). Someone writing in the reign of Constantius I could hardly have devised the prefecture in question, while also inventing the regional prefectures themselves. This example probably involves an administrative anachronism, which sets the life in question (the *Tyranni Triginta*) at least four decades after its putative date. The terminology used throughout the lives in discussing the diocese of Thrace raises further issues. The author almost invariably uses the plural form *Thraciae* in referring to this region. Zawadzki pointed out that the plural form *Thraciae* occurs only in documents and sources from the last decades of the fourth century onwards ([55]). Since Thrace itself had been divided into several provinces from an early date, it is not immediately clear what substantive change may underlie this change in terminology. Nevertheless, the pattern that Zawadzki discerned is visible in the literary sources, and may indicate the presence of an anachronism of some kind.

Chastagnol advanced an interesting and influential argument based upon what appears to be a catalogue of the Italian provinces in a biographical notice on the usurper Tetricus ([56]). According to our author, Aurelian suffered Tetricus to continue his public career even after his defeat :

> But overcome by a sense of shame, this excessively rigorous man made him over whom he had celebrated a triumph the governor of all Italy (that is Campania,

appointments : T 18, 11. The author criticised the fact that soldiers engaged in civilian occupations while allegedly in service : Max. 8, 4.

(52) T 18, 5 ; Barnes 1987 ; Seeck 1894. Some have suggested that Ausonius and his son may have jointly governed some such administrative monstrosity for a brief period : Chastagnol 1994 : cxvii-cxviii.

(53) Barnes 1987 : 23.

(54) According to Syme, "regional prefectures did not emerge until the late years of Constantine." Syme 1978 : 177.

(55) Zawadzki 1976. The plural form is very common in the *HA* : PN 5, 6 ; Cc. 5, 8 ; Gd. 26, 4 ; MB 7, 2 ; Gall. 5, 6 ; T 12, 13 ; 29, 1 ; 33, 5 ; A 10, 2 ; 17, 2 ; 22, 2 ; 32, 2 ; 41, 8 ; Pr. 16, 3 ; 18, 1 ; Q 5, 1 ; 15, 5 ; Car. 9, 4. The databases (*BTL* and *CLCLT*) include occurrences of the plural in Ammianus, Jerome, Rufinus and Orosius. The plural occurs frequently in the *Notitia Dignitatum*, although the singular is also found. In Barnes' transcription, one manuscript of the Verona list apparently reads *Diocensis tracoae*, probably a genitive singular : Barnes 1982 : 201-208. For various views, see : Desbordes and Ratti 2000 : 55 ; Paschoud 1996 : 87-88 ; Chastagnol 1994 : cxxi.

(56) Chastagnol 1963 ; Idem 1955.

Samnium, Lucania-Bruttium, Apulia-Calabria, Etruria and Umbria, Picenum and Flaminia and all the *regio annonaria*) and he allowed Tetricus not only to live, but also to maintain the supreme dignity ([57]).

This passage contrasts the six *regiones suburbicariae* (Campania, Samnium, Lucania-Bruttium, Apulia-Calabria, Etruria and Umbria, Picenum and Flaminia), administered from Rome, with the *regio annonaria*, governed from Milan. The passage in question is almost certainly anachronistic. Chastagnol noted that the first reference to the *regiones suburbicariae* came in a law of 359, while the first allusion to the *regio annonaria* occurred in Ammianus Marcellinus, with reference to the events of 364 ([58]). But Chastagnol went further than this, arguing that the passage on Tetricus provided a *terminus ante quem* for the composition of the *Tyranni Triginta*. Based on his reconstruction of the provincial administration of Italy, Chastagnol claimed that this passage must have been written before the end of 398 ([59]). According to Chastagnol, this catalogue must have been written before Flaminia was split from Picenum, to become part of the *regio annonaria* (allegedly at the end of 398), and also before the new province of Valeria was created (apparently before December 399) ([60]).

Following Chastagnol, one could argue that the enumeration of the provinces of Italy found in the *Tyranni Triginta* was written long after the putative dates of the lives, but before the end of the year 398 ([61]). While it would be most convenient to believe that the *HA* was completed around 398, Chastagnol's argument is open to numerous objections ([62]). We cannot necessarily assume that the author intended to offer an accurate and exhaustive catalogue of the administrative divisions of the *regiones suburbicariae* ([63]). Perhaps our impostor was thinking instead of vague geographical regions. After all, he omitted to mention the islands of Sicily, Sardinia and Corsica, also administered from Rome in this peri-

(57) T 24, 5 : *pudore tamen uictus uir nimium seuerus eum, quem triumphauerat, conrectorem totius Italiae fecit, id est Campaniae, Samni, Lucaniae Brittiorum, Apuliae Calabriae, Etruriae atque Vmbriae, Piceni et Flaminiae, omnisque annonariae regionis ac Tetricum non solum uiuere, sed etiam in summa dignitate manere passus est.* Note that here both Hohl and Chastagnol print *Lucaniae Brittiorum*, which is not a standard form.

(58) Chastagnol 1960 : 27 ; *CTh* XI, 16, 9 (359) ; Amm. XXVII, 3, 1. Chastagnol argued that this catalogue of the provinces followed administrative reforms undertaken in the second half of the fourth century : Syme 1971b : 46-47 ; Chastagnol 1955 : 173-180.

(59) Chastagnol 1963 : 375-379 ; Idem 1955 : 176-180.

(60) Chastagnol 1963 : 353. On the bifurcation of Flaminia and Picenum, he claimed (at p. 360-362) : *Cette réforme était déjà accomplie le 19 novembre 400, et nous avons proposé de la dater de 398.*

(61) Barnes accepted this argument : Barnes 1978 : 18.

(62) He himself seems to have placed the lives slightly later than 398.

(63) What Chastagnol called *une situation administrative precise*. Chastagnol 1964 : 146.

od. The author's reference to *Etruria et Vmbria* differs from many other documents, which use the term *Tuscia et Vmbria* for this province ([64]). A rather vague discussion of "all the cities of Campania, Etruria and Umbria, Flaminia, Picenum" in the *Gordiani Tres* raises further doubts ([65]). The failure to mention the province of Valeria cannot be considered a reliable indication of date. That province is surprisingly poorly attested, omitted from many administrative documents and also apparently absent from the epigraphic record ([66]). Even if all of these technical arguments were overcome, other objections would remain. There is always the possibility that our author based his discussion of the provinces of Italy on some obsolete or composite document ([67]).

The above discussion covers only a few examples of the administrative anachronisms detected in the *HA*. It would be possible to elaborate upon yet further cases. A reference to the state carriage (*iudiciale carpentum*) of the urban prefect in the preface to the *Diuus Aurelianus* has attracted a great deal of attention from critics ([68]). Nor should the urban prefect Iunius Tiberianus be described as a *uir illustris* ([69]). There can be no suggestion that the *HA* realistically depicts the administrative arrangements of the third century. Whatever the date of the

(64) *Tuscia* : *CTh* XII, 1, 61 (364) ; Amm. XXVII, 3, 1. This form is also used in an extract from the Council of Serdica (343 AD), quoted by Chastagnol : Chastagnol 1960 : 33. The *Tabula Peutingeriana* reads *Etruria*.

(65) Gd. 4, 6 : *Cordus dicit in omnibus ciuitatibus Campaniae, Etruriae et Vmbriae, Flaminiae, Piceni de proprio illum per quadriduum ludos scaenicos et iuuenalia edidisse*. Chastagnol suggested that : *[C]es régions d'Italie correspondent à des provinces du IV*[e] *siècle : Campagnie, Tuscie-Ombrie, Flaminie-Picénum, les trois qui sont les plus proches de Rome*. Chastagnol 1994 : 708, n. 5. Modern editors tend to separate the references to Flaminia and Picenum in this passage with a comma, which could be considered somewhat problematic. Nevertheless, Chastagnol suggested that the conjunction *et* can be omitted in presenting the double-barrelled names of provinces, as in the case of the provinces of Lucania-Bruttium and Apulia-Calabria, already mentioned above : Chastagnol 1963 : 376.

(66) The province is omitted from the earliest version of the work of Polemius Silvius : Pol. Silv., *Lat.* 2 [*MGH AA* IX, 1, 535]. (Sometimes this fact is used to provide a date for Polemius Silvius' source, which seems a dangerous procedure.) Chastagnol knew of no governor of Valeria : Chastagnol 1963 : 129.

(67) Some might argue that our scholarly impostor omitted a glaringly anachronistic reference to a recent administrative change, in order to avoid exposure. But in my opinion, he did not think in this way.

(68) Bruggisser 1996 ; Idem 1991 ; Chastagnol 1994 : cxvii ; Idem 1960 : 203-205 ; Idem 1955 : 182 ; den Hengst 1981 : 99-101 ; Johne 1976 ; Alföldi 1938. The most important piece of evidence appears in the *Relationes* : Symm., *Ep.* X, 4, 1. The phrase *iudiciale carpentum* occurs otherwise only in Ammianus, so that the term itself is perhaps an anachronism : Amm. XXIX, 6, 7 ; *TLL* III, col. 490, 31 ; *BTL* ; *CLCLT*.

(69) Chastagnol placed the introduction of this title in the reign of Valentinian I, arguing that it first occurred in a law of 368/369 : Chastagnol 1960 : 206-213.

lives themselves, their administrative terminology is often inauthentic. Moreover, the technical language found throughout the *HA* almost certainly justifies us in rejecting the dedications to Diocletian and private individuals under Constantius I. It is striking how many Roman institutions are apparently first attested in the *HA*, generally in dubious contexts. Some anachronisms discussed in this section suggest a date towards the end of the fourth century, or perhaps even later. The evidence of administrative terminology is always problematic, but nevertheless far greater problems would be created were we to accept as genuine all the references to the army, provinces and offices found in the text.

Some Allusions to Events. The administrative terminology of the *HA* suggests that it was written towards the end of the fourth century (or even around the turn of the fifth century). More precision is clearly needed, and here knowledge of political events is helpful. The author of the *HA* was tempted to introduce allusions to events from the recent past into his narrative of the history of the third century. These allusions, discussed extensively by Chastagnol and Syme, provide valuable indications of the date of the text ([70]). Nevertheless, we must exercise some caution in dealing with arguments of this kind, since not all parallels are equally compelling as evidence, and indeed some rather weak affinities have been pressed into service on this front. The clearest and most specific allusions to recent events serve to place the *HA* after about 395 ([71]). Many of the supposed intimations of events after that point are rather nebulous, although some may well find them persuasive.

One could argue that the usurpation of Eugenius (August 392 - September 394), a traumatic period for the Western elite, figures in the lives. There is a Greek rhetorician called Eugamius, allegedly tutor to the son of Maximinus Thrax ([72]). Although the form Eugamius may pun on the name of Eugenius, Syme himself did not rely on this coincidence : “Let it be waived, for discretion” ([73]). There are differing reports on Eugenius’ profession : either a grammarian or a rhetorician at Rome ([74]). The author erroneously claimed that the usurper Proculus had been proclaimed at Lyon, where Eugenius launched his rebellion in 392 ([75]). Perhaps the sudden storm that caused the defeat of the Gordians in Africa (an invention) prefigured the miraculous wind that propelled

(70) Chastagnol 1970b ; Idem 1969 ; Idem 1955. See also : Hartke 1951 ; Idem 1940.

(71) Syme’s judgement retains its validity : “None the less, with all caution and reservations, it seems permissible to assume the impact of various historical transactions of the age of Theodosius, notably what happened between 392 and 394.” Syme 1968a : 215.

(72) Max. 27, 5. Note also Tac. 4, 4 : *ecquis melius quam litteratus imperat ?*

(73) Syme 1968a : 78.

(74) *PLRE* I, 293, Fl. Eugenius 6. Our author also introduced some dubitation concerning the profession of the usurper Bonosus’ father : Q 14, 1 ; Syme 1968a : 77.

(75) Q 13, 1 ; Syme 1968a : 77.

Theodosius to victory at the battle of the river Frigidus (6 September 394), although portentous events of this kind are hardly unheard of elsewhere in ancient literature ([76]). A speech attributed to the spurious consular "Maecius Faltonius Nicomachus" may express some of the reasons that drove Virius Nicomachus Flavianus to support the regime of Eugenius, ultimately at the cost of his own life ([77]). Two further passages are of interest. The next chapter will discuss an allusion to Symmachus' lost speech against the reintroduction of the censorship, possibly delivered during the usurpation of Eugenius, and circulated in manuscript in the years 397 or 398. It will also touch upon a suppositious prophecy that the descendants of the Emperor Probus would occupy all the offices in the state. In this suspect vaticination one might see an allusion to the joint consulship of the sons of Petronius Probus in 395.

Attempts to find allusions in the lives to events after the death of Theodosius (395) are extremely speculative ; the parallels invoked are often vague and generic. Themes developed throughout the lives (notably the castigation of boy emperors and invective against their eunuch ministers) would have been topical during the reigns of the Western Emperor Honorius (395-423) and Arcadius (395-408) ([78]). But both Arcadius (in 383) and Honorius (in 384) attained the title of Augustus during their father's reign. Moreover, the unfortunate Gratian (367-383) and Valentinian II (375-392) were emperors at an early age. Chastagnol argued that the author referred to the circumstances surrounding the rebellion of Gildo in Africa (397-398) ([79]). In the summer of 397, the Senate (responding to an extraordinary request from Stilicho) declared Gildo a public enemy and ordered his property confiscated. There are similar acts of condemnation in the *HA* : the Senate declared Avidius Cassius a public enemy and confiscated his property ; Severus compelled the Senate to declare public enemies all those who had corresponded with Clodius Albinus (seizing their property) ; and the Senate declared Maximinus Thrax and his son public enemies on account of their cruelty ([80]). Even assuming that all these declarations of the Senate are fictional, there is no very strong reason to associate them with the denunciation of Gildo. The Western government embarked a large force for operations against Gildo

(76) Gd. 16, 2. As Syme wrote, "Treachery and a great tempest suddenly blowing down from the mountain (as happens in that region) decided the issue." Syme 1968a : 72.

(77) Tac. 5, 3 ; Honoré 1989 : 42.

(78) On the depiction of eunuchs, see Yanguas 1977. Syme claimed that "the hostility to boy princes acquires a startling relevance." Syme 1968a : 79.

(79) Chastagnol 1955 : 182.

(80) AC 7, 6 : *senatus illum hostem appellauit bonaque eius proscripsit.* Cl. A 12, 3-4 : *omnesque illos, quorum epistolas repperit, hostes iudicari a senatu fecit ; nec his pepercit, sed et ipsos interemit et bona eorum proposuit atque in aerarium publicum rettulit.* Max. 15, 2 : *ubi haec gesta sunt, senatus magis timens Maximinum aperte ac libere hostes appellat Maximinum et eius filium.*

early in 398. The author wrote in a digression in the *Probus* : "Now let them come, those who prepare soldiers for civil wars, those who arm the right hands of brothers to kill their relations, those who incite sons to wound their fathers !" ([81]). The expedition was a success, and Gildo was dead by the end of March. The usurper Saturninus claimed : "Indeed, it is I who have restored the Gallic provinces, I who have returned Africa from the possession of the Moors, I who have pacified Spain" ([82]). Chastagnol sought to associate these passages in he lives of Probus and Saturninus with the defeat of Gildo. These arguments cannot be considered decisive. It is difficult to see the connection between what are generic rhetorical exclamations and the concrete events of the rebellion of Gildo. While the passages cited above may reflect events, these allusions are really much too weak to bear the weight of argument placed upon them.

The passages allegedly concerning the rebellion of Gildo proved too vague to permit any definite conclusion. Also of interest is a passage concerning the usurper Bonosus (found in the *Quadrigae Tyrannorum*). In a spurious letter to Gallonius Avitus, a fictitious legate of Thrace, the Emperor Aurelian claimed : "But also, since it pleases us that Hunila be given in marriage to Bonosus, you shall give to him all the things that we have decreed in the list written out below. You shall also celebrate the wedding at public expense" ([83]). The author described Hunila as "a royal maiden" and "an exceptional woman of a noble family, although one of the Gothic tribe" ([84]). Aurelian arranged the alliance so that "through Bonsosus he might learn everything from the Goths" ([85]). One naturally thinks of the marriage of the Emperor Honorius and Maria, the daughter of Stilicho, conducted in February 398 ([86]). The marriage of Bonosus and Hunila certainly belongs in a context in which Romanised generals of barbarian extrac-

(81) Pr. 23, 5 : *eant nunc, qui ad ciuilia bella milites parant, in germanorum necem arment dexteras fratrum, hortentur in patrum uulnera liberos.*

(82) Q 9, 5 : *ego certe instauraui Gallias, ego a Mauris possessam Africam reddidi, ego Hispanias pacaui.* Note also Q 5, 4 : *canon Aegypti, qui suspensus per latronem inprobum fuerat, integer ueniet.* Gildo had cut off the grain supply from North Africa to Rome.

(83) Q 15, 7 : *nunc tamen, quoniam placuit Bonoso Hunilam dari, dabis ei iuxta breuem infra scriptum omnia, quae praecipimus ; sumptu etiam publico nuptias celebrabis.*

(84) Q 15, 4 : *femina singularis exempli et familiae nobilis, gentis tamen Gothicae.* Q 15, 5 : *erat enim illa uirgo regalis.* Hunila is a man's name, the name of a general mentioned in Jordanes : Domaszewski 1918 : 22. Note also the manly Samso : Q 12, 3. Syme detected a joke : "In climax of mockery, women are endowed with masculine names." Syme 1968a : 174.

(85) Q 15, 4 : *ut per eum a Gothis cuncta cognosceret.*

(86) See *PLRE* II, 720, Maria 1. Claudian celebrated these nuptials with Fescennine verses (*Fescennia dicta Honorio Augusto et Mariae*) and an epithalamium (*Epithalamium dictum Honorio Augusto et Mariae*).

tion could marry into the governing elite and even into the imperial house. The family of Stilicho provides other examples of favourable alliances. Maria herself was the child of a mixed marriage, in that her father Stilicho had married Serena, an adopted niece of the Emperor Theodosius ([87]). Stilicho was the product of a union between a Roman woman and a Vandal officer ([88]). Given that marriage between Romans and barbarians was a well established practice, the marriage of Bonosus and Hunila cannot be used as evidence of the exact date of the *HA*, although it does indicate the general context in which the text was written.

Chastagnol suggested that there was a parallel between the spectacles described in the *Carus et Carinus et Numerianus* and a passage in Claudian's panegyric on the consulship of Flavius Mallius Theodorus (recited 1 January, 399) ([89]). Syme viewed the correspondence as generic, suggesting that this kind of display might have been common in the late fourth century ([90]). Given that our author had an interest in games, there is every chance that he hit upon this phraseology independently ([91]). There is also a possibility that our impostor may have alluded to the consulship of one Aurelianus (400), which seems to have been subsidised by the government ([92]). We are unreliably informed that the Emperor Valerian bore the cost of Aurelian's consular games ([93]). Nevertheless, obscure birth and meritorious poverty were commonplaces where so-called military emperors were concerned. Moreover, the costs of high office naturally appalled our author, since they disturbed the solidarity of the elite ([94]). Vopiscus' claims that Emperor Aurelian's descendants continued in high office in the reign of Constantius need not be significant, since he made similar claims about almost every significant figure of the third century ([95]). Once again, these parallels are potentially interesting, without being conclusive. Some readers may find

(87) *PLRE* I, 824, Serena. She was Stilicho's wife from 384 until 408.

(88) *PLRE* I, 853-858, Fl. Stilicho.

(89) Chastagnol 1976 : 75-80 ; Idem 1970b. Chastagnol noted that the words *pegma*, *flammae* and *scaena* appear in the same order and context in both works. Car. 19, 2 : *pegma praeterea, cuius flammis scaena conflagrauit*. Compare Claud., *Pan. dict. Mall. Theod. Cons.* 325-327 : *mobile ponderibus descendat pegma reductis | inque chori speciem parcentes ardua flammas | scaena rotet*. None of these words is especially rare, and indeed the words *flamma* and *scaena* are almost ubiquitous.

(90) Syme 1968a : 195.

(91) He mentioned reading a *libellus munerarius*, describing the upcoming games of one of his friends : Cl. 5, 5.

(92) *PLRE* I, 128-129, Aurelianus 3 ; Paschoud 1996 : 91-92. Our author was not usually interested in figures from the Eastern Empire, although perhaps he made an exception in this case.

(93) A 12, 1-2. Before his elevation, Aurelian was not a senator.

(94) A 15, 4-6 ; Car. 20, 4-6.

(95) Cl. A 4, 2 ; Gd. 20, 6 ; MB 16, 1 ; Gall. 19, 8 ; T 14, 3-8 ; 25, 2 ; 27, 2 ; 33, 5 ; A 1, 3 ; 44, 5 ; Tac. 15, 2-5 ; 16, 4 ; Pr. 24, 1-3 ; Q 13, 5

them convincing, and such arguments are the stuff of learned controversy. It is worth making one final observation on the issue of date. Some unpleasant incidents of the first decade of the fifth century, notably the irruption of Radagaisus (405/406) and Alaric's sack of Rome (410), have left no obvious traces in the lives. Whenever he wrote, our impostor still fantasised about reducing Germany to a province, perhaps reflecting his astonishingly conservative cultural formation.

The allusions to recent events discussed above might reveal our impostor's limitations, his failure to understand the past on its own terms. On the other hand, we could conceive of such references as an illustration of a synchronic sensibility. The past is recast in the image of the present, while the present is explained by reference to ancient prototypes. We noted above in our discussion of possible administrative anachronisms that the description of the Roman administration found in the *HA* seems to belong to all periods and to none in particular. Our author may have creatively reworked and appropriated the past in a form comprehensible to a late antique audience. Perhaps our mentality, formed by the heroic industry of nineteenth-century criticism, cannot easily embrace this once plausible synthesis of past and present.

Conclusion. Any discussion of the *HA* must begin with a recognition that the attributions of authorship to Spartianus, Capitolinus, Lampridius, Gallicanus, Pollio and Vopiscus are an elaborate hoax. Equally spurious are the dedications to Diocletian, Constantine and private individuals under Constantius I. Evidence found throughout the corpus suggests that the *HA* was written at some point after about 395. Source critical studies (mentioned above in the introduction) corroborate this finding, since the author drew upon the works of Aurelius Victor, Eutropius and possibly also Eunapius. Nevertheless, one important issue remains unresolved : the date before which our author wrote. We cannot rule out the possibility that the *HA* was written after 400, although no evidence points to this conclusion.

CHAPTER THREE

Context

Introduction. The previous chapter examined two sources of information on the date of the *HA* : its administrative terminology and allusions to recent events. We suggested on this basis that the lives were written after about 395, placing the corpus early in the reign of the Western Emperor Honorius (395-423). This chapter seeks to describe the context in which the *HA* first appeared, based upon internal and external evidence. The lives contain spurious genealogies that celebrate the great families of the Roman aristocracy, most notably the Ceionii. At the same time, suppositious documents throughout the corpus bolster the pretensions of the senatorial elite. Clearly, our impostor sought out readers among the great houses of the Roman aristocracy, among the senatorial order, and among scholars and teachers associated with these groups. We can confidently situate our impostor within networks of cultural production established around the great Roman families in the last decades of the fourth century. Arguably, he responded to this audience's strong interest in works of imperial biography (denounced by the historian Ammianus).

Bogus Names and Spurious Genealogies. The bogus names of senators and high officials found throughout the *HA* have long engaged the interest of prosopographers, including scholars such as Dessau, Barnes, Syme and Schwartz ([1]). These writers have argued that the bogus names reflect the nomenclature of individuals and families prominent among the aristocratic elite of the city of Rome late in the fourth century. It is understandable that the author would model spurious senators and office holders on the great men of his own day ([2]). Such arguments, although sometimes persuasive, are vulnerable to criticism. Similar names tend naturally to appear throughout successive generations of the same families, while the pedigrees of some Roman aristocrats of the age of Theodosius can be traced back to the reign of Constantine (or even earlier) :

> Undoubtedly there are a great many bogus names in the *HA*. But it is another matter whether they have any bearing on the date of the work. The fact remains that we sim-

(1) Schwartz 1987 ; Syme 1976 ; Idem 1966 ; Barnes 1972 ; Dessau 1889 : 349-359.
(2) Syme 1978 : 189 ; Idem 1968a : 156.

ply do not have the material to warrant confident *ex silentio* inferences that families were not prominent half a century or more before we happen first to hear of them ([3]).

Given the considerable gaps in our knowledge, we require more than nomenclature alone to establish that the text was written late in the fourth century. Nevertheless, some spurious genealogies can be used in conjunction with other information to provide evidence of date. For example, it can be argued that a prophecy in the *Probus* refers to the joint consulship of the sons of Petronius Probus (in 395) ([4]). The intermarriage of the Postumii and the Ceionii, apparently envisaged in the *Vita Clodii Albini*, may well have occurred after the death of Constantine ([5]). Both of these examples are discussed further below.

Despite these qualifications, spurious names can provide valuable evidence on the intended audience of the *HA*. Allusions such as these could be understood as genealogical compliments on the part of the author : "[H]e wished to pay a delicate tribute to birth and rank by the evocation of illustrious ancestors from the distant past" ([6]). An honourable mention in the *HA* might help in establishing a pedigree, by suggesting that the noble lineage of prominent families stretched back into the second or third centuries. Indeed, the game of genealogies was part of the culture of the late Roman elite : "Gross genealogical fantasies proliferated in the last age" ([7]). Ammianus complained that the aristocrats thought themselves important because of their celebrated names : the Reburri, Flavonii, Pagonii, Gereones, Dalii, Tarracii and Ferasii ([8]). There were just as many great houses among the plebs, their names derived from low occupations : the Messores, Statarii, Semicupae, Serapini, Cicymbrici, Gluturini, Trullae, Lucanici, Porclacae and Salsulae. If only they had shoes ([9]). Ausonius, himself a great patron, who held the highest offices in the state, lauded the pedigree of Petronius Probus in extravagant language ([10]). He converted the undistinguished birth of some of the grammarians and rhetoricians of Bordeaux into druidic ancestry ([11]). Jerome's epitaph for Paula traced her origins back to the Gracchi

(3) Cameron 1999 : 480. Ammianus claimed that the Anicii had been accumulating wealth since the reign of Constantine : Amm. XVI, 8, 13. Cameron (at p. 501) suggested that they may have been prominent "since Severan times."

(4) Pr. 24, 1-3.

(5) Cl. A 4, 1-2. "A link can be surmised between Postumii and Ceionii, but not until late in the fourth century." Syme 1968a : 155.

(6) Syme 1968a : 154. See also A. Birley 2003 : 128-129 ; 141-143.

(7) Syme 1968a : 163.

(8) Amm. XXVIII, 4, 7. The scribes have corrupted these names : Syme 1968a : 150-151.

(9) Amm. XXVIII, 4, 28.

(10) Aus., *Epist.* 9a ; b.

(11) Aus., *Prof.* 4, 7-10.

and the Scipios ([12]). The aristocrat Toxotius was (like many other Romans) a putative descendent of Aeneas ([13]). Macrobius supplied a very long etymological and genealogical interpretation of the name Praetextatus, replete with antiquarian detail, which might well have been considered a model of scholarly accuracy ([14]). In a later period, Sidonius Apollinaris claimed that one of his correspondents was descended from the historian Tacitus ([15]). Cassiodorus appropriated for himself the dynastic mystique of Q. Aurelius Memmius Symmachus and Boethius (after their execution on the orders of Theoderic) ([16]). Cassiodorus could claim that he had restored to prominence the Amal line, while showing that no fewer than seventeen generations of Athalaric's family had held royal office. Our author may not have transgressed standards of genealogical research normal in his own day. Indeed, the many apparently spurious genealogies in the *HA* were in fact characteristic of late antique scholarship, which often devoted its ingenuity to wild or collusive conjecture ([17]).

Genealogies have always played a significant role in legitimating authority and constructing identity, and so it is not surprising to find that the late Roman aristocracy encouraged this mode of cultural production. There is an especially

(12) HIER., *Ep.* 108, 1 : *Gracchorum stirps, suboles Scipionum.* See : *PLRE* I, 674-675, Paula 1. Furia seems to have claimed descent from the Gracchi and from Camillus : HIER., *Ep.* 54, 1 ; 77, 2 ; *PLRE* I, 375-376, Furia. According to the *HA*, Gordian I traced his ancestry from the Gracchi on his father's side and from Trajan on his mother's side (she was called Ulpia Gordiana) : Gd. 2, 2. "Maecius Marullus," spurious father of Gordian I, may imitate Furius Maecius Gracchus 3 (*PLRE* I, 400) : SYME 1966 : 268.

(13) HIER., *Ep.* 108, 4. A Toxotius appears in the *HA* : Max. 27, 6 ; CHASTAGNOL 1994 : 351 ; SYME 1968a : 158 ; DESSAU 1889 : 351. Toxotius (who died in 380) was the husband of Paula. His son, the younger Toxotius, married Laeta, daughter of the pontifex Albinus, around 390.

(14) MACR., *Sat.* I, 6. The discussion seems to supply Vettius Agorius Mavortius Praetextatus with ancestors among the senators of the Republic : MACR., *Sat.* I, 6, 26.

(15) SID., *Ep.* IV, 14, 1-2. Compare Tac. 10, 3.

(16) This fragment (*Excerpta ex libello Cassiodori Senatoris ... quem scripsit ad Rufium Petronium Nicomachum ex consule ordinario patricium et magistrum officiorum*) is reproduced in Mommsen's edition of the *Variae* : MOMMSEN 1961a [first ed. 1894] : v.

(17) The examples cited above involve the pedigrees of private individuals. The public rhetoric of their respective regimes connected Constantine to Claudius II and Theodosius to Trajan : SYME 1971b : 89-112. Our author suggested that Licinius claimed descent from Philip the Arab, a no less plausible connection : Gd. 34, 4. According to the author, Alexander Severus attempted to derive his ancestry from the Metelli, although apparently unconvincingly : AS 44, 3. Ulpius Crinitus, a spurious descendant of the great conqueror Trajan, allegedly adopted the young Aurelian : A 10, 2-3 ; 11, 7 ; 14, 6. According to our author, Zenobia claimed descent from Cleopatra (T 27, 2 ; 30, 2 ; Cl. 1, 1), the usurper Piso was descended from the Calpurnii Pisones (T 21, 1 ; 32, 5), the enigmatic Domitianus sought to associate himself with the Emperor Domitian (12, 14) and the usurper Regilianus was connected to the Dacian chieftain Decebalus (10, 8).

significant genealogical compliment in the *Vita Clodii Albini*. The author claimed that Clodius Albinus was descended from three families of Rome :

> But to return to Albinus, he was, as I have said, born in Hadrumentum, but he was of noble rank among his own people and he traced his descent from the Roman families, namely the Postumii and the Albini and the Ceionii. This family, which was advanced greatly by Gallienus and the Gordians, is also most noble today, and it has been exalted by you and deserves to be exalted further, greatest Constantine ([18]).

The Ceionii were the only family praised in this manner, and naming them in an apostrophe to the Emperor Constantine increased yet further their prominence. The author included further allusions to the Ceionii throughout the lives, perhaps hinting at a relatively close affiliation ([19]). It seems reasonable to suggest that the Ceionii were among the connections of the author, given their well attested interest in scholarship, which persisted throughout several generations. Priscian cited a work on Roman history in verse ascribed to an Albinus (apparently identified as Ceionius Rufius Albinus, consul in 335) ([20]). Servius dedicated his tract *de Centum Metris* to another Albinus, a young man whose ancestors had been heavily involved in literature ([21]). Writing some decades later, Macrobius introduced two members of this family, "Furius Albinus" and "Caecina Albinus," as disputants in his dialogues on Virgil ([22]). He described them as the most learned men of their era ([23]). Perhaps no mere savant, however erudite, could have merited this distinction in Macrobius' eyes. Scholarship alone could not compete with an aristocratic cultural formation, which was accessible only to a minority among the literate.

The *HA* also contains a probable allusion to the family of Petronius Probus. Certain prophets had claimed that the descendants of the Emperor Probus would be pre-eminent in the Senate :

(18) Cl. A 4, 1-2 : *Sed ut ad eum redeam, fuit, ut dixi, Albinus Hadrumetinus oriundo, sed nobilis apud suos et originem a Romanis familiis trahens, Postumiorum scilicet et Albinorum et Ceioniorum. quae familia hodie quoque, Constantine maxime, nobilissima est et per te aucta et augenda, quae per Gallienum et Gordianos plurimum creuit*. It seems unlikely that a contemporary of the Emperor Constantine would give advice of this kind, which is almost impertinent, in that it concerns appointments that have not yet been made.

(19) Chastagnol 1994 : xvi ; Barnes 1972 : 146 ; Dessau 1889 : 353-355. "Clodius Celsinus," a spurious relation of Clodius Albinus (S 11, 3 ; Cl. A 9, 6 ; 12, 9) calls to mind Clodius Celsinus signo Adelphius 6 (*PLRE* I, 192-193). "Faltonius Probus," an invented proconsul of Africa (A 40, 4) may have taken his name from Faltonius Probus Alypius 13 (*PLRE* I, 49), the son of Clodius Celsinus Adelphius.

(20) Prisc., *Inst.* VII, 22 [*GL* II, 304] ; *PLRE* I, 37, Ceionius Rufius Albinus 14.

(21) Serv., *de Cent. Metr.* [*GL* IV, 456] : *Clarissimo Albino*. He is described as *praetextatorum decus*.

(22) Macr., *Sat.* I, 2, 15-16 ; 4, 1.

(23) Macr., *Sat.* VI, 1, 1.

> The descendants of Probus, moved either by hate or by fear of inspiring jealousy, fled the Roman state, and established themselves in Italy near Verona and the Lakes Benacus and Larius [Garda and Como] and in that district. Indeed, I cannot avoid mentioning the fact that, when a statue of Probus in the region of Verona was struck by lightning in such a fashion that the colours of its bordered toga were altered, the soothsayers predicted that future generations of his family would rise to such distinction in the Senate and that they would all hold the highest posts. As yet, however, we have seen none, and moreover it would seem that the "future generations" have an eternity, not a time limit ([24]).

This passage may refer to Petronius Probus, who traced his origins to North Italy. He was a successful and flagrant nepotist, who established his relations and associates in positions of authority throughout the Western empire ([25]). The prophecy that the descendants of the Emperor Probus would hold the highest honours was fulfilled in 395, when Anicius Probinus and Anicius Olybrius (Petronius Probus' sons) were joint consuls ([26]). Since the prophecy seems to refer to the events of 395, we might well conclude that the author wrote after this date. Petronius Probus (in about 371) received copies of works of Nepos and Iulius Titianus from Ausonius, who must have hoped that the magnate would appreciate his gift ([27]). He may also have received the dedication of the *Ora Maritima* of Rufius Postumius Festus Avienus. Petronius Probus dedicated verses to the Emperor Theodosius, which included his own compositions, as well as those of his father and grandfather ([28]).

Petronius Probus had married into one of the most splendid families of the late antique world. The Anicii were heavily involved in scholarship in the last decades of the fourth century. The consuls Anicii received the dedication to

(24) Pr. 24, 1-3 : *Posteri Probi uel odio uel inuidiae timore Romanam rem publicam fugerunt et in Italia circa Veronam ac Benacum et Larium atque in his regionibus larem locauerunt. sane quod praeterire non potui cum imago Probi in Veronensi sita fulmine icta esset, ita ut eius praetexta colores mutaret, aruspices responderunt huius familiae posteros tantae in senatu claritudinis fore, ut omnes summis honoribus fungerentur. sed adhuc neminem uidimus, posteri autem aeternitatem uidentur habere, non modum.*

(25) Barnes 1978 : 18 ; Syme 1966 : 267 ; Chastagnol 1955 : 182 ; Hartke 1951 : 346-347 ; Seeck 1912 : 604 ; Dessau 1889 : 355-356. On the career of Petronius Probus, see : Cameron 1985 ; Novak 1980. On the North Italian connections of the Anicii, see Lizzi Testa 2007 : 283-284.

(26) Chastagnol 1994 : xcviii. The poet Claudian celebrated the happy event with a panegyric (*Panegyricus dictus Probino et Olybrio Consulibus*). There may be another allusion to this circumstance elsewhere in the *Probus*, where the Emperor Valerian bestows a military tribunate on the excellent youth "although he was almost beardless." Pr. 3, 5 : *adulescens Probus corporis uiribus tam clarus est factus, ut Valeriani iudicio tribunatum prope inberbis acciperet.*

(27) Aus., *Ep.* 9a.

(28) *Anth. Lat.* I, 783-785 ; *PLRE* I, 736-740, Sex. Claudius Petronius Probus 5.

Arusianus Messius' *Exempla elocutionum* in 395, and Claudian dedicated a verse epistle to each brother ([29]). Anicius Probinus was himself a poet, who had some of his verses included in the *Epigrammata Bobiensia* ([30]). Modern scholars ascribe the *Cento Virgilianus de laudibus Christi* either to Faltonia Betitia Proba, wife of Clodius Celsinus signo Adelphius (urban prefect 351), or to Anicia Faltonia Proba, the wife of Petronius Probus ([31]). An otherwise unknown Anicius exchanged epigrams with an obscure grammarian on the theme of noble ancestry, probably in the course of the fifth century ([32]). Anicius Manlius Torquatus Severinus Boethius, one of the great philosophers of the West, was related in some way to this line.

The spurious genealogies found throughout the lives suggest that the author conceived of members of the great Roman houses, notably the Ceionii and possibly also the Anicii, as privileged readers of the text. By praising these families, the author sought to associate himself with the most prestigious guardians of high culture. This stance may have attracted yet further readers among the Western elite, while also helping to ensure the dissemination of the text and its transmission to future generations. Although these spurious genealogies may appear fanciful or even ridiculous to us, they may well have conformed to prevailing scholarly standards. They were also socially appropriate.

Suppositious Documents. The genealogical compliments scattered throughout the *HA* suggest that our scholarly impostor engaged with some of the most important aristocratic families of his day. By contrast, many of the spurious documents found throughout the lives (the letters, speeches, harangues, decrees and acclamations) seem to bolster the pretensions of the senatorial class as a whole. Extraordinary privileges are granted to the senatorial order ; an unscrupulous antiquarianism fabricates the necessary precedents in a masterpiece of improvisation. One cannot discount the persuasive force of documentation in establishing social primacy, justifying political influence or vindicating usurped rights.

(29) Claud., *Carm.* 40-41.

(30) *Epig. Bob.* 65.

(31) Barnes 2006 : 254-256 ; *PLRE* I, 732, Faltonia Betitia Proba 2 ; 732-733, Anicia Faltonia Proba 3. Faltonia Betitia Proba was the mother of Faltonius Probus Alypius, perhaps the inspiration for 'Faltonius Probus,' a spurious proconsul of Africa named at A 40, 4.

(32) *Anth. Lat.* I, 772a.

(33) The common source of the epitomes seems to have described the brief reign of Tacitus and Florianus as little more than an interregnum (compare Tac. 14, 5 : *quasi quidem interreges inter Aurelianum et Probum*). It was Aurelius Victor who first misinterpreted this claim, in order to produce an improbable interregnum between the reigns of Aurelian and Tacitus : Aur. Vic., *Caes.* 35, 9-12 ; 36, 1 ; *Epit.* 35, 9. Our author transformed this error into an elaborate fantasy of senatorial government : A 40, 1-41, 15 ; Tac. 1, 1-9, 6 ; 12, 1-2.

One might argue that many of the fabrications of the *HA* arose from a desire to establish the supremacy of the senatorial order on a solid evidentiary basis. These spurious documents certainly flattered the corporate vanity of readers among the senatorial elite, in a period in which members of that order were active in the high politics of the Western empire. But we might also interpret these documents in antiquarian terms. Confronted with ancient models, the author and his readers may have readily believed that the Senate formerly exercised considerable power and influence. We have already seen how easily our author accepted glaring anachronisms, fanciful genealogies, literary typologies and etymological explanations. Perhaps our impostor simply believed that, in the absence of any evidence to the contrary, the Senate of the third century ought to be patterned on the great council of the Republic.

The author presented spurious documents purporting to demonstrate that the Roman Senate of the third century enjoyed extraordinary authority and jurisdiction. Indeed, these documents suggest that the Senate acted independently at key moments, notably in the selection of emperors. The lives ascribed to Flavius Vopiscus Syracusius provide striking models of senatorial intervention in the government of the empire. The alleged interregnum between the reigns of Aurelian and Probus arose as a misunderstanding in Aurelius Victor ([33]). Our scholarly impostor corroborated this error with apposite forgeries on the election of the Emperor Tacitus, "exuberant fabulation … extolling the restoration of the Senate's dignity" ([34]). A letter from the Roman Senate to the provinces boasts that the state has been returned to its ancient condition, that the Senate now rules, that it chooses the emperors, makes the laws and directs the foreign policy of the empire ([35]). The municipal council of Carthage is informed that the rights of granting the imperial power, naming an emperor and giving the title of Augustus have reverted to the Senate ([36]). The same letter makes the extraordinary claim that all appeals should now be made to the urban prefect ([37]). The citizens of Trier, Antioch, Milan, Alexandria, Thessalonica, Corinth and Athens allegedly received similar correspondence ([38]). An appendix of private letters between senators elaborates upon the same themes in rapturous tones ([39]). Senatorial corre-

(34) Syme 1978 : 179.
(35) Tac. 12, 1-2.
(36) Tac. 18, 2-4. The relevant phrase (at 18, 2) is *ius imperii, appellandi principis, nuncupandi Augusti*.
(37) Tac. 18, 3 : *omnis prouocatio*. The Roman aristocracy had every reason to seek to extend the jurisdiction of the urban prefecture, since it was an office over which they were in a position to exercise considerable influence : Syme 1978 : 182. Moreover, Symmachus' official correspondence with the Emperor Valentinian II reveals that genuine disputes might eventuate over the jurisdiction of the urban prefect.
(38) Tac. 18, 6.
(39) Tac. 12, 2 ; 19, 1-5.

spondence, speeches and proceedings consume almost all of the *Tacitus*, probably an indication of the importance the author placed upon these materials, although arguably there was little else to write about this brief reign.

The Emperor Probus hardly owed his elevation to the Senate, and nothing in the historical tradition could be made to suggest that he did. Nevertheless, documents were produced. In one letter, Probus submitted himself to the Senate and asked them to regularise his acclamation by the army ([40]). He styled the senators "rulers of the universe" (*mundi principes*) and predicted that their descendants would hold the same title ([41]). In another communication, Probus granted the Senate the right to hear appeals from the highest judges, the right to appoint proconsuls and their legates, to give the rank of praetor to governors and to sanction his own laws by decree ([42]). Yet another document ascribed to Probus encouraged senators to participate actively in public life ([43]). When he came to the reign of Carus, the author displayed his inventiveness in a new way. A spurious letter establishes that Carus' ancestors were Roman, while a speech delivered before the Senate reveals that he was a member of that assembly prior to his elevation to the purple ([44]). The fantasy of senatorial power has reached its apogee in the election to the imperial office of a senator allegedly born in the city of Rome. The cumulative effect of the fabricated documents found throughout the corpus was to establish a dubious precedent for senatorial engagement in the government of the empire.

That our impostor invented documents is not in itself unusual. The fabrication of documents was a very common practice in Late Antiquity, although it was usually associated with confessional purposes. Our author lived in an age that credited the supposititious correspondence of Seneca and Paul, the risible letters between the toparch Abgarus and Jesus, as well as the alleged rescript of the Emperor Marcus Aurelius concerning the miracle of the Thundering Legion, to give only the most egregious examples ([45]). Various productions concerning the trial and execution of Christ circulated in the fourth century ([46]). Many fourth-century writers cited documentary sources of impossible antiquity, apparently derived from the Early Republic ([47]). False documents are often produced to

(40) Pr. 9, 4.

(41) Pr. 9, 2 : *estis mundi principes et semper fuistis et in uestris posteris eristis*. Note also A 41, 2 : *sancti et uenerabiles domini*.

(42) Pr. 13, 1.

(43) Car. 6, 1.

(44) Car. 4, 6-8 ; 5, 1-3.

(45) Eusebius claimed that he had translated from the Syriac the correspondence of Jesus and Abgarus the toparch, found in the official archives of Edessa : Eus., *Hist. Ecc.* I, 13.

(46) Eus., *Hist. Ecc.* I, 9.

(47) Baudou 1998 ; Drews 1988 ; Rawson 1971.

establish the illustrious pedigree of prominent individuals, to assert the privileges of towns or corporations, or to support outrageous claims of jurisdiction. But we should remember that our concept of forgery is itself historically conditioned, constructed by the polemics of the Reformation and the Enlightenment, and brought to arid perfection in the scholarship of the nineteenth century. An ancient scholar might not have accepted (or even understood) the notion that writing about the past should be autonomous from contemporary social realities. Moreover, the fabrication of plausible sources may have been a tolerable approach where authentic documentation concerning a whole period was absent. Evidence had to be produced, genuine or otherwise. Our author understood that imperial biography in the manner of Suetonius and Marius Maximus demanded some show of research ([48]). His inventions would naturally reflect the shared understandings and cultural preconceptions of the period in which they were written.

On a slightly different note, at least two spurious documents found in the corpus seem to imitate interventions plausibly associated with Roman aristocrats of the fourth century. Some scholars have noted a verbal parallel between some criticism of the Emperor Carus and a sanguinary law against male prostitution enacted in 390, perhaps the work of Virius Nicomachus Flavianus himself ([49]). The law against male prostitution, replete with blandishments of style, was promulgated in the Forum of Trajan in 390. There it might have attracted the notice of the rhetoricians, whose schools were established in that quarter towards the end of the fourth century. A speech declining the offer of the censorship, falsely ascribed to Valerian, probably imitates Symmachus' oration against the restoration of that office, most likely delivered during the usurpation of Eugenius. Four extant letters, written between about 397 and 398, refer to the circulation of this lost speech among members of the Western elite ([50]). This particular example of

(48) Marius Maximus seems to have included long extracts from original documents in his lives, going well beyond his predecessor in this respect. One of the few genuine documents in the corpus, an extract from the proceedings of the Senate quoted in the *Commodus Antoninus*, is derived from Marius Maximus : C 18-19.

(49) Car. 16, 1-5 ; Honoré 1998 ; Idem 1989 ; Chastagnol 1976. The relevant law survives in two distinct forms : *CTh* IX, 7, 6 [forum of Trajan, 6 August 390] ; *Coll. Mos. Rom. Leg.* V, 3 [Hall of Minerva, 14 May 390]. Ratti claimed that the parallel in question established *l'identité de personne entre les deux rédacteurs* (the legislator, who may have been Virius Nicomachus Flavianus, and our impostor). Ratti 2007 : 312.

(50) Val. 5, 4-6, 9 ; Symm., *Ep.* IV, 29 ; 45 ; V, 9 ; VII, 58 ; Chastagnol 1995 ; Cristo 1975 ; Hartke 1940 : 85-88 ; Seeck 1961 [first ed. 1883] : vii. Chastagnol argued that the offer to restore the censorship may have been made under Theodosius, Eugenius or even Stilicho. Seeck and Hartke both suggested that the speeches in question were circulated towards the end of 397 or the beginning of 398. The *Valeriani Duo* seems to imitate the one and only phrase from the lost speech quoted in Symmachus' surviving letters. Val. 6, 9 : *cui tempora sic repugnant.* Compare Symm., *Ep.* IV, 29 : *hanc partem : 'quae temptes-*

imitation could also be seen as an honorific allusion. Arusianus Messius and Servius both inserted citations of Symmachus into their grammatical treatises, suggesting in this manner that the great senator was a model of style comparable to the ancients ([51]). This mode of flattery may have been conventional in dealings with some members of the Roman elite.

Biography, Emperors and Usurpers. The cultural networks associated with the Roman aristocracy of the last decades of the fourth century provide a meaningful context for a scholarly project involving the lives of the emperors. Indeed, our author may have responded to an interest in works of this kind among his intended audience. The historian Ammianus Marcellinus complained in his second urban digression that the Roman aristocrats of his day read nothing except Juvenal and Marius Maximus ([52]). Writing at Rome after 395, the anonymous redactor of the *Epitome de Caesaribus* drew upon material probably derived from Marius Maximus, but not otherwise preserved in the tradition ([53]). Nevertheless, the influence of Marius Maximus was not restricted to historians, biographers and the compilers of epitomes. One can perhaps detect the influence of imperial biography in an even more unlikely place : a cookery book ascribed to the notorious gourmand Apicius (the *de Re Coquinaria*) ([54]). Some comments in Jerome's letters may suggest that the extant version of the cookery book was compiled by an anonymous scholar active at Rome towards the end of the fourth century ([55]). Traces of this work have been detected in the *Aelius* and *Antoninus*

tate resecata est' totius ordinis nostri antetulit auctoritas. Symmachus' letters refer to five different individuals who received copies of his speech against the censorship, only four of whom are named. Protadius, an imperial official who hoped to write a history of Gaul, was one of these. Flavius Mallius Theodorus was another.

(51) Arus. Mess. 85 [*GL* VII, 458] ; 354 [489] ; Serv., *Explan. in Artem Donati* [*GL* IV, 488].

(52) Amm. XXVIII, 4, 14 ; Syme 1968a : 84-88. Kulikowski argued that Marius Maximus was known "well beyond the eccentric confines of the *HA* :" Kulikowski 2007 : 244.

(53) The imperial biographies of Suetonius and Marius Maximus were known to the author of the common source of Aurelius Victor and Eutropius, probably writing in the first half of the fourth century.

(54) There are many modern editions, of which the most significant are André 1974 and Milham 1969. I cite the most recent version (Grocock and Grainger 2006), noting where it diverges from André. Numbers in square brackets also refer to André's edition. Perhaps interesting is the edition and English translation of Flower and Rosenbaum, since its preparation contributed towards two subsequent articles on the *HA* itself : Flower and Rosenbaum 1958. The second author of this translation (under the name Alföldi-Rosenbaum) was the first to explore the connection between the *HA* and the cookery book.

(55) Hier., *Ep.* 29, 1 (384) ; 33, 3 (385) ; Chastagnol 1994 : 74, n. 1. There is every possibility that several works on the subject of cookery were ascribed to Apicius in Late Antiquity. Note, for instance, the excerpts compiled by Vinidarius. The cookery book represents a wholly different branch of the tradition : André 1974 : xvii. The scholia on

Heliogabalus ([56]). Moreover, the cookery book includes some epithets plausibly associated with Roman emperors. The cookery book describes some of its recipes using the terms *Vitellianus*, *Traianus*, *Commodianus* and *Vardanus* ([57]). The first three of these epithets almost certainly refer to the Emperors Vitellius, Trajan and Commodus, while the latter may allude to Elagabalus. It is certainly interesting to see that the cookery book should refer to emperors whose lives were written by Suetonius and Marius Maximus, perhaps reflecting an interest in the period covered by these authors.

The scholia on Juvenal cite Marius Maximus on the informers of the reign of Domitian, and the quotation must almost certainly come from a lost life of Nerva ([58]). This citation corroborates in a striking manner Ammianus' complaint about the reading habits of the Roman aristocracy (Juvenal and Marius Maximus). The extract from Marius Maximus preserved in the scholia also resembles in its phraseology some passages in the *Vita Marci Antonini Philosophi* and the

Juvenal (*Schol. Iuu.* IV, 23) refer to a treatise *de iuscellis*. The claim that an Apicius wrote a treatise on sauces is reported in at least two texts of the fifth century. The Vatican Mythographer (II, 225) and a gloss on the play *Querolus* (at III [42]) employ the phrase *de condituris* (both texts reproduced in André's edition at p. xxviii). Tertullian had used the phrase *condimentis Apicianis et Lurconianis* : Tert., *de Anima* 33, 4 [*CCSL* II, 833, 27].

(56) Mader 2005 : 141 ; Alföldi-Rosenbaum 1972a ; Idem 1972b. Apicius is named several times, as an object of emulation : Hel. 18, 4 ; 20, 5 ; 24, 4. There is also a reference to a cookery book : Ael. 5, 9. A recipe for seafood rissoles attributed to Elagabalus closely parallels a recipe in the cookery book itself : Hel. 19, 6 ; Apic. II, 1, 1 [42] ; André 1974 : 143-144. Note also some references to rose petals : Ael. 5, 7 ; Apic. I, 4 [4]. Both passages use the word *album* to refer the white inner part of the flower : *TLL* I, col. 1509, 47. The word *hydrogarum* appears in both texts : Hel. 29, 5 ; Apic. II, 2, 1 [49] ; 5 [53] ; *TLL* VI, 3, col. 3134, 71 ; *BTL* ; *CLCLT* ; Moes 1980 : 67. Found otherwise in two glossaries.

(57) *Vitellianus*, from Vitellius : Apic. V, 3, 5 [190] ; 9 [194] ; VIII, 7, 7 [373]. See : V 4, 6 ; Suet., *Vit.* 13, 4-5 ; André 1974 : 177-178. *Traianus*, from Trajan : Apic. VIII, 7, 16 [382]. *Commodianus*, from Commodus : Apic. V, 4, 4 [198] ; C 14, 3. The epithet *Commodianus* generally occurs in prose authors in the collocation *Thermae Commodianae*. Apparently only the cookery book and the *HA* apply the term more generally than this : *TLLO* II, col. 550, 38. *Vardanus*, potentially a corrupt reading for *Varianus* : Apic. VI, 8, 11 [247] ; André 1974 : xi ; 186 ; Alföldi-Rosenbaum 1972b : 5, n. 1. André and others have accepted the reading *Vardanus*, because an M. Vitruvius Vardanus is attested, although not in a context associated with cookery : André 1974 : xi ; 186. Nevertheless, it is still extraordinarily tempting to emend the passage to read *Varianus*. The word *Varianus* appears in the preface to the *Diuus Aurelianus*, with reference to the Emperor Elagabalus : A 1, 2. This adjective *Varianus* is derived from the name Varius, a genuine element of the nomenclature of the Emperor Elagabalus : Hel. 2, 1-2. Given Elagabalus' reputation in Late Antiquity, he would have merited inclusion in any recipe collection.

(58) *Schol. Iuu.* IV, 53(2) : *Potentes apud Domitianum hi : Armillatus, Demosthenes et Latinus archimimus, sicut Marius Maximus scribit.*

Verus, presumably derived from the same biographical source ([59]). The most obvious indication of the date of the scholia on Juvenal is their reference to the urban prefecture of Neratius Cerealis, which fell in the years 352-353 ([60]). The text of Juvenal seems to have appeared at Rome towards the end of the fourth century, where it was received with some enthusiasm ([61]). The scholia are closely affiliated with the so-called Codex Pithoeanus, on which modern texts of Juvenal heavily depend ([62]). There was also close association between the Roman schools and the so-called vulgate recension of the *Saturae*, generally considered an inferior derivative of the tradition represented by the Codex Pithoeanus and the scholia. Ancient subscriptions preserved in two medieval manuscripts suggest that an individual called Niceus was involved in correcting a manuscript of Juvenal at the house of a Serbius or Servius ([63]). The celebrated grammarian Servius innovated by quoting from Juvenal in his commentary on Virgil, almost certainly adding these quotations to the materials he inherited from the scholastic tradition ([64]).

The production of the scholia, the subscription of Niceus and the quotations from Juvenal in the commentary of Servius probably reflect ongoing interest in this poet in learned circles associated with the Roman schools in the decades around the turn of the fifth century. Our impostor clearly knew the great satirist ([65]). Moreover, some passages in the *HA* may draw upon aspects of the ancient exegetical tradition imperfectly preserved in the scholia on Juvenal. A description of a riot at Alexandria, incorporated in a biographical entry on the usurper Aemilianus, imitates Juvenal's lurid account of a cannibal orgy among the Egyptians ([66]). The scholia supply the gloss *uicina furori* for the phrase

(59) MA 15, 2 : *multum sane potuerunt liberti sub Marco et Vero Geminus et Agaclytus*. V 9, 3 : *liberti multum potuerunt apud Verum, ut in uita Marci diximus, Geminas et Agaclytus, cui dedit inuito Marco Libonis uxorem.*

(60) *Schol. Iuu.* X, 24. A scholar writing for an audience outside of the city of Rome might not have referred to the urban prefecture to provide a date.

(61) Symmachus alluded to the first satire in a letter to Protadius, a senator active in the imperial administration, perhaps a member of the same literary sect : Symm., *Ep.* IV, 34, 3 ; Iuv. I, 18 ; Highet 1954 : 298, n. 8. Seeck placed this letter in 395, Callu in 397. The poet Claudian drew inspiration from Juvenal, especially in his invectives against the eunuchs Eutropius and Rufinus.

(62) Modern editors sometimes rely upon the lemmata of the scholia in establishing the text of the satires.

(63) Velaza 1999 : 294 ; Tarrant 1983 ; Zetzel 1984 [diss. Harvard, 1973] : 237 ; Pecere 1986 : 37-38 (with plates 10-11). Some critics have suggested that this otherwise unknown Niceus was himself responsible for the vulgate recension : Friedländer 1969 : 50.

(64) Kaster 1978.

(65) Cameron 1964a.

(66) Iuv. XV, 61-68 ; T 22, 3.

domestica seditione, found in Juvenal, while the entry concerning Aemilianus includes the phrase *familiari furore* at this point ([67]). The author of the *HA* introduced a spurious proconsul of Africa called "Vibius Passienus" ([68]). He conflated the nomenclature of two different figures, Q. Vibius Crispus and C. Sallustius Passienus Crispus ([69]). The scholia on Juvenal make a similar error, when they explain a reference to a Crispus in Juvenal (Vibius Crispus was intended), with biographical material concerning Passienus Crispus ([70]). Syme conceded that since the "actual names" Vibius and Passienus did not occur in the scholia "as preserved" then "derivation may be contested" ([71]). Nevertheless, the scholia "as preserved" can hardly be considered a full representation of the late antique exegetical tradition on Juvenal. From a slightly different perspective, our impostor used several otherwise rare words, which also occur in the scholia on Juvenal, notably *boletar*, *diasyrticus*, *dextrocherium* and *dulcium* ([72]). This evidence may not be sufficient definitively to prove that the author of the *HA* drew upon the scholia on Juvenal. Nonetheless, these scholia retain considerable importance as a source of evidence on the context of the corpus. We have already noted the connections between the text of Juvenal, its exegetical apparatus and the school associated with the grammarian Servius, who dedicated one of his treatises to a scion of the Ceionii, and appeared alongside two members of the same clan in Macrobius' imaginary dialogue. The redactor of the cookery book, probably one of the "learned men" castigated by Jerome, may have emerged from the same context as the late antique commentator on Juvenal.

Usurpers in Ausonius. At the risk of tiring the reader, we have shown how the works of Suetonius and Marius Maximus influenced not only minor histori-

(67) *Schol. Iuu.* XV, 64(d) ; T 22, 3.

(68) T 29, 1.

(69) *PIR* V 379, Q. Vibius Crispus ; *PIR* P 146, C. Sallustius Passienus Crispus.

(70) *Schol. Iuu.* IV, 81 ; Schwartz 1966 ; Syme 1966 : 263. Jerome mentioned a Passienus Crispus (called Passienus), but there are no further references to this figure in the literature of the fourth century.

(71) Syme 1968a : 87.

(72) *Boletar* (plural *boletaria*), a kind of dish : Cl. 17, 5 ; *Schol. Iuu.* XI, 137 ; Apic. V, 2, 1-2 [183-184] ; 3, 4 [189] ; VI, 2, 5 [216] ; VIII, 7, 13 [379] ; *TLL* II, col. 2066, 46 ; *BTL* ; *CLCLT* ; Moes 1980 : 87-88. Found otherwise in Martial, the Old Latin (Vetus Itala) version of the Bible and the *Latin Anthology*. *Dulcium* (generally appears in the plural), sweetmeats : Hel. 27, 3 ; Tac. 6, 5 ; *Schol. Iuu.* VI, 202(2s) ; Apic. VII, 11, 1-6 [296-301] ; *TLL* V, 1, col. 2198, 46. Found otherwise in Martial, the scholia on Juvenal, Macrobius and Isidore. *Dextrocherium*, bracelet : Max. 6, 8 ; 27, 8 ; T 14, 4 ; *Schol. Iuu.* IX, 50(d) ; *TLL* V, 1, col. 938, 13 ; *BTL* ; *CLCLT* ; Moes 1980 : 75. Found otherwise in Lucifer, the pseudo-Ambrose, the *Itineraria Antonini Placentini*, Priscian and a glossary. *Diasyrticus*, satirical, mocking : Cc. 10, 5 ; *Schol. Iuu.* V, 44 ; *TLL* V, 1, col. 955, 57 ; *BTL* ; *CLCLT* ; Syme 1968a : 184. The word *diasyrticus*, admittedly borrowed from Greek, appears frequently in scholarly commentaries produced in the Roman schools of the same period, or in authors such as Jerome who had been educated in these schools.

cal writers, but also the authors of various scholarly productions. We might now examine a slightly different theme. One of the most remarkable features of the *HA* is its inclusion of lives of usurpers. Indeed, the *HA* can be described as a parallel series of the lives of emperors and usurpers. The decision to include the lives of usurpers was a significant departure from the tradition, since neither Suetonius nor Marius Maximus had attempted anything like this ([73]). Other authors active late in the fourth century may have shared this curious interest. Ausonius wrote a double series of monostichs and tetrastichs on the Roman emperors starting from Caesar (the *Caesares*), which breaks off abruptly in the middle of a quatrain on Elagabalus. These verses clearly drew upon material derived from the tradition of imperial biography, including both Suetonius and Marius Maximus ([74]). Ausonius may also have written a series of poems on usurpers, which is no longer extant. The medieval scholar Giovanni Mansionario transcribed a catalogue of the works of Ausonius, which includes the following entries :

> Item ad hesperium filium suum de ordine imperatorum.
> Item ad eundem de imperatoribus res nouas molitis a decio usque ad dioclecianum uersu iambico trimetro iuxta libros eusebij nanetici ystorici ([75]).

This series of epigrams on usurpers from Decius to Diocletian (*de imperatoribus res nouas molitis*) calls to mind those lives in the *HA* attributed to Pollio and Vopiscus, which include two books on usurpers : the *Tyranni Triginta* and the *Quadrigae Tyrannorum*. A parallel series of epigrams on the emperors and usurpers up to Diocletian, published by Ausonius in the last years of his life, would do much to explain the subsequent appearance of the *HA*. It may also be

(73) Q 1, 1-2 ; Syme 1968a : 53-59.

(74) Scholars have noted parallels between these verses and the *HA* : Thomson 2008 ; Green 1991 : 559 ; Idem 1981 ; Cazzaniga 1972 : 149-151 ; Schwartz 1972 ; Syme 1968a : 90, n. 1 ; Barnes 1967 : 66, n. 11. The bulk of these affinities probably reflect common use of Marius Maximus. Nevertheless, our author did refer to some verses that are suspiciously similar to those written by Ausonius : OM 7, 7-8. Moreover, there is a parallel between these verses and a line of verse in the *Opilius Macrinus* : Aus., *Caes.* 138-139 ; OM 14, 2(2).

(75) Reproduced in Green's edition of Ausonius. The catalogue is discussed in Green's commentary and in two articles : Green 1991 : 720 ; Reeve 1977 : 115-120 ; Weiss : 1971. Reeve (at p. 119) commented that the poem on usurpers "can hardly have been anything but a genuine work of Ausonius." Ausonius demonstrated an interest in the usurpers of the fourth century. He mentioned Victorinus and the Tetrici at *Parent.* 4, 8-10. Note also Aus., *Ordo* 67-70 : ... *sed magis illud | eminet, extremo quod te sub tempore legit, | solueret exacto cui sera piacula lustro | Maximus, armigeri quondam sub nomine lixa.* The full title of the seventh poem in Green's edition was *Pater ad filium, cum temporibus tyrannicis ipse Treueris remansisset et filius ad patriam profectus esset. hoc incohatum neque impletum sic de liturariis scriptum.*

relevant to note that Paulinus of Nola, a student and correspondent of Ausonius, composed a series of verses on the foreign kings mentioned in Suetonius ([76]). This poem, manifestly a virtuoso composition, demonstrates a fascination with marginal historical figures and an interest in the genre of imperial biography.

A work from a slightly later period provides another example of scholarship concerning usurpers. Polemius Silvius compiled his *Laterculus* in the third decade of the fifth century, drawing on an earlier source. The section of the *Laterculus* that deals with administrative matters had its origins in an earlier period, and Polemius seems to have copied it out without fully appreciating its contents. Polemius Silvius appended to each month of this calendar information of interest to scholars, mostly in the form of lists on various subjects : the emperors, the provinces, the animals, the buildings of Rome, some myths, animal noises, the poetic metres, the philosophical sects, a chronology, a table of weights and measures and a method for calculating the date of Easter ([77]). Alone among the compilers of chronicles, Polemius Silvius included among his list of emperors notices of certain usurpers ([78]). His otherwise unidentified source must have taken considerable care over these minor figures ([79]).

The genre of imperial biography clearly influenced the literary culture of the Roman elite in the last decades of the fourth century. An anonymous epitomator, the scholiast on Juvenal, the obscure redactor of a cookery book, not to mention Ausonius, all drew upon the works of Marius Maximus in this period. Ammianus was perhaps justified in grumbling about standards. Perhaps he encountered related cultural developments, and complained about them to his Roman friends.

(76) Paul. Nol., *Carm.* 3.

(77) Pol. Silv., *Lat.*, praef. [*MGH AA* IX, 1, 518-519].

(78) He included Camillus under Claudius, Vindex and Clodius under Nero, Antonius under Domitian, Cassius under Antoninus Pius (!), Pescennius Niger and Clodius Albinus under Septimius Severus, Marcellus, Sallustius, Uranius, Seleucus and Taurinus under Elagabalus, the two Gordians under Maximinus, Iotabianus under Philip, Priscus and Valens under Decius, under Gallienus, Ingenuus, Regalianus, Postumus, Laelianus, Marius, Macrinus, Quietus, Odaenathus, Aureolus, under Aurelian, Victorinus, Vabalathus, Zenobia, Antiochus, Felicissimus, the Tetrici and Faustinus, under Probus, Saturninus, Proculus and Bonosus and so the catalogue continues down to the consulship of Postumianus and Zeno. See Burgess 1993.

(79) Burgess suggested that references to usurpers in both Ausonius and Polemius Silvius reflect in some way the *Kaisergeschichte* : Burgess 1993 : 494. Burgess even ascribed the *Kaisergeschichte* to Eusebius of Nantes, the alleged source of Ausonius' lost verses on usurpers. Sivan strongly criticised this identification : Sivan 1992. There is surely a danger in allowing a lost source to consume almost every minor work on an historical theme written in Latin in the fourth century. Burgess recently argued that Jerome, Eutropius, Festus, Ammianus and the *Epitome de Caesaribus* shared a common source in the period between 358 and 378, which he once again associated with the *Kaisergeschichte* : Burgess 2005. Note also Kelly 2009.

We noted already in Chapter One that an extant collection of panegyrics associated with Pacatus (the *Panegyrici Latini*) may have provided a model for the attributions of authorship and dedications to Diocletian, Constantius I and Constantine found throughout the *HA*. Moreover, what we call hagiography was an increasingly prominent genre towards the end of the fourth century. Jerome, the learned biblical scholar, fabricated the lives of three hermits, to provide Western asceticism with spiritual forefathers ([80]). Meanwhile, Nicomachus Flavianus prepared a version of Philostratos' *Life of Apollonius of Tyana*, the over-celebrated wonderworker ([81]). Eunapius subsequently published his *Lives of the Philosophers and Sophists*, which included supernatural episodes and some apocryphal material. Surely the moment was right for an even more audacious production.

Conclusion. This chapter has argued that the *HA* emanated from networks of cultural production centred upon the aristocratic elite of the city of Rome, from which its intended audience was drawn. Many of the bogus names found throughout the lives reflect the nomenclature of Roman aristocrats active late in the fourth century. The presence throughout the lives of what appear to be genealogical compliments connects the author to the great houses of the Roman aristocracy, notably the Ceionii. The author asserted the status and prestige of the senatorial order, furnishing precedents for senatorial government by fabricating large numbers of documents. The literary culture of the Roman aristocracy provides an appropriate context for the elaboration of a vast series of imperial biographies, given the interest attested in the works of Marius Maximus during the last decades of the fourth century. A bewildering array of correspondences and parallels, evidence of complicated relationships of filiation between texts of various genres, suggest that our impostor belonged within this milieu.

(80) See the recent edition with French translation : Leclerc et al. 2007. There is a strong possibility that our author imitated the preface to Jerome's *Vita Hilarionis* in his preface to the *Probus* : Schmeidler 1927.

(81) Sid., *Ep.* VIII, 3, 1. Our author may have known of this work : A 24, 9 ; 27, 6 ; Syme 1968a : 111 ; Hartke 1940 : 18-19 ; Geffcken 1920 ; Hohl 1920 : 296-299. The minor senator Tascius Victorianus, a literary factotum for the Symmachi, may have brought out a posthumous recension of Nicomachus Flavianus' opus.

CHAPTER FOUR

Naucellius

Iunius or Iulius Naucellius. The previous chapters have established that the *HA* was the work of one author, a learned impostor writing in the last years of the fourth century, active within a cultural milieu associated with the Roman aristocracy and their adherents. We can now explore some connections between the *HA* and a particular individual : namely Iunius or Iulius Naucellius, a poetaster and antiquarian, a correspondent of Symmachus and an imitator of Ausonius (1). There are three principal sources of evidence concerning this curious writer : (i) a series of short poems, known collectively as the *Epigrammata Bobiensia* (2) ; (ii) the seven letters that Symmachus addressed to Naucellius

(1) *PLRE* I, 617-618, Iulius Naucellius ; 1028-1029, Anonymus 159. The manuscripts report two different first names for Naucellius : Iunius and Iulius. *Epig. Bob.* 5, 3 : *Iunius Ausoniae notus testudinis ales*. *Epig. Bob.* 7, 1 : *Iulius Ausonia notus testudine uates*.

(2) I quote Giordano Rampioni's text of the *Sulpiciae conquestio* (*Epig. Bob.* 37) and Speyer's text of the other epigrams : Giordano Rampioni 1982 ; Speyer 1963. There is an earlier edition of the Bobbio poems : Munari and Campana 1955. Two further editions of the *Sulpiciae conquestio* deserve mention : Fuchs 1968 ; Lana 1949. The secondary literature on the *Epigrammata Bobiensia* concentrates on questions of textual criticism : Dihle 1994 : 580-581 ; Pascucci 1986 ; Skutsch 1982 ; Ballaira 1975 ; Hemer 1973 ; Alfonso 1972 ; Kuijper 1964 ; Idem 1960 ; Veyne 1964 ; Bloch 1963 : 211-212 ; Mariotti 1962 ; Idem 1956 ; Browning 1961 ; Schmid 1960 ; Terzaghi 1960 ; Weinreich 1959 ; Zicàri 1959 ; Idem 1958 ; Munari 1958 ; Dahlmann 1956 ; Enk 1956. The extant collection has an elaborate tradition, and its survival is associated with the monastery established by the followers of St Columban at Bobbio in 614 : Giordano Rampioni 1982 : 11-20 ; Lana 1949 : 3-22. It was here in 1493 that G. Galbiati, the amanuensis of Giorgio Merula, discovered a cache of manuscripts of late Roman authors, many of which were copied at the end of the seventh or the beginning of the eighth century : Reeve 1983 : 405-406 ; Ferrari 1973 ; Idem 1970. The manuscript of the *Epigrammata Bobiensia* found in 1493 has long since disappeared, although many of the poems appeared in early printed editions of Ausonius (where they were often attributed to Ausonius himself, further confusing matters). This unhappy state of affairs persisted until 1950, when Campana discovered almost all the epigrams in a humanist miscellany of the fifteenth or sixteenth century, a copy of the lost Bobbio manuscript (Codex Vaticanus latinus 2836). This manuscript is reproduced in facsimile in Speyer's Teubner edition. It lacks some of the extant epigrams.

some time between the years 396 and 400 ([3]) ; and (iii) a fragmentary inscription, which may be Naucellius' epitaph ([4]). These sources, which are at once tantalising and somewhat frustrating, offer insights into the career of an unconventional figure whose life spanned most of the fourth century. Some indications may connect Naucellius with the spurious Flavius Vopiscus Syracusius, while also hinting that he inhabited the same context as our scholarly impostor. Nevertheless, the available evidence does not permit us definitively to identify Naucellius as the author of the *HA*. Instead, this chapter explores some plausible connections and circumstantial associations in the hope of encouraging further research.

Our sources on Naucellius emerge from the last period of his life (between about 396 and 400), after he had withdrawn from Rome to his villa at Spoleto, in order to enjoy a cultured retirement ([5]). He well deserved this period of repose, since he was more than ninety years old at the time. It is unfortunate that we know so little about Naucellius' life before this point. The only explicit reference to his public career in the *Epigrammata Bobiensia* is his claim that he was *parcus amator opum, blandorum uictor honorum* ([6]). He had become a member of the Senate ([7]). Naucellius enjoyed a more or less familiar correspondence with Symmachus, while the *Epigrammata Bobiensia* include two poems addressed to Nonius Atticus Maximus (consul in 397) and another attributed to Anicius Probinus (consul in 395) ([8]). The fragmentary inscription identified as Naucellius' epi-

(3) Symm., *Ep.* III, 10-16 ; Pellizzari 1998 : 83-102 ; Monaco 1987-1988. Seeck in his edition placed these letters in the year 400. Callu preferred a date between 396 and 400. One further letter may have been addressed to Naucellius : Symm., *Ep.* IX, 110 ; *PLRE* I, 1028-1029, Anonymus 159 ; Roda 1981 : 241-246 ; Syme 1968a : 109 ; Cameron 1964b. In the notes to his edition of Symmachus, Callu suggested that Virius Nicomachus Flavianus may have been the addressee of this letter.

(4) *ILCV* 725 ; *ICVR* I, 957b ; *ICVR* n.s. II, 5017 ; Champlin 1982. The editor described this piece as *tabulae marmoreae opisthographae fragmenta quattuor fere coniuncta.* The inscription on the other face is dated to 511 or 512. The fragment in question is associated with the epitaph of the jurist Floridus, set up in 427 : *ICVR* II, 4886 ; *ICVR* I, 654. Champlin wrote (at p. 184) : "Everything suggests that this is the epitaph of the poet, composed by himself or a close imitator : content above all, but also metre, vocabulary (not just *ex atauis*, but possibly *lare* in line one), the fragmentary name (first suggested by Diehl), and the date (De Rossi emphatically connected the lettering of this inscription with that of *ICVR* 1.654, also from St Paul's, dated to 427."

(5) *Epig. Bob.* 2 ; 7, 3-4 ; 8a, 8 ; 37, 58-63 ; 57, 11-15 ; Symm., *Ep.* III, 12, 2.

(6) *Epig. Bob.* 5, 1.

(7) Symm., *Epist.* III, 12, 2.

(8) *Epig. Bob.* 48, 6 : *balnea quae consul Nonius instituit.* 57 tit. : *Ad Nonium Atticum de opere suo*. In this poem (*Epig. Bob.* 57, 2) Naucellius addressed Atticus as *columen Vrbis*. He may still have been consul when this poem was written. The title of the sixty-fifth poem in the series names as author Anicius Probinus, and although this attribution cannot be authenticated by any other evidence, one is constrained to accept the witness of

taph alludes in obscure terms to some sort of fame among the Germans and to the Northern Ocean, and one might infer from this allusion that he was active at the court at Trier or in campaigns against barbarians on the Rhine frontier at an earlier stage in his career ([9]). Repetitious criticism of grammarians throughout the epigrams may possibly reflect academic malice, a disease endemic in schools ([10]). Naucellius' frequent imitation of Ausonius throughout his poems may also be significant, given the important role that the imperial tutor played in the careers of many provincials during the period of his political ascendancy ([11]). Indeed, Naucellius and Ausonius were almost exact contemporaries. There can be no doubt that Naucellius came from outside the traditional orbit of the Roman aristocracy. Naucellius, a man apparently without notable ancestors or descendants, a man who did nothing to disguise his provincial origins, must surely have attained office through some form of patronage.

Flavius Vopiscus Syracusius. As we have noted many times before, the last five lives of the *HA* (the *Diuus Aurelianus*, *Tacitus*, *Probus*, *Quadrigae Tyrannorum* and *Carus et Carinus et Numerianus*) are ascribed to a spurious author known as Flavius Vopiscus Syracusius. In the prefaces to these lives, Vopiscus almost speaks with an independent voice, especially when he engages in dialogues with Roman notables. The prefaces assigned to Vopiscus were probably intended to be the high point of the collection, displaying the full powers, ingenuity and erudition of the author himself. These prefaces include dialogues on learned subjects, a long digression on the origins of the interregnum, a medita-

the text and the tradition on this point, noting that the *Epigrammata Bobiensia* were found together with a work dedicated to Anicius Probinus and his brother Anicius Olybrius (Arusianus Messius' *Exempla elocutionum*). Our author may possibly have flattered these boys, under the guise of praising the young Probus : Pr. 3, 5 ; 4, 2.

(9) *ILCV* 725 ; *ICVR* I, 957b ; *ICVR* n.s. II, 5017 ; Champlin 1982 : 184. The fifth and six lines of this inscription read : [... nomen] GERMANIS NOBILE C[unctis] | [... term]INAT OCEANVS. Epigram eight, in which the order of the verses is confused, may omit some lines at a point corresponding to these lines in the inscription. Champlin noted : "[T]he connection with Germany, prompted perhaps by the civil or military service there of Naucellius or one of his Sicilian ancestors." He claimed : "With a man of letters, one thinks immediately of an association with Ausonius and the court at Trier."

(10) Two poems (*Epig. Bob.* 46 ; 64) criticising incompetent grammarians (*in grammaticos indoctos, in grammaticos imperitos*) should be grouped together. Both couplets begin with the salutation *Salue, Grammatice, salue*, and end with the quotation *Arma uirumque cano*. Another poem on a similar theme (*Epig. Bob.* 47) also refers to Virgil through the sentence *Arma uirumque cano*.

(11) Speyer noted parallels between the *Epigrammata Bobiensia* and almost all the poems of Ausonius : the *Epicedion in Patrem*, *Parentalia*, *Commemoratio Professorum Burdigalensium*, *Epitaphia Heroum*, *Epigrammata*, *Eclogae*, *Griphus*, *Mosella*, *Caesares*, *Ordo Vrbium Nobilium* and *Epistulae*. Naucellius frankly admitted that he strummed an "Ausonian lyre" (*Ausonia testudo*) : *Epig. Bob.* 5, 3 ; 7, 1. This is not a direct reference to Ausonius, although a pun may be intended.

tion on fame and a brief synopsis of the history of the Roman empire. Some strange correspondences serve to associate Vopiscus with Naucellius, although admittedly the evidence could be explained in various different ways.

Naucellius was by origin and ancestry a Syracusan. He claimed that his parents were Syracusans and that his home city was Syracuse : *et pater et genetrix larque Syracosius* ([12]). An inscription in verse identified as Naucellius' epitaph includes the word fragment [...]*racusis*, likely another reference to Syracuse ([13]). It is interesting to find that Vopiscus and Naucellius shared these origins, and proclaimed them in a similar manner. Devices of this kind are occasionally attested in ancient literature as a means of identifying authorship ([14]). There may be another parallel between these two figures. There is strong evidence to suggest that Naucellius was in his nineties towards the end of the fourth century ([15]). In the very poem that disclosed his Syracusan origins, Naucellius compared two pictures of himself, painted at different stages of his life. In one of these paintings he was "seven decades old" and in another "almost nine and a half decades old" ([16]). These words were written late in the fourth century, most likely around 397, since two of the *Epigrammata Bobiensia* address the consul of that year (Nonius Atticus Maximus), celebrating his construction of a bath complex at Rome ([17]). Although we cannot know the exact date either of the painting or of the poem, there is a reasonable possibility that Naucellius was born in the vicinity of the year 304 ([18]). The dubious Vopiscus first appears in the state carriage of

(12) *Epig. Bob.* 8b, 4. Naucellius employed the form *Syracosius* for metrical reasons.

(13) The second and third lines of the inscription read [... Sy]RACVSIS | [... Nau]CELLIVS HOC FV[it ...].

(14) A subtle reference to Madaura hints that Apuleius was the author of the *Metamorphoses*, ostensibly ascribed to Lucius of Corinth : Apul., *Met.* XI, 27. The pseudonym Dictys Cretensis, applied to an account of the Trojan War, may point to the geographical origin of the author himself, sometimes identified with the scholar Serenus Sammonicus : Keyser 1994 : 375-378 ; Champlin 1981 ; Cameron 1980.

(15) Naucellius claimed that he was more than ninety (*Epig. Bob.* 9, 1-2) : *Tres orbes, Saturne, tuos, pater optime, uixi | aetatis nullo crimine conspicuus.* Comments in Symmachus' letters corroborate the notion that Naucellius was a man of advanced age by the end of the fourth century : Symm., *Ep.* III, 11, 1 ; 13, 2 ; 15, 2.

(16) *Epig. Bob.* 8a, 7-8 : *septima huic aeui fuerat decas, huic fuerat tunc | nona fere ac decimae dimidium decadis.*

(17) The theme of baths and bathing features prominently in the Bobbio collection. Naucellius offered an aetiological explanation of the Aquae Maternae : *Epig. Bob.* 1, 1-2. An explanation of the Aquae Mammaeanae appears in the *Alexander Severus* : AS 26, 9. Both the *HA* and the *Epigrammata Bobiensia* refer to the cold water from the Claudian aqueduct : AS 30, 4 ; *Epig. Bob.* 48, 2 ; *TLLO* III, col. 477, 61.

(18) According to an exclusive reckoning, someone born in the year 304 would have turned ninety-five between 1 January and 31 December 399. According to an inclusive reckoning, a person born in the year 304 would have turned ninety-five between 1 January and 31 December 398.

the urban prefect Iunius Tiberianus (12 September 303 and 4 January 304) ([19]). The etymology of the name Vopiscus is somewhat peculiar : a *uopiscus* is a child, born alive after the miscarriage of its twin. For this reason, Vopiscus would be an appropriate name for a fictitious author introduced to mark the date of someone else's birth ([20]).

An oblique allusion to an individual like Naucellius would not be out of place in the context of the *HA*, given that allusions to office-holders active late in the fourth century are found throughout the lives. Moreover, critics have noted that some of the spurious authorities cited in the corpus take their names from writers active in the fourth century. Flavius Vopiscus Syracusius may belong alongside dubious doubles of Aurelius Victor, Festus, Eutropius, Ausonius, Ammianus Marcellinus and Virius Nicomachus Flavianus ([21]). But of course the matter is not nearly so simple. We noted above in Chapter One some arguments that may sufficiently explain the pseudonym Flavius Vopiscus Syracusius. The name Flavius refers to the imperial dynasty and the name Vopiscus to the disputant in Cicero's *de Oratore*, while his association with Syracuse reflects a stereotype about Sicilian humour. Moreover, Naucellius was not the only Syracusan active in scholarship in the fourth century ([22]). Although it seems likely that Naucellius was born in about 304, we can never hope to know the exact date of his birth.

(19) Chastagnol 1962 : 40-41. Another man of the same name held an earlier urban prefecture. Naming Iunius Tiberianus probably served to authenticate the suppositious date of the preface. Crude research of this kind was conducted at Rome around the turn of the fifth century. An anonymous epitomator produced the name of the consul and urban prefect Pomponius Bassus to fill a perceived gap in the tradition : *Epit.* 34, 3. Any decision to mark a date using the tenure of an urban prefect would have been unusual, although not entirely unprecedented. The scholia on Juvenal refer to the urban prefecture of Neratius Cerealis (352-353) in this manner : *Schol. Iuu.* X, 24. The *Chronography of 354* provides a catalogue of urban prefects, including Iunius Tiberianus.

(20) Pliny the Elder wrote (*N.H.* VII, 10(8) 47) : *Vopiscos appellabant a geminis, qui retenti utero nascerentur, altero interempto abortu.* Quintilian compiled a list of names derived from accidents at birth (*Inst.* I, 4, 25) : *ex casu nascentium (hic Agrippa et Opiter et Cordus et Postumus erunt), et ex iis quae post natos eueniunt, unde Vopiscus.* The name Cordus may somehow participate in this learned game.

(21) Paschoud 1995. Aurelius Verus (AS 48, 6) and Aurelius Victor Pinius (OM 4, 2) probably imitate the epitomator Aurelius Victor. A Festus appears alongside Aurelius Victor Pinius : OM 4, 4. Fabius Marcellinus (A 48, 6 ; Pr. 2, 7) and Valerius Marcellinus (MB 4, 5) may impersonate the great historian. Nicomachus, an interpreter for the usurper Zenobia (A 27, 6), is probably a version of Virius Nicomachus Flavianus, who translated or revised a work on Apollonius of Tyana. (Nearby, the author announced his own intention of translating a life of the same figure : A 24, 9.) The fictive senator Autronius (Tac. 19, 1) may represent an archaising deformation of 'Ausonius,' although the name itself is probably derived from Sallust.

(22) Ausonius commemorates a Syracusan called Citarius, who taught grammar at Bordeaux. He prospered and married a Gallic woman, but died childless : Aus., *Prof.* 13.

The placement of the preface to *Diuus Aurelianus* in the year 304 may be associated in some way with the subsequent abdication of Diocletian in 305, which provoked considerable change in the tetrarchic system and eventually a new round of internal conflicts. Moreover, the decision to end the *HA* with the accession of Diocletian (284) could have been made independently of any connection with Naucellius. We have already noted a possible connection between the dedications and the *Panegyrici Latini*, which includes speeches in praise of Diocletian, Maximian and Constantine. Ausonius too terminated some lost verses on usurpers with the reign of Diocletian.

Some circumstantial considerations may serve to associate Naucellius more closely with our learned impostor, without necessarily suggesting that they were one and the same person. We might begin with literary output. According to Symmachus, Naucellius had translated into Latin a Greek work on ancient constitutions ([23]) ; our impostor shared this antiquarian enthusiasm ([24]) ; he too was a translator, who turned to Herodian, Dexippus and perhaps Eunapius when his other sources failed him ([25]). Our impostor feared that "the day, the hour or the minute" might snatch him away with its "fatal necessity," although perhaps such words were merely commonplace ([26]) ; he cogitated on the maximum span of a human life, a theme Symmachus touched upon delicately in his letters to Naucellius ([27]). The sources suggest that Naucellius was active between about

(23) SYMM., *Ep.* III, 11, 3. Syme speculated on the contents of this lost book in the following terms : "If some graces of style be conceded, the content of the work is not reassuring : erudite fiction may be surmised." SYME 1968a : 109.

(24) The monarchy, the interregnum and the Republic, the Sibylline books, the wars against the Gauls, Spaniards and Carthaginians, Marius, Sulla and Catiline all appear in the *HA*. Ael. 2, 3-5 : etymology of the name Caesar. Cc. 7, 3-5 : gender of the god Luna. OM 12, 2 : decimation and centimation. Max. 33, 2 : Venus Calva. Gd. 12, 1-4 : *senatus consultum tacitum*. MB 8, 5-7 : origin of gladiatorial shows. MB 11, 4-7 : definition of hecatomb. Tac. 1, 1-2, 2 : the *interregnum*.

(25) As his next project, if he lived long enough, the author intended to translate a life of Apollonius of Tyana : A 24, 8-9. Naucellius was involved in translating epigrams from Greek into Latin, often recasting Ausonius' earlier versions with close reference to the original. One of the characteristic follies of the author of the *HA* was to invent or appropriate Latin verses, all the while claiming that these wretched offerings were translations from Greek originals : PN 12, 5-6 ; OM 11, 3-7 ; Max. 27, 4 ; T 11, 5-7. But the model was probably Suetonius. "The reason for the device is patent. The author would have liked to insert Greek quotations after the fashion of Suetonius, but nothing was available." SYME 1968a : 197.

(26) Tac. 16, 7 : *haec ego in aliorum uita de Probo credidi praelibanda, ne dies, hora, momentum aliquid sibi uindicaret in me necessitate fatali ac Probo indicto deperirem.*

(27) SYMM., *Ep.* III, 15, 2 : *nolo annos ad calculum uoces : fiducia salutis in uiribus est. quas cum uitet expendere tutela morum tuorum, spera confecturos deos, ut maneas uitae integer in metas, quas ueterum definitio dedit saeculo.* Cl. 2, 4 : *doctissimi mathematicorum centum uiginti annos homini ad uiuendum datos iudicant neque amplius cui-*

396 and 400, the period in which our author likely wrote. He too engaged an audience among the high aristocracy of the city of Rome. Both the *HA* and the *Epigrammata Bobiensia* address a mysterious Bassus (perhaps the same Bassus, although the name is widely attested) ([28]). Naucellius clearly entrusted copies of his works to Symmachus, probably hoping that the magnate would circulate them among the elite ([29]) ; perhaps the only reference to the *HA* in late antique literature occurs in a fragment of a lost work of Q. Aurelius Memmius Symmachus (consul in 485), a direct descendant of Symmachus himself ([30]). The *Epigrammata Bobiensia*, which preserve Naucellius' unfortunate effusions, survived through a manuscript held in the monastery of St Columban at Bobbio. Some scholars have suggested that the lost original of the *HA* persisted for centuries in the same milieu ([31]).

Sulpiciae conquestio. Some doubts persist over the authorship of the constituent elements of the Bobbio collection. Speyer argued that the *Epigrammata Bobiensia* were the work of the circle of Naucellius, implying that the extant series includes anonymous poems by some of Naucellius' friends and acquaintances ([32]). The attribution of poems two through nine to Naucellius is certain,

quam iactitant esse concessos. Note also Tac. 15, 4 (ever so possibly a hint) : *non magna haec urbanitas haruspicium fuit, qui principem talem post mille annos futurum esse dixerunt, quia, si post centum annos praedicerent, forte possent eorum deprehendi mendacia ... pollicentes, cum uix remanere talis possit historia*. The text is slightly corrupt. Symmachus, with mock insistence, summoned Naucellius back to Rome, alleging that the Senate needed him. Symm., *Ep.* III, 12, 2 : *sat temporis Spoletio datum, bonae urbi et optimorum ciuium matri, intellegenti tamen, quod nostrae curiae uiros usucapere non possit.* Such importunate demands occur in an appendix of private letters between senators found in the *Tacitus*. The spurious senator Autronius Tiberianus wrote to his father Autronius Iustus (Tac. 19, 2) : *fac igitur ut conualescas, curiae interfuturus antiquae*. Claudius Sapilianus wrote to Cereius Maecianus (Tac. 19, 5) : *abice Baianos Puteolanosque secessus, da te urbi, da te curiae*. One of the Bobbio poems opens (*Epig. Bob.* 48, 1) : *Cedite deliciae Baiarum, cedite Bauli.*

(28) *Epig. Bob.* 70 ; Q 2, 1. A Bassus appears in the preface to the *Quadrigae Tyrannorum*, in a scholarly controversy between Marcus Fonteius, Rufius Celsus, Ceionius Iulianus, Fabius Sossianus and Severus Archontius. "Some of these friends of 'Vopiscus' may have been assigned, deliberately, names borne by historical friends or patrons of the real author." Syme 1968a : 193. The name Bassus is widely attested among the descendants of Anicius Auchenius Bassus 11 (*PLRE* I, 152-154) and Clodius Celsinus signo Adelphius 6 (*PLRE* I, 192-193). Paschoud notes at least thirty men with this name attested in the period between 260 and 395 : Paschoud 2001 : 205-206.

(29) Symm., *Ep.* III, 11, 4 (involving a process of revision and expansion). Compare : T 31, 8.

(30) Discussed below in Chapter Six.

(31) Discussed below in Chapter Six.

(32) Speyer 1959. Speyer's theory seems to have lost ground in recent times. It was accepted by the editors of the *Prosopography of the Later Roman Empire*, but is rejected in the latest edition of the *Oxford Classical Dictionary*. One poem is unambiguously

since his names appear throughout this autobiographical series ([33]). Moreover, it seems fairly certain that Naucellius wrote the two poems addressed to the consul of 397, Nonius Atticus Maximus (48, 57), and also three poems on the Aquae Maternae which are present in the collection (1 ; 38 ; 58) ([34]). Given that Naucellius seems to have written at least five otherwise anonymous poems interspersed throughout the collection, he may well have written other epigrams preserved within the same manuscript. Symmachus claimed that he had received a collection of poems from Naucellius, possibly the *Epigrammata Bobiensia* themselves or some related anthology ([35]). One could devote many further pages to the dozens of shorter poems in the extant collection, some of which are no more than couplets. But perhaps little is to be gained from prosecuting such minor points.

Undoubtedly the most significant element of the Bobbio collection is a work described as the *Sulpiciae conquestio de statu rei publicae et temporibus Domitiani*. The *Sulpiciae conquestio* purports to be a diatribe against the government of Domitian, written by a poet called Sulpicia. The conventional view is that there were two poets called Sulpicia : the Sulpicia whose verses are preserved in the *Corpus Tibullianum*, active in the reign of Augustus, and another Sulpicia, active in the reign of Domitian ([36]). An incident reported in Suetonius provides the scenario of the *Sulpiciae conquestio* ([37]). The tyrant has ordered the

ascribed to the young Anicius Probinus (*Epig. Bob.* 65), the consul of 395. There are much more dubious attributions of authorship to the poets Sulpicia (37) and Domitius Marsus (39-40), as well as the suggestion that two poems in the series (42-43) were copied from tombs on the Via Latina.

(33) *Epig. Bob.* 2, 1 ; 6, 1.

(34) Speyer himself conceded that Naucellius probably wrote the two poems addressed to Nonius Atticus Maximus (*Epig. Bob.* 48 ; 57). One of these poems describes its author as a *uates*, an appellation appropriated by Naucellius on no fewer than three occasions in the autobiographical series : *Epig. Bob.* 2, 1 ; 6, 1 ; 7, 1 ; 57, 16. The author also blames his choice of writing materials on his situation in the country, a circumstance consistent with Naucellius' retirement to a villa : *Epig. Bob.* 57, 11-15. The three poems on the Aquae Maternae found throughout the collection (1 ; 38 ; 58) show similarities both with each other and also with the poem that Naucellius wrote on his private baths. Note the parallel between (*Epig. Bob.* 1, 8) *et sacer in uitreis ignis anhelat aquis* and (*Epig. Bob.* 38, 5) *fontibus immixtus uitreis sacer ignis anhelat*. The first of these lines can be compared with a description of Naucellius' baths near Spoleto (*Epig. Bob.* 2, 3-4) : *sed quae | larga riget uitreis lympha perennis aquis*.

(35) Symm., *Ep.* III, 11, 4. These letters also refer to Naucellius' decision to leave Rome for his villa near Spoleto in Umbria, a recurring theme of the epigrams : *Epig. Bob.* 2 ; 7, 3-4 ; 8, 8 ; 57, 11-5 ; Symm., *Ep.* III, 12, 2.

(36) References to the second Sulpicia occur in various late authors : Aus., *Cent. Nupt.* concl. ; *Schol. Iuu.* VI, 537 [Valla] ; Sid., *Carm.* 9, 261-266 ; Fulg., *Myth.* I, 4 ; 23. There is a small literature on the second Sulpicia : Schmidt 2003 : 1095-1096 ; Waterhouse 1993 ; Hallett 1992 : 120-123 ; Parker 1992 ; Richlin 1992 ; Merriam 1991.

(37) Suet., *Dom.* 10.3 : *cuius criminis occasione philosophus omnis urbe Italiaque summouit*.

expulsion from Rome of the philosophers, and Sulpicia and her husband Calenus have been caught up in the purge. As she leaves Rome, Sulpicia invokes the Muse Calliope, rails against Domitian and his vices, and offers moralising digressions on aspects of Roman history. It goes without saying that this diatribe is not a genuine work of the Flavian period. Modern scholars assign the *Sulpiciae conquestio* various dates in the decades around the turn of the fifth century ([38]). At the centre of the Bobbio collection is an imposture, or at best an impersonation, allegedly belonging to the age of the emperors and apparently drawing on a close reading of imperial biography.

Sulpicia's diatribe elaborates upon a minor incident recorded in Suetonius, drawing some phraseology and thematic material from Juvenal and his scholarly parergon. The scholia on Juvenal contain the only known fragment of the poet known as the second Sulpicia ([39]). The claim that Sulpicia wrote in iambic trimeter, found in the *Sulpiciae conquestio*, is corroborated by the presence of an otherwise unknown erotic fragment in this measure in the scholia ([40]). Moreover, the second part of the title *Sulpiciae conquestio de statu rei publicae et temporibus Domitiani* may be derived from the phrase *tempora Domitiani tyranni*, featured prominently in the scholia ([41]). The Sulpicia of the *Epigrammata Bobiensia* adopts a characteristically 'Juvenalian' stance in denouncing the abuses of Domitian (*grauiter carpsit* as the scholiast put it). The basic scenario of the *Sulpiciae conquestio* may have been taken from Juvenal's third satire, in which the weary Umbricius explains his decision to leave Rome for his place of retirement at Cumae. The notion that Juvenal himself was persecuted and exiled during his lifetime (naturally by Domitian) was present in the exegetical tradition, and may have informed the diatribe ascribed to Sulpicia. There is no evidence anywhere else in the tradition that either Calenus or Sulpicia endured exile at any stage in their lives. Faced with the *Sulpiciae conquestio*, one naturally thinks of

(38) Fuchs argued that the *Sulpiciae conquestio* was written after the *de Reditu Suo* of Rutilius Namatianus (which appeared in 417), although arguments based exclusively upon verbal parallels of this kind are not always compelling : Fuchs 1968. Giordano Rampioni concluded that the poem was written *non anteriore alla fine del IV secolo*. Giordano Rampioni 1982 : 34. Lana argued that this diatribe contained some lines reminiscent of Claudian's *de Bello Gildonico* (first recited at Milan in April 398), perhaps suggesting that the diatribe appeared in or after the year 398 : Lana 1949 : 72-74. It is worth remembering in this context that Chastagnol discerned some (rather vague) similarities between passages in the *Bellum Gildonicum* (398), the *Probus* and the *Quadrigae Tyrannorum* : Chastagnol 1970b : 444-463.

(39) *Schol. Iuu.* VI, 537 [Valla].

(40) *Epig. Bob.* 37, 5.

(41) *Schol. Iuu.* I, 1 [sup. et s] : *ea tempora Domitiani tyranni, quibus etiam ipse uixit, eo quod in aula ipsius plus histriones quam bonae uitae homines possent, grauiter carpsit.* Perhaps coincidentally, the phrase *Ser. Sulpici conquestio* occurs in Cicero's speech in defence of Murena : Cic., *pro Mur.* 3, 7.

the notorious letter of Hadrian criticising the Alexandrians (presented in the *Quadrigae Tyrannorum*), in which phraseology taken from Juvenal embellishes a spurious account of an episode probably reported in the lost works of Marius Maximus ([42]). The same constellation of connections appears. The fact that the only known quotation from the second Sulpicia occurs in the scholia on Juvenal, which also happen to contain the only express quotation of Marius Maximus outside the *HA*, indicates the narrow basis of the tradition.

There is a case to be made for ascribing the *Sulpiciae conquestio* to Naucellius, who is heavily associated with many of the other poems in the Bobbio collection. The dramatic setting of the diatribe coheres with a central theme of the autobiographical series in the *Epigrammata Bobiensia* : Naucellius' retreat from Rome to his delightful villa, where he enjoyed a sadly too fruitful retirement among his books. When Sulpicia invokes the *optima Musa ... sine qua mihi nulla uoluptas uiuere*, one naturally thinks of Naucellius' desire to cultivate learning and leisure, or to enjoy *quodque uoluptati est* on his estate ([43]). Naucellius had quit Rome for a retirement near Spoleto. His personal connection with Umbria might well explain an otherwise obscure reference to a mythical emigration. In a corrupted passage, Sulpicia alludes to an emigration associated with "the Lydian" and the city of Smyrna ([44]). These verses probably refer to the legendary prince Tyrrhenus, who led some Lydian refugees from Smyrna, allegedly founding the Etruscan civilisation ([45]). Perversely, the Sulpicia of the *Epigrammata*

(42) Q 7, 6-8, 10. Our author claimed to have found the letter in a work of the imperial freedman Phlegon (Q 7, 6), discussed earlier in a genuine context in the *de Vita Hadriani* (H 16, 1). Servianus, a senator obliged to suicide by Hadrian (H 15, 8 ; 23, 2-3 ; 8 ; 25, 8), appears as the recipient (Q 8, 1-10). The *de Vita Hadriani* mentions unrest at Alexandria, caused by the appearance of Apis, while Cassius Dio suggested that the emperor Hadrian wrote to the Alexandrians, rebuking them for rioting : H 12, 1 ; Cass. Dio LXIX, 8, 1. The spurious missive echoes a well known line of Juvenal on the multifarious occupations of the Greekling. Q 8, 3 : *nemo illic archisynagogus Iudaeorum, nemo Samarites, nemo Christianorum presbyter non mathematicus, non haruspex, non aliptes*. Compare Iuv. III, 76-78 : *grammaticus, rhetor, geometres, pictor, aliptes, | augur, schoenobates, medicus, magus, omnia nouit | Graeculus esuriens*. Note also *Schol. Iuu.* VI, 557 (1) : *magorum, haruspicum aut mathematicorum*. Moreover, the letter may take its theme from the title of the fifteenth satire as it appears in the Codex Pithoeanus (*de religionibus aegypti*). Clausen omitted this title, reported in an otherwise obsolete edition : Owen 1907.

(43) *Epig. Bob*. 37, 58-60. Compare *Epig. Bob*. 5, 2 : *hic studia et Musis otia amica colo*. Note also 5, 4-6 : *quodque uoluptati est, hinc capio atque fruor : | rura, domus, rigui genuinis fontibus horti | dulciaque imparium Marmora Pieridum.*

(44) *Epig. Bob*. 37, 60-61. The text of this passage is not entirely clear. Giordano Rampioni read *uti quondam Zmyrna Lydusque peribat | nunc itidem migrare uelit*, and translated the phrase with *come quando un tempo Smirna e il Lido scomparvero per sempre, che ora allo stesso modo voglia emigrare anche lui.*

(45) Her. I, 94 ; Giordano Rampioni 1982 : 102-103.

Bobiensia may echo the words of a much earlier poetess of the same name, compelled to leave Rome for a dreary country estate near Arezzo ([46]). The reference to the foundation myth of the Etruscan civilisation in the *Sulpiciae conquestio* seems to combine antiquarian learning and literary allusion in an eccentric fashion. Other passages in the diatribe touch upon the Roman reception of Greek laws and institutions, a subject known to have been of interest to Naucellius himself ([47]). It is surely more than a coincidence that the Sulpicia of the *Corpus Tibullianum*, the Sulpicia of the *Epigrammata Bobiensia* and the elderly Naucellius all alluded to a retreat in approximately the same region of Italy.

There are some affinities between the *Epigrammata Bobiensia* and the *HA*, in addition to the curious connections between Naucellius and Vopiscus. The historical digressions in the *Sulpiciae conquestio* resemble in some respects the often confused declamations that grace the prefaces ascribed to Flavius Vopiscus Syracusius. Lana, Speyer and Giordano Rampioni noted a parallel between the *Sulpiciae conquestio* and the preface to the *Carus et Carinus et Numerianus*. Sulpicia claimed :

> … duo sunt quibus extulit ingens
> Roma caput, uirtus belli et sapientia pacis.
> Sed uirtus, agitata domi et socialibus armis,
> in freta Sicaniae et Carthaginis exilit arces
> ceteraque imperia et totum simul abstulit orbem ([48]).

> There are two things by which Rome raised her great head : vigour in war and wisdom in peace. But vigour (trained at home and in wars with allies) sprung upon the straits of Sicily and the citadel of Carthage, and it at once snatched away the other powers and the whole world.

Elaborating on a similar theme, the *HA* includes the following :

> Then the state grew great, after Carthage was conquered and the empire was extended across the seas (*trans maria missis imperiis*), but afflicted by conflict with its allies (*socialibus adfecta discordiis*), having lost its sense of good fortune, it wasted away, afflicted by civil wars until the time of Augustus. Then it was restored by Augustus, if one may say that it was restored, when it gave up its freedom. But somehow, although

(46) Tib. IV, 8, 3-4 : *dulcius urbe quid est ? an uilla sit apta puellae | atque Arretino frigidus amnis agro ?*. I owe this observation to Ann Moffatt. Umbria and Etruria are geographically proximate. Moreover, in the fourth century, these regions were part of a conjoined administrative unit, called "Etruria et Umbria." Gd. 4, 6 : *Etruria et Vmbria*. T 24, 5 : *Etruria atque Vmbria*.

(47) *Epig. Bob*. 37, 29 : *ipsa domi leges et Graia inuenta retractans*. Compare Symm., *Ep*. III, 11, 3 : *arma a Samnitibus, insignia ab Tuscis, leges de lare Lycurgi et Solonis sumpseramus*. Also noteworthy is a reference to the Sabines : *Epig. Bob*. 37, 63. The name Sabinus ran in Naucellius' family.

(48) *Epig. Bob*. 37, 20-24 ; Lana 1949 : 39-40. Lana sought to differentiate the historical schemata involved.

it was unfortunate at home (*tristis domi*), it flourished among foreign peoples. Next, after it suffered so many Neros, it lifted its head (*extulit caput*) under Vespasian ([49]).

There are some parallels between these two passages. The *Sulpiciae conquestio* juxtaposes the capture of the straits of Sicily (at the beginning of the First Punic War) and the destruction of Carthage, while the preface to the *Carus et Carinus et Numerianus* contrasts the fall of Carthage and the extension of Roman power over the seas. The phrase *extulit ingens Roma caput* appears in the diatribe, while the preface contains the phrase *extulit caput* (with the implied subject *Romana res publica* or *nostra res publica*) ([50]). The phrase *agitata ... socialibus armis*, found in the diatribe, echoes the phrase *socialibus adfecta discordiis* in the preface. One would not want to assert too much on the basis of these two passages, although the comparison is interesting. While their language is in some ways close, much of the verbiage involved is probably formulaic. Moreover, the claim that the Roman state began to decline after the fall of the old enemy Carthage was obviously a commonplace ([51]).

There are a few further affinities between the *Sulpiciae conquestio* and the prefaces of the *HA*. Commenting on the strength of the Romans when faced with difficult circumstances, Sulpicia repeated one of "the holy sayings of the ancient Cato" (*prisci sententia dia Catonis*), which she quoted without acknowledgment from Aulus Gellius ([52]). We know that the preface to the *Probus* repeated another saying of Cato the Elder preserved in the same compilation ([53]). There are also

(49) Car. 3, 1-2 : *creuit deinde uicta Carthagine trans maria missis imperiis, sed socialibus adfecta discordiis extenuato felicitatis sensu usque ad Augustum bellis ciuilibus adfecta consenuit. per Augustum deinde reparata, si reparata dici potest libertate deposita. tamen utcumque, etiamsi domi tristis fuit, apud exteras gentes effloruit ; passa deinceps tot Nerones, per Vespasianum extulit caput.* Magie translated the phrase *trans maria missis imperiis* "having ... extended its empire over the seas," while Chastagnol writes *en étendant son empire au-delà des mers*, but there is perhaps also the possibility that the author alluded to the establishment of overseas commands.

(50) On the use of the phrase *extulit caput* in a metaphorical sense with reference to Roman power, see : GIORDANO RAMPIONI 1982 : 77 ; *TLL* V, 2, col. 145, 42. Note also some comments of Scipio Africanus on the perfection of the Roman state after the defeat of Carthage : MB 17, 8.

(51) Note, for example : CLAUD., *de Cons. Stilich.* III, 140 : *haec obuia fatis | innumeras uno gereret cum tempore pugnas, | Hispanas caperet, Siculas obsideret urbes | et Gallum terris prosterneret, aequore Poenum, | numquam succubuit damnis et territa nullo | uulnere post Cannas maior Trebiamque fremebat | et, cum iam premerent flammae murumque feriret | hostis, in extremos aciem mittebat Hiberos | nec stetit Oceano remisque ingressa profundum | uincendos alio quaesiuit in orbe Britannos.* Some similar ideas also occur in the *Bellum Gildonicum* (76-95).

(52) *Epig. Bob.* 37, 49-51. Compare GELL. VI, 3, 14.

(53) Pr. 1, 1 : *Certum est, quod Sallustius Crispus quodque Marcus Cato et Gellius historici sententiae modo in litteras rettulerunt.* Compare GELL. III, 7, 19. Note also : H 5, 3 ; 16, 6.

parallels in language between the *HA* and the *Sulpiciae conquestio*. The diminutive *fabella* (meaning "account, short account") occurs twice in the poem and six times in the *HA* ([54]). Both works use the verb *frequentare* to mean "celebrate, make famous" ([55]). The usage, themes and concerns of the *Sulpiciae conquestio* reflect in some respects those of the prefaces of the lives ascribed to Vopiscus. These parallels are intriguing, although they would not necessarily make a case for close filiation. It is perhaps surprising that we should find any similarities at all, given the small number of extant verses associated with the name of Naucellius.

Conclusion. Hypotheses concerning the authorship of the *HA* generally suffer a grim fate. It would be unwise to make exaggerated claims based upon the material presented in this chapter. Parallels in phraseology and language, unless utterly damning, are unlikely to support an identification of authorship, especially across texts of different genres. Merely circumstantial considerations, such as those discussed above, may suggest that two authors worked in close proximity, without proving anything more definitive. Nonetheless, some arguments stand out. The fact that Naucellius and Vopiscus shared an affiliation with Syracuse, openly publicised in the same circles at the same time, is perhaps significant. Moreover, the connections between the *Sulpiciae conquestio*, the scholia on Juvenal and Marius Maximus, important points in a constellation of cultural references, may be relevant. Taking all the evidence into account, one might conclude that Naucellius and the dreadful verses of the *Epigrammata Bobiensia*

(54) *Epig. Bob.* 37, 2 ; 58 ; MA 19, 1 ; Cc. 8, 6 ; AS 38, 6 ; Max. 31, 4 ; Gd. 10, 6 ; Car. 14, 1 ; *TLL* VI, 1, col. 6, 69 ; *BTL* ; *CLCT* ; Giordano Rampioni 1982 : 66-67. The *TLL* lists only nine further occurrences in Latin literature of the word *fabella* with this meaning : one in Cicero, two in Horace, one in Tibullus, one in Pliny the Younger, one in Apuleius, one in Jerome, one in Augustine and one in Martianus Capella. The *CLCT* lists about a dozen further examples from Augustine, some of which probably fall into the category *narratio commenticia, incredibilis* : *TLL* VI, 1, col. 7, 1. The dimunitive *fabella* is more common with specialised meanings, associated with poetry, fable or myth : *TLL* VI, 1, col. 7, 3 (*de poetarum et scriptorum fabulis*). Nonetheless, Glare's entry for the word *fabella* differs markedly from that found in the *TLL* (although it does not deal with the material from the later period) : Glare 1968-1982 : 664. Giordano Rampioni claimed that the verb *texere* and compound verbs derived from *texere* (notably *contexere*) often governed the words *fabula* or *fabella* in the literature of the fourth century. Nevertheless, she cited four examples, only one of which involved the word *fabella* (MA 19, 2 : *fabellam ... contexere*) : Giordano Rampioni 1982 : 66-67.

(55) *TLL* VI, 1, col. 1309, 232 ; Giordano Rampioni 1982 : 66. *Epig. Bob.* 37, 1 : *Musa, quibus numeris heroas et arma frequentas.* A 1, 5 : *'ergo Thersiten, Sinonem ceteraque illa prodigia uetustatis et nos bene scimus et posteri frequentabunt : diuum Aurelianum, clarissimum principem, seuerissimum imperatorem, per quem totus Romano nomini orbis est restitutis, posteri nescient ?'* A 24, 3 : *ueterem philosophum, amicum uere deorum, ipsum etiam pro numine frequentandum.*

were somehow associated with Flavius Vopiscus Syracusius and the works of our impostor. This possible connection is ingenious and interesting. Moreover, we can think beyond the narrow confines of an 'authorship hypothesis' when describing any association between Naucellius and our impostor. Naucellius was a figure of merely parochial interest, and so any decision to celebrate or deride him would represent a strong indication of context. It is conceivable, for example, that an amanuensis, relative, disciple, imitator or detractor assumed the identity of Naucellius for some obscure purpose. The *HA* might be interpreted as a work compiled under the aegis of an elderly master, as a perverse homage to an aged scholar, or even as a savage parody of an ancient don. There is also the possibility that Naucellius' death at an advanced age prompted some reverent or unscrupulous person to assume his mantle.

It is worth noting that an association between our impostor and Naucellius would be broadly consistent with some received interpretations of the *HA*. Many scholars have argued that the corpus reflects the values, concerns and interests of the Roman aristocracy and the senatorial class more generally. Naucellius was a minor senator, apparently affiliated with several prominent families, including the Nicomachi-Symmachi. One could argue that Naucellius undertook antiquarian projects to glorify the great aristocrats with whom he was associated. Indeed, interventions of this kind were most likely to emanate from individuals at the fringes of the elite, who had been conditioned to engage with influential benefactors through scholarship. At the same time, aspects of Naucellius' character bring to mind Syme's devious and capricious "rogue scholar." The pedantic background of the *Epigrammata Bobiensia*, as well as their connections to the scholia on Juvenal, are consistent with this hypothesis. Moreover, the species of erudite bricolage demonstrated throughout the *Sulpiciae conquestio* should already be familiar to readers of the *HA*. The notion that a nonagenarian Syracusan was somehow implicated in the most notorious imposture in Latin literature is wonderfully perverse. Nevertheless, Naucellius himself remains an enigmatic figure, and much concerning his motives and background is obscure. The purpose of this chapter has been to provoke debate, rather than to propose a definitive solution to the problem of authorship. Hopefully there is room for further discussion ([56]).

(56) I would like to thank Doug Kelly for his astute criticisms of an earlier version of this chapter.

SVLPICIAE CONQVESTIO DE STATV REI PVBLICAE ET TEMPORIBVS DOMITIANI

Musa, quibus numeris heroas et arma frequentas,
fabellam permitte mihi detexere paucis.
Nam tibi secessi, tecum penetrale retractans
consilium ; quare neque carmine curro Phalaeco
nec trimetro iambo nec qui pede fractus eodem
fortiter irasci discit duce Clazomenio ;
cetera quin etiam, quot denique milia lusi
primaque Romanos docui contendere Graiis
et salibus uariare nouis, constanter omitto
teque quibus princeps et facundissima calles
aggredior : precibus descende clientis et audi.
Dic mihi Calliope : quidnam pater ille deorum
cogitat ? an terras et patria saecula mutat
quasque dedit quondam morientibus eripit artes
nosque iubet tacitos et iam rationis egenos
non aliter, primo quam cum surreximus aruo,
glandibus et purae rursus procumbere lymphae ?
an reliquas terras conseruat amicus et urbes,
sed genus Ausonium Romaeque exturbat alumnos ?

This reconstruction follows the text of Giordano Rampioni's edition. The *Sulpiciae conquestio* falls into four parts : the first invocation of the Muse (1-19), the first historical digression (20-38), the second historical digression (39-57) and the second invocation of the Muse (58-70). There are indications that these four sections conform to the page divisions of the (lost) autograph manuscript. The first, second and third sections contain nineteen lines of verse each, while the fourth section occupies thirteen lines, leaving exactly six lines for the next poem in the series (*Epig. Bob.* 38). Admittedly, one must exclude the title of poem 37 from these calculations, but include the title of poem 38.

Quid ? reputemus enim : duo sunt quibus extulit ingens
Roma caput, uirtus belli et sapientia pacis.
Sed uirtus, agitata domi et socialibus armis,
in freta Sicaniae et Carthaginis exilit arces
ceteraque imperia et totum simul abstulit orbem.
Deinde, uelut stadio uictor qui solus Achaeo
languet et immota secum uirtute fatescit,
sic itidem Romana manus, contendere postquam
destitit et pacem longis frenauit habenis ;
ipsa domi leges et Graia inuenta retractans
omnia bellorum terra quaesita marique
praemia consilio et molli ratione regebat.
Stabat in his, neque enim poterat constare sine ipsis :
aut frustra uxori mendaxque Diespiter olim
»imperium sine fine dedi« dixisse probatur.
Nunc igitur qui rex Romanos imperat inter,
non trabe sed tergo prolapsus et ingluuie albus,
et studia et sapiens hominum nomenque genusque
omni abire foras atque Vrbe excedere iussit.

There appear to be parallels between the first historical digression and the second historical digression. These are parallels in the literal sense of the word, since the second and third sections can be placed side by side, one mirroring the other. So, for example, we find *quid ? reputemus* at line twenty, opposite to *quid facimus ?* at line thirty-nine (remembering here that the punctuation is a modern convention). The noun *Roma* appears at line twenty-one, while the adjective *Romana* appears at line forty. The past participle *agitata* occurs at line twenty-two, alongside the present participle *turbante* at line forty-one. The word *manus* occurs at line twenty-seven and also at line forty-seven. The verbs *stare* and *constare* are applied to the Roman state at line thirty-two, while the verb *stare* occurs in a similar context at line fifty. The noun *uxor* appears at line thirty-three and at line fifty-two. The use of *uxor* at line thirty-three is perhaps surprising, since Jupiter is meant to have addressed his prophecy on the greatness of Rome to Venus (and not to Juno) : VIRG., *Aen.* I, 278-279.

Quid facimus ? Graios hominumque relinquimus urbes,
ut Romana foret magis his instructa magistris :
nunc, Capitolino ueluti turbante Camillo
ensibus et trutina Galli fugere relicta,
sic nostri palare senes dicuntur et ipsi
ut ferale suos onus exportare libellos.
Ergo Numantinus Libycusque errauit in isto
Scipio, qui Rhodio creuit formante magistro,
ceteraque illa manus bello facunda secundo
quos inter prisci sententia dia Catonis
scire deos magni fecisset, utrumne secundis
an magis aduersis staret Romana propago.
Scilicet aduersis : nam, cum defendier armis
suadet amor patriae et captiua penatibus uxor,
conuenit, ut uespis, apium domus arce mouente,
turba rigens strictis per lutea corpora telis ;
ast ubi apes secura redit oblita fauorum
plebs regesque una somno moriuntur obeso.
Romulidarum igitur longa et grauis exitium pax.

Hoc fabella modo pausam facit. Optima, posthac,
Musa uelim moneas, sine qua mihi nulla uoluptas
uiuere, uti quondam Zmyrna Lydusque peribat,
nunc itidem migrare uelis : uel denique quiduis
ut dea quaere aliud : tantum Romana Caleno
moenia iucundes pariterque auerte Sabinos.
Haec ego : tum paucis dea me dignarier infit :
»pone metus aequos cultrix mea : summa tyranno
haec instant odia et nostro periturus honore est.
Nam laureta Numae fontisque habitamus eosdem
et comite Egeria ridemus inania coepta.
Viue, uale. Manet hunc pulchrum sua fama dolorem :
Musarum spondet chorus et Romana Apollo«.

CVISDAM IN AQVAS MATERNAS

Corniger has quondam pedibus pulsauit harenas
taurus et undantis expressit rupibus ignis.
admiranda fides dictu : duo corpora rerum
inter se aduersis semper pugnantia fatis,
fontibus immixtus uitreis sacer ignis anhelat.

What appears to be a transition formula (*Hoc fabella modo pausam facit*), as well as the renewed invocation of the Muse (*optima ... Musa*), mark a clear point of discontinuity at line 58.

The three poems on the Aquae Maternae (*Epig. Bob.* 1 ; 38 ; 58), probably written by Naucellius himself, may have helped to structure the collection, or they may have been added merely to fill the available space. The first poem on this theme introduces the biographical series (*Epig. Bob.* 2-9), while the third occurs immediately after a poem addressed to the consul of 397 (57).

CHAPTER FIVE

Redaction

Introduction. In the introduction to his English translation of the *HA*, Magie wrote scathingly about the "method of composition" of the lives :

> The literary, as well as the historical, value of the *Historia Augusta* has suffered greatly as a result of the method of its composition. In the arrangement in categories of the historical material, the authors did but follow the accepted principles of the art of biography as practised in antiquity, but their narratives, consisting often of mere excerpts arranged without regard to connexion or transition, lack grace and even cohesion. The over-emphasis of personal details and the introduction of anecdotal material destroy the proportion of many sections, and the insertion of forged documents interrupts the course of the narrative, without adding anything of historical value or even of general interest. Finally, the later addition of lengthy passages and brief notes, frequently in paragraphs with the general content of which they have no connexion, has put the crowning touch to the awkwardness and incoherence of the whole, with the result that the oft-repeated charge seems almost justified, that these biographies are little more than literary monstrosities (1).

No doubt many other readers of the *HA* react negatively to its awkwardness and incoherence. Nevertheless, it may be best to put aside aesthetic objections of this kind, which contribute very little to our understanding of the text. By concentrating upon the evidence of the manuscript tradition, one can develop a greater appreciation of the processes that contributed to the present structure and form of the corpus. The received text appears to be the result of a process of redaction undertaken long before the earliest extant manuscripts. Arguably, the basic organisation of the corpus reflects the manner in which it was composed and redacted, and not the accidents or interventions of the scribal tradition (2).

The discussion of redaction that follows differs from previous approaches to the subject. There have been various attempts to describe the sequence in which the individual lives were composed, and to assign these lives individual dates,

(1) Magie 2006 : I, xxiii-xxiv.

(2) We cannot rule out the involvement of an amanuensis in this process of redaction, if only because the author himself mentions that he employed dictation in his haste : T 33, 8 ; Schlumberger 1976b.

although such efforts have produced mutually contradictory results ([3]). There is also a traditional classification, based largely upon source critical considerations, which divides the lives into primary, secondary, intermediate and final groups ([4]). This typology, although generally accurate, rests upon too narrow a foundation. The new approach adopted in this chapter seeks to describe the original form of the corpus on the basis of all the available evidence. We can gain a full understanding of the question by analysing the sources, citations (including spurious citations), attributions and dedications found throughout the lives, as well as the evidence present within the manuscript tradition. This approach reduces the obscuring influence of modern editorial conventions, while revealing new patterns within the corpus. Otherwise apparently intractable problems (notably the lacuna and other discontinuities in the text) can be put into a new perspective.

The Order of the Lives. Before discussing the redaction of the corpus, it is important to establish the order in which the thirty lives appeared in the original version of the text. This problem has not been recognised by previous scholars, who have assumed (naturally enough) that the lives were presented to their first readers more or less in the order in which the various emperors and usurpers

(3) Chastagnol 1994 : xlvi-li ; Syme 1972b. Some scholars also attempt to place the lives in a relative order, and then to assign absolute dates to individual lives : Callu 1992 : xiv-lxx ; Honoré 1987 : 157-165. Many scholars seem to assume that the lives were written one after the other, as discrete units. But the author may well have redacted the lives all together, progressively adulterating his sources with layer after layer of spurious materials. Consistent with this theory are the great number of false endings in the text : AC 13, 8 ; PN 9, 1 ; MB 7, 7 ; 15, 3 ; Tac. 16, 5 (among other examples). Contradictory statements in the *Gallieni Duo* reflect two different stages in the evolution of the *Tyranni Triginta*. There are three references to a collection of twenty tyrants in the *Gallieni Duo* : Gall. 16, 1 ; 19, 6 ; 21, 1. The same life also mentions a collection of thirty tyrants : Gall. 19, 7. The *Tyranni Triginta* contains a core of about twenty entries (probably T 3, 1-22, 14), which has been padded with further material. The accretion of marginalia might explain the disorganisation of many of the lives.

(4) Chastagnol 1994 : xxxvii-xlii. The primary lives (the *de Vita Hadriani*, *Antoninus Pius*, *Vita Marci Antonini Philosophi*, *Verus*, *Commodus Antoninus*, *Heluius Pertinax*, *Didius Iulianus*, *Seuerus* and *Antoninus Caracallus*) essentially paraphrase the biographical tradition (i.e. Marius Maximus), although not without adulteration, interpolation and truncation. The secondary lives (the *Aelius*, *Auidius Cassius*, *Pescennius Niger*, *Vita Clodii Albini* and *Antoninus Geta*) derive their genuine content from lives of Hadrian, Marcus Aurelius or Severus preserved within the biographical tradition. Herodian, sometimes supplemented by Dexippus, provided the framework for the intermediate lives (*Opilius Macrinus*, *Diadumenus Antoninus*, *Antoninus Heliogabalus*, *Alexander Seuerus*, *Maximini Duo*, *Gordiani Tres* and *Maximus et Balbinus*). The so-called final lives are derived from Dexippus (*Valeriani Duo*, *Gallieni Duo*, *Tyranni Triginta* and *Diuus Claudius*) and an unnamed Greek historian (the *Diuus Aurelianus*, *Tacitus*, *Probus*, *Quadrigae Tyrannorum* and *Carus et Carinus et Numerianus*).

reigned. Nevertheless, in discussing this problem we should begin with the evidence preserved in the manuscript tradition. It is well known that some of the lives appear out of their proper place throughout all the most significant manuscripts. The *Auidius Cassius*, *Didius Iulianus*, *Vita Clodii Albini*, *Opilius Macrinus*, *Diadumenus Antoninus* and *Antoninus Heliogabalus* appear out of their chronological order in the Codex Palatinus latinus 899 (P), the basis of our tradition. The same might be said of another early witness to the text. During his stay at Liège in the middle of the ninth century, Sedulius Scottus quoted some passages from a lost manuscript of the lives (a manuscript in some respects superior to P) ([5]). Based upon the order of his excerpts, it seems that Sedulius Scottus drew upon a manuscript in which the *Commodus Antoninus* appeared before the *Auidius Cassius*, while the *Antoninus Heliogabalus* appeared before the *Opilius Macrinus* : features clearly exemplified in P and its descendants. The *Vita Clodii Albini*, *Opilius Macrinus, Diadumenus Antoninus* and *Antoninus Heliogabalus* also appear in reverse order in an important group of humanistic manuscripts (Σ), although here the *Didius Iulianus* and *Auidius Cassius* have been returned to their proper chronological position. We can conclude on this basis that the *Auidius Cassius*, *Didius Iulianus*, *Vita Clodii Albini*, *Opilius Macrinus*, *Diadumenus Antoninus* and *Antoninus Heliogabalus* must have appeared out of their chronological sequence in the archetype of the manuscript tradition. On this basis, we can contrast the order in which the lives appeared in the lost archetype of the manuscript tradition (their manuscript order) with their chronological sequence (the order in which the various dynasties, emperors and usurpers reigned). The terms "manuscript order" and "chronological sequence" will be used throughout the following discussion.

Modern editors generally return the *Auidius Cassius*, *Didius Iulianus*, *Vita Clodii Albini*, *Opilius Macrinus*, *Diadumenus Antoninus* and *Antoninus Heliogabalus* to their proper chronological position without much comment or explanation. These editors seem to assume that the manuscript order of the lives was a result of an accident in the tradition, which affected the lost archetype of the extant manuscripts ([6]). Nonetheless, it is difficult to see how a random accident could have rearranged the lives in the manuscript order, without causing catastrophic damage to the corpus. Moreover, when the lives are placed in their manuscript order, meaningful patterns emerge. Most obviously, it seems that lives ascribed to Spartianus (the *Seuerus*, *Pescennius Niger*, *Antoninus*

(5) There are modern editions of the *Collectaneum* and an edition and a translation of the *de Regibus Christianis* : Simpson 1988 ; Doyle 1983 ; Hellman 1906. On the place of the excerpts in the *Collectaneum* in the tradition of the *HA*, see : Velaza 1998 ; Callu 1985 : 125 ; Ballou 1914 : 76-79 ; Hohl 1914 ; Mommsen 1878.

(6) This assumption is rarely stated. Pecere, however, refers to "the serious damage" at some stage in the transmission of the text : Pecere 1995 : 331.

Figure One : The Manuscript Order of the Lives (I-XVIII)

P	**Sedulius Scottus**	**Σ**	**Archetype (reconstructed)**
de Vita Hadriani	*de Vita Hadriani*	*de Vita Hadriani*	*de Vita Hadriani*
Aelius	–	*Aelius*	*Aelius*
Antoninus Pius	*Antoninus Pius*	*Antoninus Pius*	*Antoninus Pius*
Vita Marci Antonini Philosophi	*Vita Marci Antonini Philosophi*	*Vita Marci Antonini Philosophi*	*Vita Marci Antonini Philosophi*
Verus	–	*Verus*	*Verus*
Didius Iulianus	–	*Auidius Cassius*	**Didius Iulianus**
Commodus Antoninus	*Commodus Antoninus*	*Commodus Antoninus*	*Commodus Antoninus*
Heluius Pertinax	–	*Heluius Pertinax*	*Heluius Pertinax*
Auidius Cassius	**Auidius Cassius**	*Didius Iulianus*	**Auidius Cassius**
Seuerus	–	*Seuerus*	*Seuerus*
Pescennius Niger	*Pescennius Niger*	*Pescennius Niger*	*Pescennius Niger*
Antoninus Caracallus	–	*Antoninus Caracallus*	*Antoninus Caracallus*
Antoninus Geta	–	*Antoninus Geta*	*Antoninus Geta*
Antoninus Heliogabalus	**Antoninus Heliogabalus**	**Antoninus Heliogabalus**	**Antoninus Heliogabalus**
Diadumenus Antoninus	–	**Diadumenus Antoninus**	**Diadumenus Antoninus**
Opilius Macrinus	**Opilius Macrinus**	**Opilius Macrinus**	**Opilius Macrinus**
Vita Clodii Albini	–	**Vita Clodii Albini**	**Vita Clodii Albini**
Alexander Seuerus	*Alexander Seuerus*	*Alexander Seuerus*	*Alexander Seuerus*

Lives out of their proper chronological sequence are marked with asterisks (*). *The order of the remaining lives (XIX-XXX) is well established.*

Caracallus and *Antoninus Geta*), Lampridius (the *Antoninus Heliogabalus* and *Diadumenus Antoninus*) and Capitolinus (the *Opilius Macrinus* and *Vita Clodii Albini*) have been placed together ([7]). Moreover, the lives as they occur in the earliest manuscripts fall naturally into three groups, which can be distinguished on the basis of their attributions of authorship, dedications and underlying sources, as well as their citations of genuine and spurious authorities. These patterns are closely bound up with the content of the text, and so they are unlikely to be the result of merely scribal initiative. The boundaries of the three groups of

(7) The final colophons to the *Pescennius Niger* (PESCENNIUS NIGER AELI SPARTIANI EXPLICIT) and the *Vita Clodii Albini* (VITA CLODI ALBINI IVLI CAPITOLINI EXPLICIT) corroborate these attributions.

lives seem to coincide with significant disruptions in the corpus itself : the absence of lives of Nerva and Trajan, the perverse arrangement of the *Vita Clodii Albini*, *Opilius Macrinus, Diadumenus Antoninus* and *Antoninus Heliogabalus*, as well as the apparent lacuna covering the period from the death of Gordian III until the capture of Valerian. Some of the patterns seen when the lives are arranged in their manuscript order disappear when they are arranged according to the chronological sequence of the dynasties, emperors and usurpers. There is considerable evidence that the author himself was responsible for the manuscript order of the lives. Arguably, future editors should restore the order of the lives found in the earliest and most informative manuscripts.

Three Groups. The first group of lives is the most difficult to describe, in part because it contains the fewest aberrant features. It includes the *de Vita Hadriani*, *Aelius*, *Antoninus Pius*, *Vita Marci Antonini Philosophi*, *Verus*, *Didius Iulianus*, *Commodus Antoninus*, *Heluius Pertinax*, *Auidius Cassius*, *Seuerus*, *Pescennius Niger*, *Antoninus Caracallus* and *Antoninus Geta*. All the lives in this group draw upon the biographical material generally associated with the name of Marius Maximus, supplemented in some places with passages extracted from the epitomators. It is worth noting that the scope of the first group corresponds almost exactly to the alleged limits of the work of the "unknown biographer" invoked by Syme and Barnes among others ([8]). The so-called primary lives (the *de Vita Hadriani*, *Antoninus Pius*, *Vita Marci Antonini Philosophi*, *Verus*, *Commodus Antoninus*, *Heluius Pertinax*, *Didius Iulianus*, *Seuerus* and *Antoninus Caracallus*) contain relatively few of the fabrications and digressions found elsewhere in the corpus. The so-called secondary lives of group one (the *Aelius*, *Auidius Cassius*, *Pescennius Niger* and *Antoninus Geta*) draw upon material related to Hadrian, Marcus Aurelius, Severus and Caracalla, much of it previously presented in the primary lives. The secondary lives are much more liberal with their inventions, "notably orations and forged documents, bogus authorities, and fabricated names" ([9]). Prefaces and epilogues only appear in the secondary lives of the first group. The first group contains all the lives ascribed to Spartianus and the only life ascribed to Gallicanus. It is the only group in which Spartianus, Capitolinus, Gallicanus and Lampridius appear together.

(8) Some references on this question appear in the introduction (at n. 9). Those who accept the theory of an unknown biographer might argue that the first group of lives relied upon his works alongside the works of Marius Maximus, while the *Antoninus Heliogabalus* (in the second group) relied upon Marius Maximus alone. Others might argue that the transition from group one to group two coincided with a change in the manner in which the author redacted the works of Marius Maximus.

(9) Syme 1968a : 93. Syme claimed that these lives "show the stigmata of the developed manner."

Figure Two : Grouping the Lives

GROUP ONE

Life	Author	Dedications	Key Citations	Sources
H	Spartianus	None	Marius Maximus : H 2, 10 ; 12, 4 ; 20, 3 ; 25, 4.	Marius Maximus
Ael.	Spartianus	Diocletian : Ael. 1, 1 ; 2, 2.	Marius Maximus : Ael. 3, 9 ; 5, 5.	Marius Maximus
AP	Capitolinus	None	Marius Maximus : AP 11, 3.	Marius Maximus
MA	Capitolinus	Diocletian : MA 19, 12.	Marius Maximus : MA 1, 6 ; 25, 10.	Marius Maximus
V	Capitolinus	Diocletian : V 11, 4.		Marius Maximus
DI	Spartianus	None		Marius Maximus
C	Lampridius	None	Marius Maximus : C 13, 2 ; 15, 4 ; 18, 2.	Marius Maximus
P	Capitolinus	None	Marius Maximus : P 2, 8 ; 15, 8.	Marius Maximus
AC	Gallicanus	Diocletian : AC 3, 3.	Marius Maximus : AC 6, 6-7 ; 9, 5.	Marius Maximus
S	Spartianus	Diocletian : S 20, 4.	Marius Maximus : S 15, 6.	Marius Maximus
PN	Spartianus	Diocletian : PN 9, 1.		Marius Maximus
Cc.	Spartianus	None		Marius Maximus
G	Spartianus	Constantine : G 1, 1.	Marius Maximus : G 2, 1.	Marius Maximus

GROUP TWO

Life	Author	Dedications	Key Citations	Sources
Hel.	Lampridius	Constantine : Hel. 34, 1.	Marius Maximus : Hel. 11, 6.	Marius Maximus, Herodian
Dd.	Lampridius		Herodian : Dd. 2, 5.	Herodian
OM	Capitolinus	Diocletian : OM 15, 4.	Cordus : OM 1, 3-5.	Herodian
Cl. A.	Capitolinus	Constantine : Cl. A 4, 2.	Marius Maximus : Cl. A 3, 4 ; 9, 2 ; 5 ; 12, 14. Herodian : Cl. A 1, 2 ; 12, 14. Cordus : Cl. A 5, 10 ; 7, 2 ; 11, 2.	Marius Maximus
AS	Lampridius	Constantine : AS 65, 1.	Marius Maximus : AS 5, 4 ; 21, 4 ; 30, 6 ; 48, 6 ; 65, 4. Herodian : AS 52, 2 ; 57, 3. Dexippus : AS 49, 3 ; 5.	Herodian, Dexippus

Max.	Capitolinus	Constantine : Max. 1, 1.	Herodian : Max. 13, 4 ; 33, 3. Dexippus : Max. 32, 3-4 ; 33, 3. Cordus : Max. 4, 1 ; 6, 8 ; 12, 7 ; 27, 7 ; 28, 10 ; 29, 10.	Herodian, Dexippus
Gd.	Capitolinus	Constantine : Gd. 1, 1 ; 34, 6.	Herodian : Gd. 2, 1. Dexippus : Gd. 2, 1 ; 9, 6 ; 19, 9 ; 23, 1. Cordus : Gd. 4, 6 ; 5, 6 ; 12, 1 ; 14, 7 ; 17, 3 ; 19, 8 ; 21, 3-4 ; 22, 2 ; 26, 2 ; 31, 6 ; 33, 4.	Herodian, Dexippus.
MB	Capitolinus	None	Herodian : MB 1, 2 ; 15, 3 ; 16, 6. Dexippus : MB 1, 2 ; 15, 5 ; 16, 3-6. Cordus : MB 4, 2 ; 5 ; 12, 4.	Herodian, Dexippus

GROUP THREE

Life	Author	Dedications	Key Citations	Sources
Val.	Pollio	Anonymous person : Val. 7, 1 ; 8, 5		Dexippus
Gall.	Pollio	Constantius I (Caesar) : Gall. 7, 1 ; 14, 3.	Dexippus : Gall. 13, 8 (as an historical actor).	Dexippus
T	Pollio	Anonymous relative of Herennius Celsus : T 11, 7 ; 22, 12. Anonymus scholar : T 31, 8-10 ; 33, 7-8.	Herodian : T 32, 1. Dexippus : T 32, 1. Templum Pacis : T 31, 10.	Dexippus, with one passage influenced by Herodian
Cl.	Pollio	Constantius I (Caesar) : Cl. 1, 1 ; 3, 1 ; 9, 9 ; 10, 7 ; 13, 2. Anonymous person (a patron of games) : Cl. 3, 1 ; 5, 5	Dexippus : Cl. 12, 6.	Dexippus
A	Vopiscus	Iunius Tiberianus : A 1, 1. Pinianus (?) : A 1, 9. Constantius I (Augustus) : A 44, 5.	Bibliotheca Ulpiana : A 1, 7 ; 10 ; 24, 7. An historical account of wars, written in Greek : A 1, 6. The archives of the urban prefect : A 9, 1.	Eunapius (?)
Tac.	Vopiscus	None	Bibliotheca Ulpiana : Tac. 8, 1.	Eunapius (?)
Pr.	Vopiscus	Celsinus : Pr. 1, 3.	Marius Maximus : Pr. 2, 7. Bilbiotheca Ulpiana, Thermae Diocletianae, Domus Tiberiana and Porticus Porphyretica : Pr. 2, 1.	Eunapius (?)

Q	Vopiscus	Bassus : Q 2, 1.	Marius Maximus : Q 1, 1-2.	Eunapius (?)
Car.	Vopiscus	A friend : Car. 21, 2-3	Bibliotheca Ulpiana : Car. 11, 3.	Eunapius (?)

SYNOPSIS

Discontinuity :	The absence of lives of Nerva and Trajan.
Group One :	H, Ael., AP, MA, V, *DI*, C, P, *AC*, S, PN, Cc., G.
Discontinuity :	The disorganisation of the lives of Elagabalus, Diadumenus, Macrinus and Clodius Albinus.
Group Two :	*Hel.*, *Dd.*, *OM*, *Cl. A*, AS, Max., Gd., MB.
Discontinuity :	The lacuna from the death of Gordian III until the capture of Valerian.
Group Three :	Val., Gall., T, Cl., A, Tac., Pr., Q, Car.

The second group includes the *Antoninus Heliogabalus*, *Diadumenus Antoninus*, *Opilius Macrinus*, *Vita Clodii Albini*, *Alexander Seuerus, Maximini Duo*, *Gordiani Tres* and *Maximus et Balbinus* ([10]). One can distinguish the range of the second group on the basis of citations alone. This group contains every citation of the spurious biographer Aelius or Iunius Cordus, who appears in the preface to the *Opilius Macrinus* and then disappears after the *Maximus et Balbinus* ([11]).

(10) One could not assert that the second group is entirely homogenous. The *Antoninus Heliogabalus* draws its account of his reign from Marius Maximus, and takes very little information from other sources : Hel. 11, 6. There are several largely worthless references to Marius Maximus in the *Alexander Seuerus*, where one might expect to find citations of the spurious biographer Cordus : AS 5, 4 ; 21, 4 ; 30, 6 ; 48, 6 ; 65, 4. Nevertheless, the *Heliogabalus* has some unusual features : its use of extensive prefaces and epilogues, as well as its long and entirely spurious digression on the theme of luxury. The account of the reign Gordian III falls outside the scope of Herodian's narrative, and so differs in an important respect from the other lives of the second group. This inconsistency can be explained by a desire to associate the life of Gordian III with the lives of Gordian I and Gordian II (in the *Gordiani Tres*).

(11) Cl. A 5, 10 ; 7, 2 ; 11, 2 ; OM 1, 3-5 ; Max. 4, 1 ; 6, 8 ; 12, 7 ; 27, 7 ; 28, 10 ; 29, 10 ; Gd. 4, 6 ; 5, 6 ; 12, 1 ; 14, 7 ; 17, 3 ; 19, 8 ; 21, 3-4 ; 22, 2 ; 26, 2 ; 31, 6 ; 33, 4 ; MB 4, 2 ; 5 ; 12, 4. Aelius or Iunius Cordus probably takes his name from a passage in the first satire of Decimus Iunius (!) Iuvenalis, who castigated the interminable plays of Cordus, written on the back and front of a book roll and still not finished : Iuv. I, 1-6. (The reading Codrus is a corruption introduced by the editor of the vulgate recension.) Common verbosity may have justified the association. Nevertheless, Sidonius Apollinaris subsequently used the same passage from the first satire to characterise a process of marginal accretion : Sid., *Ep.* VIII, 16, 1 : *iam uenitur ad margines umbilicorum, iam tempus est, ut satiricus ait, Orestem nostrum uel super terga finiri*. Note also : Sid., *Ep.* VIII, 1, 1 ; IX, 1, 4. We might imagine that our impostor introduced into the margins of his work material ascribed to Cordus.

This group also includes all the citations of Herodian in the corpus, with the exception of one reference in a biographical entry on the usurper Titus (which appears out of its proper chronological place in an addendum to the *Tyranni Triginta*) ([12]). Interestingly, our impostor's accounts of the lives of Marcus Aurelius, Commodus, Didius Iulianus, Pertinax, Severus, Pescennius Niger, Caracalla and Geta (all found in the first group) do not draw on Herodian, even though these lives fall within the period covered by Herodian's narrative. Moreover, the end of the second group is distinguished by a development in the attributions and dedications : the authors Capitolinus and Lampridius, as well as the dedications to Diocletian and Constantine, are abandoned in favour of Pollio and Vopiscus, allegedly writing during the reign of Constantius I. That the author himself intended this arrangement is clear from his comments in the preface to the life of Aurelian ([13]). The preface to the *Opilius Macrinus* (the first life in chronological sequence) may have marked the opening of the second group, before the lives fell into their manuscript order ([14]).

The third group is relatively easily distinguished from the lives that precede it. This group contains the *Valeriani Duo*, *Gallieni Duo*, *Tyranni Triginta*, *Diuus Claudius*, *Diuus Aurelianus*, *Tacitus*, *Probus*, *Quadrigae Tyrannorum* and *Carus et Carinus et Numerianus*. This group includes all the lives attributed to Pollio and Vopiscus and dedicated to private individuals of the reign of Constantius I. Where once the author purported to draw upon the suppositious biographer Cordus as a source of authority, he now names libraries and other places in Rome associated with scholarship (notably the Temple of Peace, the Ulpian Library, the Porphyry Portico, the Palace of Tiberius and the Baths of Diocletian) ([15]). The end of the second group coincides with the last event in Herodian's historical narrative : the deaths of Maximus and Balbinus. By contrast, the author turned to Dexippus as the main source of the lives ascribed to Pollio, while the lives ascribed to Vopiscus draw upon an unnamed Greek historian, often identified as Eunapius. For this reason, it seems that the divisions between the first, second and third groups coincide with changes in the underlying sources of the lives.

(12) Cl. A 1, 2 ; 12, 14 ; Dd. 2, 5 ; AS 52, 2 ; 57, 3 ; Max. 13, 4 ; 33, 3 ; Gd. 2, 1 ; MB 1, 2 ; 15, 3 ; 16, 6 ; T 32, 1 (out of chronological sequence). Herodian is three times cited under the name Arrianus : Max. 33, 3 ; Gd. 2, 1 ; MB 1, 2.

(13) A 2, 1.

(14) The first words of this preface seem to echo the full title of the corpus (see introduction, n. 1). Moreover, the preface appears to introduce the spurious authority Cordus to a credulous readership.

(15) Aulus Gellius also mentioned some of these archives. Temple of Peace : T 31, 10 ; Gell. V, 21, 9 ; XVI, 8, 2. Bibliotheca Ulpia : A 1, 7 ; 10 ; 8, 1 ; 24, 7 ; Tac. 8, 1-2 ; Pr. 2, 1 ; Car. 11, 3 ; Gell. XI, 17, 1. Domus Tiberiana : Pr. 2, 1 ; Gell. XIII, 20, 1. References in the *HA* cannot be trusted as evidence on the libraries of Rome late in the fourth century, since they may to be modelled on literary sources.

It is interesting to note that some of the patterns observed above disappear once the lives are returned to their proper chronological order. The *Vita Clodii Albini* appears outside of its chronological sequence in all the manuscripts, and one might speculate that the displacement of this life has somehow disrupted the order of the lives immediately before it (those of Macrinus, Diadumenus and Elagabalus). Nonetheless, the *Vita Clodii Albini* includes citations of the historian Herodian and the spurious biographer Cordus, features otherwise exclusively associated with the period from Macrinus to Maximus and Balbinus, and entirely absent from the earlier lives, including the *Pescennius Niger* ([16]). There is surely no chance that an accident in the tradition could have caused the *Vita Clodii Albini* to assume the characteristic features of the lives of the second group. One can only suspect that the author himself, as he revised the second group in its manuscript order, contaminated his account of the usurpation of Clodius Albinus in this curious manner. It is difficult to see how else citations of Herodian and Cordus could have appeared in the *Vita*, which draws most of its genuine materials from Marius Maximus' biography of Severus.

We have now seen how the manuscript order of the lives coincides with patterns in their attributions, dedications, sources and citations. Three distinct groups of lives emerge. It is intriguing to note that the divisions between these three groups coincide with significant discontinuities in the corpus. The collection begins abruptly with Hadrian. One would expect lives of Nerva (96-98) and Trajan (97/98-117), which ought to connect the corpus with the works of Suetonius (Caesar to Domitian) ([17]). Our impostor clearly had access to good sources on these reigns ([18]). Moreover, comments in the *Aelius* seem to suggest that the collection once included lives of emperors before Hadrian ([19]). The manuscript order of the first four lives of the second group (the *Antoninus Heliogabalus*, *Diadumenus Antoninus*, *Opilius Macrinus* and *Vita Clodii Albini*)

(16) Cordus : Cl. A 5, 10 ; 7, 2 ; 11, 2. Herodian : Cl. A 1, 2 ; 12, 14. The *Pescennius Niger* and the *Vita Clodii Albini* are nevertheless clearly companion pieces : "He draws a contrast between the harsh Niger, a stern man necessary to the state, whom he assigns to Spartianus, and the amiable Albinus, a favourite of the senate, who even want to restore senatorial rule, and is assigned to Capitolinus." Honoré 1987 : 171.

(17) Meckler attempted to find thematic reasons for a decision to begin the corpus with Hadrian : Meckler 1996. See also Chastagnol 1994 : xxxv. Interestingly, the *Epitome* (*Epit.* 14, 11) claimed that Hadrian's military, administrative and provincial reforms were the basis of the contemporary Roman state.

(18) The extant lives sometimes refer to persons or events of the reigns of Nerva and Trajan : Schlumberger 1976a ; Idem 1974 : 126.

(19) The author claimed that he had already written lives of emperors "up to the divine Hadrian" (*usque ad diuum Hadrianum*) : Ael. 1, 1. In the postscript to the *Aelius*, the author suggested that he had set out to write lives of all those who had attained the rank of Caesar or Augustus, whether by adoption or inheritance, from the reign of Caesar onwards : Ael. 7, 5.

reflects some sort of disorganisation. Many critics have argued that the lacuna covering the period from the death of Gordian III until the capture of Valerian is a fraudulent device of the author ([20]). This controversial and suspect lacuna mars the beginning of the third group of lives. Certainly, the problem of the lacuna takes on a different aspect when it is seen in the context of the other apparently regular patterns in the corpus. Although it is difficult to be certain on these matters, it seems entirely possible that all these discontinuities are the result of the activities of the author. He may have been a negligent and incompetent redactor of his own work. Alternatively, he may have applied his talents to the creation of learned dilemmas. It is more than a little suspicious that the end product consists of exactly thirty books : a round number already seen in the *Tyranni Triginta*.

The traces of a division into three parts are visible throughout the corpus. While it would be futile to speculate on exactly how the text assumed its present form, perhaps we can make some general observations. The language used in the prefaces suggests that our author produced a codex or codices and not a series of book rolls ([21]). There seems to be an association between the introduction of lives of usurpers into the text and various disruptions in the coherence of the corpus. The *Didius Iulianus* and *Auidius Cassius* have been transposed, while the manuscript order of the *Opilius Macrinus*, *Diadumenus Antoninus* and *Antoninus Heliogabalus* perhaps owes something to the insertion of the *Vita Clodii Albini* within the second group. One wonders whether there is not some connection between the presence of the lives of Aelius, Avidius Cassius, Pescennius Niger and Geta in the first group and the absence of lives of Nerva and Trajan. One might well connect the absence of lives covering the period from the death of Gordian III to the capture of Valerian and the appearance of the *Tyranni Triginta* and the *Quadrigae Tyrannorum*. The notion that the author operated under severe constraints of space is not entirely fanciful. Indeed, this hypothesis might help to explain his avowed concern with brevity, the crude paraphrase and jumbled arrangement of his sources, as well as the absence of whole blocks of lives from the corpus. There are signs that point in this direction. For example, the chronological narratives of the *de Vita Hadriani* and the *Seuerus* both break off well before the end of the reigns of these emperors ([22]). Moreover, there are indications of other constraints of space, operating on a larger scale. When one removes the *Vita Clodii Albini* from consideration, a strange parallel emerges.

(20) The relevant references appear in the introduction (n. 2).

(21) The author used words *liber* and *uolumen* as exact synonyms to describe the individual lives that made up his corpus : Max. 1, 1 ; Gd. 1, 3 ; T 31, 8. This equation, found in Jerome and other ecclesiastical authors, reflects the general demise of the book roll. It implies that the word *uolumen* had already lost its primitive meaning : Haelst 1989 ; Arns 1953 : 118 ; 122.

(22) H 14, 8 ; S 17, 5.

The lives from *Opilius Macrinus* to *Maximus et Balbinus* occupy 175 pages in Hohl's edition, while the lives of group three occupy 176 pages ([23]). The notion that our author (or perhaps an amanuensis) adopted increasingly desperate measures to constrain the corpus within certain limits may help to explain some of the aberrations of the received text.

Further Considerations. Some evidence preserved in P may provide further insights into the various problems of redaction ([24]). The *index uitarum* found in P erroneously ascribes the *Valeriani Duo*, *Gallieni Duo* and *Tyranni Triginta* to Capitolinus (instead of Pollio). This mistake is most probably derived from an ambiguity in the colophons ([25]). The colophon to the *Valeriani Duo* does not name Pollio as the author. Instead it reads INCIPIT EIVSDEM VALERIANI DVO. The colophon to the *Maximus et Balbinus* names Capitolinus, and this attribution has been mistakenly carried over due to the ambiguity of the following sequence of attributions :

INCIPIVNT MAXIMINI DVO IVLI CAPITOLINI FELICITER.
INCIPIT GORDIANVS. GORDIANVS TERTIVS EXPLICIT.
INCIPIT MAXIMVS. MAXIMVS SIVE PVPPIENVS ET BALBINVS IVLI CAPITOLINI EXPLICIT.
INCIPIT EIVSDEM VALERIANI DVO.
INCIPIT EIVSDEM GALLIENI DVO.
INCIPIT EIVSDEM TYRANNI TRIGINTA.
INCIPIT EIVSDEM DIVVS CLAVDIVS FELICITER VENTVM EST AD PRINCIPEM CLAVDIVM. EXPLICIT TREVELLI POLLIONIS DIVVS CLAVDIVS.
INCIPIT FLAVI VOPISCI SYRACVSII DIVVS AVRELIANVS.

(23) The lives of group one and the lives of group two occupy approximately the same amount of space in Hohl's edition : 184 pages and 189 pages respectively. These figures are slightly skewed, because group one probably once contained material equivalent to the *index uitarum* found in P (not included in the above calculation).

(24) The following paragraphs rely heavily upon the evidence reported in Hohl's edition, as well as the comments and facsimiles of Pecere : Pecere 1995 ; Hohl et al. 1971. I have not been able to consult P directly.

(25) Although the index is erroneous in this respect, not all the information it contains is necessarily wholly derivative. The index accurately reports the general title of the corpus, which also appears in the final colophon to P. Perhaps more significantly, only the index notes the proper title of the collective biography of the Gordians (*Gordiani Tres*), which is reflected in the wording of the relevant preface : Gd. 1, 4. The index reports at least some accurate information not found in the colophons, possibly suggesting that it is an independent source, although one cannot wholly discount scribal ingenuity as a potential explanation in this case. The spelling of the proper names mentioned in the index is often irregular, so that Vulcacius Callicanus appears for Vulcacius Gallicanus, Victuria for Victoria, Ticus for Titus, Treuellius Pollio for Trebellius Pollio and Charinus for Carinus. These orthographical confusions (especially C for G, C for T and U for B) might have resulted from the misinterpretation of a manuscript written in minuscule letters (a manuscript earlier than P). Nonetheless, the spelling Treuellius also appears in the colophons, which are apparently in capitals.

This error may point to the authenticity of the lacuna, since the colophon to the *Valeriani Duo* seems to refer to a lost colophon introducing the name of Pollio. Nevertheless, a discontinuity of this kind may instead reflect the negligence or incompetence of the author in redacting his own work. Indeed, one wonders whether the colophon to the *Valeriani Duo* should appear at all, given that a lacuna has apparently engulfed the beginning of the text. The colophon itself, as well as the *index uitarum*, express what is manifestly an accurate title for the life, analogous to the titles *Maximini Duo*, *Gordiani Tres*, *Gallieni Duo* and *Philippi Duo*. One might not expect such an apposite title from a medieval scribe confronted with a genuinely lacunose manuscript.

The colophons also seem to reflect some of the problems surrounding the manuscript order of the lives. The colophons of the lives from the *Seuerus* to *Antoninus Geta* appear as follows in P :

INCIPIT DIDIVS IVLIANVS AELI SPARTIANI FELICITER. DIDIVS IVLIANVS EXPLICIT.
INCIPIT AELI SPARTIANI SEVERVS. AELI SPARTIANI SEVERVS EXPLICIT.
INCIPIT PESCENNIVS NIGER. PESCENNIVS NIGER AELI SPARTIANI EXPLICIT.
INCIPIT ANTONINVS CARACALLVS. ANTONINVS CARACALLVS EXPLICIT.
INCIPIT ANTONINVS GETA FELICITER. ANTONINVS GETA EXPLICIT.

It should be immediately apparent that the attributions of the *Antoninus Caracallus* and the *Antoninus Geta* follow the attribution of the *Pescennius Niger*. But restoring the *Vita Clodii Albini* to its proper chronological place disrupts this pattern :

INCIPIT DIDIVS IVLIANVS AELI SPARTIANI FELICITER. DIDIVS IVLIANVS EXPLICIT.
INCIPIT AELI SPARTIANI SEVERVS. AELI SPARTIANI SEVERVS EXPLICIT.
INCIPIT PESCENNIVS NIGER. PESCENNIVS NIGER AELI SPARTIANI EXPLICIT.
INCIPIT VITA CLODII ALBINI IVLII CAPITOLINI. VITA CLODI ALBINI IVLI CAPITOLINI EXPLICIT.
INCIPIT ANTONINVS CARACALLVS. ANTONINVS CARACALLVS EXPLICIT.
INCIPIT ANTONINVS GETA FELICITER. ANTONINVS GETA EXPLICIT.

One must now ascribe the lives of Caracalla and Geta to Capitolinus ([26]). For this reason, the practice of modern editors is at least inconsistent, since they ascribe the *Antoninus Caracallus* and the *Antoninus Geta* to Spartianus, while arranging the colophons in a manner incompatible with these attributions of authorship. Since almost all the attributions of authorship rely on the colophons,

(26) We cannot place the *Vita Clodii Albini* before the *Pescennius Niger*, since the former cites the latter : Cl. A 1, 4.

this inconsistency is a serious enough matter. However one chooses to resolve this particular dilemma, it is not possible to maintain both the chronological sequence of the lives and the attributions of authorship proposed by modern editors.

The scribal marks preserved in P, despite their accuracy and antiquity, cannot resolve all the problems surrounding the redaction of the corpus. The evidence of the colophons confirms the view that the *Vita Clodii Albini* occupies an anomalous position in the corpus, although no more definite conclusion can be drawn on this basis. Nor can the colophon to the *Valeriani Duo* answer the questions concerning the authenticity of the so-called lacuna. One senses that the redaction of the corpus was an untidy process crudely performed.

Conclusion. This chapter has proposed some new approaches to the problems surrounding the redaction of the *HA*. By examining the evidence of the earliest manuscripts, we can establish the original order the lives, which differs in many respects from the order adopted by modern editors. The lives can be divided into three groups, based upon patterns in their attributions, dedications, sources and citations. This kind of analysis helps to reveal some of the underlying structural features of the received text. Naturally, evidence of correlation can be subjected to various interpretations. Nevertheless, some serious disruptions in the corpus, generally ascribed to accidents in the tradition, were probably the result of the inept efforts of the author to redact his own work, perhaps in order to accommodate the lives of usurpers and other minor figures. Mere deviousness may also account for the disposition of the lives, if our impostor deliberately fabricated lacunae and other difficulties. Whatever explanation one prefers, it seems most likely that the corpus attained essentially its present form during the lifetime of the author : a new and surprising conclusion. Perhaps the arrangement preserved in the earliest manuscripts should be preferred to the rationalising emendations of modern editors. The next chapter will attempt to trace the reception and transmission of the *HA* in the period before our earliest manuscripts.

CHAPTER SIX

Reception

Introduction. It now remains for us to discuss the reception and transmission of the *HA* in the era before our earliest extant manuscripts : a period stretching from about 400 until about 800 AD. This task is complicated by the fact that almost no evidence is available to us. Perhaps only one passage in late antique literature draws upon the *HA* : a fragment of the lost *Historia Romana* of Q. Aurelius Memmius Symmachus (consul in 485), originally derived from material in the *Maximini Duo*. This citation is clearly consistent with the evidence presented elsewhere in this study on the intended audience of the *HA*, since Q. Aurelius Memmius Symmachus was probably the great-grandson of Q. Aurelius Symmachus. Many scholars have attempted to find further allusions to the lives in ancient literature, but with only equivocal success. Nor is it easier to locate the text in the early medieval period, although there are some indications, admittedly tenuous, that the tradition may have been transmitted through a manuscript held at the monastery of Bobbio. The first allusion to the *HA* in medieval literature, not previously noted, may occur in Einhard's *Vita Karoli Magni*, a work written soon before our earliest extant manuscripts were copied.

A Fragment in Jordanes. Perhaps the only reference to the *HA* in ancient literature is a fragment of the lost *Historia Romana* of Memmius Symmachus (preserved in two different forms in the *Getica* and *Romana* of the sixth-century historian Jordanes) (1). This fragment repeats some fabrications familiar from the *Maximini Duo* in the *HA*. It describes Maximinus' barbarian background, his wrestling matches, his great height, his interview with the Emperor Severus and his military service under Caracalla, Macrinus, Elagabalus and Alexander Severus. The fragment even mentions Maximinus' supposed parents Micca and Ababa, whose names appear nowhere else in the tradition (2). These figments were among the eccentric inventions of our scholarly impostor, and so all this

(1) Iord., *Rom.* 281 [*MGH AA* V, 1, 36, 23] ; *Get.* 15(83-88) [78, 9] ; Baldini 2007 ; Zecchini 1993 : 45-49 ; Croke 1987 : 123-124 ; Hartke 1951 : 427-439 ; Hohl 1920 : 298. Memmius Symmachus is cited at the beginning and end of the fragment. Iord., *Get.* 15(83) [78, 11] ; (88) [80, 10]. On Memmius Symmachus, see : *PLRE* II, 1044-1046, Q. Aurelius Memmius Symmachus Iunior 9 ; IIIb, 1212, Symmachus 1 ; Chadwick 1981 : 6-16 ; Courcelle 1948 : 257-312.

(2) Burian 1988 ; Hohl 1942.

material must originally descend from the *Maximini Duo*. No alternative source could have provided this information, since it had no basis in either fact or tradition. Memmius Symmachus, writing during the reign of the Gothic king Theoderic, had a strong motive for celebrating the achievements of a purportedly barbarian emperor such as Maximinus Thrax. He seems to have omitted the fierce criticism of Maximinus found throughout the life.

The dubious claims about the Emperor Maximinus found their way into the works of Jordanes by a circuitous route, since they passed from the *HA* to Memmius Symmachus' *Historia Romana*, then to Cassiodorus' lost history of the Goths and then finally to Jordanes' epitomes of Roman and Gothic affairs. Unfortunately, there is an ongoing controversy over the extent to which Jordanes depended upon Cassiodorus' lost work. My own view is that Jordanes was heavily dependent upon Cassiodorus (and here the source-critical arguments advanced by Mommsen are still compelling) ([3]). Whatever position one adopts on this matter, however, it is likely that Jordanes' quotation from the Memmius Symmachus' *Historia Romana* was derived from Cassiodorus. Cassiodorus himself mentioned this lost work in his account of the literary activities of his alleged forebears (the only such reference outside of the works of Jordanes) ([4]). Moreover, Jordanes probably extracted many of his recondite citations (including references to Livy, Tacitus, Josephus, Claudius Ptolemaeus and Ablavius) from Cassiodorus' earlier work ([5]). The evidence suggests that neither Cassiodorus nor Jordanes knew the *HA* directly. Instead, Jordanes drew upon Cassiodorus, who drew upon Memmius Symmachus, who drew in turn upon the *Maximini Duo* ([6]).

The appearance of clearly spurious material from the *HA* in a work ascribed to Memmius Symmachus is of considerable significance. The fragment preserved in Jordanes helps to establish new connections between the *HA* and the Roman aristocracy. The Q. Aurelius Memmius Symmachus active around the turn of the sixth century was a direct descendant (probably the great-grandson) of Q. Aurelius Symmachus ([7]). There is a direct link between the milieu in which

(3) CHRISTENSEN 2002 : 84-123 ; MOORHEAD 1999 ; ZECCHINI 1993 : 193-209 ; HEATHER 1989 : 127-128 ; SCHWARTZ 1983 ; LUISELLI 1976 ; GIUNTA 1952 : 159-163 ; ENSSLIN 1949 ; MOMMSEN 1961b [first ed. 1882] : xxiii-lxvii.

(4) CASS., *Libell.* [*MGH AA* XII, v, 6].

(5) All these authors are cited in Cassiodorus' extant works. Livy : IORD., *Get.* 2(10) [*MGH AA* V, 1, 56, 6] ; CASS., *Inst.* I, 17, 1. Tacitus (called Cornelius) : IORD., *Get.* 2(13) [*MGH AA* V, 1, 57, 3] ; CASS., *Var.* V, 2, 2 [*CCSL* XCVI, 183 (15)]. Josephus : IORD., *Get.* 4(29) [*MGH AA* V, 1, 61, 6] ; CASS., *Inst.* I, 17, 1. Claudius Ptolemaeus : IORD., *Get.* 3(16) [*MGH AA* V, 1, 58, 1] ; 3(19) [58, 15] ; CASS., *Inst.* I, 25, 2. Ablavius : IORD., *Get.* 4(28) [*MGH AA* V, 1, 61, 5] ; 14(82) [78, 4] ; 23(117) [88, 12] ; CASS., *Var.* X, 22, 2 [*CCSL* XCVI, 405 (15)].

(6) There is no need to transport either Memmius Symmachus' history or an early manuscript of the *HA* to Constantinople, despite Callu's comments : CALLU 1985 : 115.

(7) CALLU 1997 : 80.

the *HA* was produced and the milieu in which it was read three generations and almost one hundred years later. We might suspect that Memmius Symmachus obtained his text of the *HA* through his family connections, which stretched back at least a century. It is not unusual to find that there are links between Roman aristocrats of the age of Theodosius and Roman aristocrats active in the cultural sphere at the beginning of the sixth century. One thinks of the corrector of manuscripts Vettius Agorius Basilius Mavortius, almost certainly a descendant of the Vettius Agorius Praetextatus who died in 384 ([8]). The consul L. Turcius Rufius Apronianus Asterius, again active as a corrector of manuscripts, was the descendant of an aristocrat known from the age of Theodosius ([9]). The number of manuscript traditions associated with these men reveals the narrow basis of classical culture in the West.

A great aristocratic house might play a significant role in the preservation of manuscripts and traditions. The subscriptions to the so-called Nicomachean recension of the first decade of Livy record the transmission of one manuscript through three generations of the Nicomachi-Symmachi (as Zetzel demonstrated) ([10]). This manuscript was the basis of the whole tradition of the first decade (with the exception of a relatively trivial papyrus fragment). Memmius Symmachus aggressively appropriated the symbolic capital amassed by his ancestors. Like his forebears, he was involved in correcting manuscripts of earlier authors. Before his consulship in 485, Memmius Symmachus (with the assistance of Macrobius Plotinus Eudoxius) emended the text of Macrobius' *Commentariorum in Somnium Scipionis* ([11]). All the evidence suggests that Macrobius had sought to enhance his respectability by identifying himself with the great families of the Roman aristocracy. His *Saturnalia* developed a sort of literary cult around elite figures such as Praetextatus, Symmachus, Virius Nicomachus Flavianus and the Ceionii. Macrobius had also dedicated to an otherwise unidentified Symmachus a treatise comparing aspects of Latin and Greek grammar (*de*

(8) *PLRE* II, 736-737, Vettius Agorius Basilius Mavortius 2 ; Velaza 1999 : 295.

(9) *PLRE* II, 173-174, Fl. Turcius Rufius Apronianus Asterius 11 (consul 494) ; Velaza 1999 : 295.

(10) In a letter written around the year 400, Symmachus claimed that he had undertaken a recension of the text of Livy : Symm., *Ep.* IX, 13, 1. He had already owned a manuscript of this work for some time : Symm., *Ep.* IV, 18, 5. The ancient colophons preserved throughout the manuscripts name three correctors, Tascius Victorianus, Nicomachus Flavianus the Younger and Appius Nicomachus Dexter : Velaza 1999 : 292 ; Reynolds and Wilson 1991 : 40 ; Pecere 1986 : 59-69 (plates 18-9) ; Zetzel 1984 : 214-215 ; Idem 1980 ; Jahn 1851 : 335-342 ; *PLRE* I, 345-347, Nicomachus Flavianus 14 ; II, 357-358, Appius Nicomachus Dexter 3. Tascius Victorianus claimed that he had corrected the text "for the lords Symmachi" (*domnis Symmachis*). The spelling of the subscription is aberrant.

(11) Velaza 1999 : 295 ; Zetzel 1984 : 217 ; Cameron 1966 : 37 ; *PLRE* II, 413, Macrobius Plotinus Eudoxius 7 ; 436, Plotinus Eustathius 13.

Differentiis et Societatibus Graeci Latinique uerbi) ([12]). Memmius Symmachus devoted his critical efforts to an author whose works enhanced the prestige of his own family. Any writer might seek posterity for his or her works by praising the ancestors of the great families, dynasties whose long continuity seemed to guarantee the perpetuation of cultural traditions into the distant future. More than mere patronage was involved in such calculations.

Some Medieval Traces. An astonishingly large number of manuscripts associated with Memmius Symmachus and his relatives appear in the library of the monastery of St Columban at Bobbio from an early date. A manuscript written at that monastery in a hand of the eighth century contains the fullest and earliest witness to Macrobius' treatise on Greek and Latin grammar (the only version to record the dedication to an otherwise unidentified Symmachus) ([13]). The same eighth-century manuscript also contains extracts from Macrobius' work on the *Somnium Scipionis*, easily the earliest witness to this text. We might speculate that Bobbio held for many centuries the manuscript of Macrobius' *Commentariorum* corrected by Memmius Symmachus at Ravenna before his consulship in 485, a manuscript near the base of the extant tradition ([14]). Furthermore, a catalogue of the manuscripts held at Bobbio, compiled in either the ninth or the tenth century, mentions three treatises that Priscian dedicated to Memmius Symmachus : the *de Figuris Numerorum*, the *de Metris Fabularum Terentii* and the *Praeexercitamina* ([15]). Moreover, Boethius' tract on arithmetic, which was also dedicated to Memmius Symmachus, was preserved at Bobbio in a manuscript copied in the sixth or seventh centuries ([16]). The library at Bobbio preserved from an early date several other manuscripts associated with Boethius ([17]).

(12) Macr., *de Diff.* [*GL* V, 631, 6] : *Theodosius Symmacho suo salutem dicit.* We do not know much about the Symmachus who was consul in 446, although he was presumably the son of Fabius Memmius Symmachus and the father of Memmius Symmachus. See also : *PLRE* II, 1102-1103, Theodosius 20 ; 1042-1043, Symmachus 3.

(13) *CLA* III, no. 397b.

(14) Our only extant manuscript of Cicero's *de Re Publica*, the text on part of which Macrobius commented, is a palimpsest from Bobbio : *CLA* I, no. 35. While the version of Macrobius' *Commentariorum in Somnium Scipionis* corrected by Memmius Symmachus must lie near the very base of the manuscript tradition, Barker-Benfield was not prepared to concede that it was "the only text-carrier ... to survive the Dark Ages." Barker-Benfield 1983 : 225.

(15) Becker 1885 : 32, no. 430, no. 431-432. Bobbio long preserved a closely related group of grammatical manuscripts, written in a quarter-uncial hand of the fifth century : *CLA* I, no. 117 ; III, no. 397a, no. 398.

(16) *CLA* IV, 450.

(17) The earliest catalogue of the contents of the monastery library also mentions Boethius' tracts on astronomy and music : Becker 1885 : 32, no. 384-387, no. 662. Gerbert, Abbot of Bobbio and later Pope Sylvester II (999-1003), suggested that Bobbio held Boethius' works on astrology : Gerb., *Ep.* 1, 8. Gerbert certainly drew on Boethius in compiling his mathematical works : Gerb., *Geom.* I, 1 [*PL* 139, col. 91 B]. It may not

The same centre may have held the only extant witness to Symmachus' speeches, a palimpsest originally copied in the sixth century, and then written over with the Acts of the Council of Chalcedon during the seventh century (probably at Bobbio) ([18]). The date assigned to the original script of this palimpsest may suggest a connection with Memmius Symmachus or perhaps with Ennodius, his ingratiating correspondent (whose name also appears in the Bobbio catalogue). One could hardly over-estimate the riches of the Bobbio collection.

There are some indications that the *HA* was preserved until the eighth century somewhere in North Italy, even perhaps in the library at Bobbio. Some palaeographers have argued that the best extant manuscript, the Codex Palatinus latinus 899 (P), was copied in North Italy early in the ninth century ([19]). Orthographic confusions found throughout the manuscripts may indicate transmission through an intermediary manuscript copied according to Insular scribal conventions ([20]). Several scholars have connected these so-called Insular symptoms with the monastery at Bobbio, an important centre of Insular influence throughout the eighth century ([21]). Moreover, there are significant similarities between the *HA* and some works held for centuries exclusively at Bobbio. Arusianus Messius' *Exempla elocutionum*, which was dedicated to Anicius Probinus and Anicius Olybrius (the joint consuls of 395), incorporated apparently honorific citations

be a coincidence that the Bobbio library catalogue also mentions Aristotle's *Categories* and Porphyry's *Isagoge*, works which Boethius himself had translated into Latin : Becker 1885 : 32, no. 392-393, no. 394, no. 405-408. A palimpsest fragment of a Latin translation of Euclid, written at the end of the fifth century and copied over at Luxeuil in the eighth century, may be close to the Boethian autograph : *CLA* IV, no. 501 (also noting Mynors' comments in his index to Lowe) ; Chadwick 1981 : 103-104. Luxeuil (595) was another foundation of St Columban, associated from an early stage with the monastery at Bobbio.

(18) *CLA* I, no. 29.

(19) Bischoff first expressed this view in his book on the manuscripts of the monastery at Lorsch (published in 1974). This work was unavailable to me. This view has won the endorsement of Callu and Marshall : Callu 1992 : xcv ; Marshall1983 : 354. Nevertheless, Bischoff expressed a slightly different opinion in a paper written soon afterwards : "Some questions about this stage in the transmission of the *Historia Augusta*, however, remain unanswered. Where was Vatican Pal. lat. 899 written ? Although this manuscript is connected with Verona, it cannot be fitted into the well known picture of the Verona scriptorium under Pacificus, yet it cannot be assigned with certainty to another centre. From what source did Fulda acquire Vatican Pal. lat. 899, the exemplar of its copy, Bamberg Class. 54 (E.III.9) ? Where did the Carolingian transmission of the text begin ? What ancient manuscripts were used ?" Bischoff 1994 : 122.

(20) Boyer 1948 : 33-39.

(21) Dumville drew the link with the Insular foundation of St Columban at Bobbio : "in fact the abbreviation-evidence … should allow the text to be situated at Bobbio in the seventh century and the ninth-century North Italian copy explained thus." Dumville 1995 : 223. See also Callu 1985 : 123, n. 122.

of Symmachus' speeches. This work survives only through an early medieval manuscript found at Bobbio in the fifteenth century ([22]). The scholarly subject matter of this text, as well as its date (395), not to mention the social background of its author (an official from outside the high aristocracy) and his connections to prominent aristocrats (the consuls Anicii and Symmachus) are all noteworthy from this perspective. These are the sort of factors that might determine the late antique reception of a work, thus influencing its fate in the early medieval period. Notable also for these reasons is a trivial collection of epigrams, whose principal author, the Syracusan Naucellius, has been connected with the bizarre Flavius Vopiscus Syracusius. These effusions, discovered in an early medieval manuscript at Bobbio in 1493, were lost once again through the industry of the humanists. Their intended audience probably included Symmachus, Anicius Probinus and the consul of 397, not to mention the scholiasts and glossators who thronged the schools at Rome. Although the mechanisms of transmission are hopelessly obscure, we see analogous results in several similar cases ; late antique reception may have conditioned early medieval transmission in ways that we do not fully understand.

The circumstantial evidence presented above may place the *HA* in North Italy in the seventh and eighth centuries, and provides some grounds for associating the manuscript tradition with the monastery of St Columban at Bobbio. Naturally, the limitations of our evidence preclude (and may always preclude) any certainty. It is not until the Carolingian period that the tradition resurfaces. The first allusion to the *HA* in medieval literature may occur in Einhard's *Vita Karoli Magni*, written during the reign of Louis the Pious (814-833). It has long been accepted that this *Vita* imitates Suetonius, adapting choice phrases culled from this model to describe Charlemagne's character and appearance. The connection between the *Vita* and the *HA* has not been noted previously ([23]). Einhard claimed that Charlemagne was "elegant and even witty" : *Adeo quidem facundus erat ut etiam dicaculus appareret* ([24]). He quite possibly took the phrase *etiam dicaculus* from a sentence in the *de Vita Hadriani* : *ioca eius plurima exstant ; nam fuit etiam dicaculus* ([25]). The adjective *dicaculus* is rather rare in both

(22) *PLRE* I, 639-640, Anicius Hermogenianus Olybrius 2 ; 734-735, Anicius Probinus 1. An entry in the library catalogue of an unidentified Francogallic king suggests that Messius' dictionary had escaped across the Alps by beginning of the ninth century, although it failed to establish a viable tradition there : Becker 1885 : 20, no. 12. The Bobbio catalogue of 1461 described it in the following terms : *Arusiani Messi vc or. comitis primi ordinis exemplaria elocutionum ex Virgilio Salustio* [sic] *Terrentio Cicerone digesta per littera alphabeti. in littera longobarda abscura* [sic]. Manitius 1935 : 125 [196].

(23) Innes 1997 ; Nicoll 1975 ; Townend 1967 : 102-106 ; Halphen 1938 : x-xi ; Idem 1921 : 91-95 ; Rand 1926 : 40-48. Casaubon first recognised some of these parallels in his edition of Suetonius.

(24) Ein., *Vit. Karl.* 25.

(25) H 20, 8.

ancient and medieval literature, although Einhard may of course have hit upon this diminutive form himself ([26]). The context, however, is important : Einhard was clearly trawling the works of Suetonius for showy words, and the suggestion that he also borrowed terminology relating to Hadrian seems plausible. Einhard's allusion to the *de Vita Hadriani* is significant because it may indicate that a manuscript of the *HA* was present in Francia at the beginning of the ninth century (although the exact date of the *Vita Karoli Magni* is not precisely known). It may be worth remembering in this context that Einhard was educated at the monastery at Fulda, which had an early association with the manuscript tradition of Suetonius ([27]). Now that we have reached Einhard and the ninth century, the question of the reception of the *HA* becomes much less pressing, and so it is appropriate to draw our account of the subject to a close. Previous scholars have exhaustively discussed the manuscript tradition of the lives, and so there is no need for a full treatment of that subject here ([28]). My only comment on the manuscript tradition would be that a fifteen word passage in the *Diuus Aurelianus*, preserved only in a group of interpolated manuscripts of humanistic date (Σ), is clearly both original and authentic ([29]). The presence of this passage provides a strong argument for the independent value of the interpolated manuscripts.

We can tentatively reconstruct the fate of the *HA*, based upon a combination of evidence, analogy and conjecture. Destined for an audience that included the Ceionii, Anicii and Nicomachi-Symmachi, the *HA* formed part of the inheritance of Memmius Symmachus. Perhaps not widely copied, the text may never have

(26) The word *dicaculus* occurs twice in Plautus (PLAUT., *As.* 508 ; *Cas.* 529), twice in Apuleius, once in the *de Vita Hadriani* in the *HA* and once in Iulianus Pomerius, a fifth-century author on asceticism (imitating Apuleius) : *TLL* V, 1, col. 957, 80 ; *BTL* ; *CLCLT*. The adverb *dicacule* occurs twice in Apuleius : APUL., *Met.* I, 9 ; VIII, 25.

(27) Bischoff (quoted above in note 19) suggested that P was present at Fulda, where a copy of it was made in the ninth century.

(28) The basic authorities on the manuscript tradition are cited in the introduction (note 1). For some questions of textual criticism, see : DESBORDES 1999 ; SOVERINI 1981.

(29) A 19, 6 : *patrimis matrimisque pueris carmen indicite. nos sumptum sacris, nos apparatum sacrificiis, nos aras tumultuarias indicemus*. The phrase *patrimis matrimisque pueris* occurs in the life of Elagabalus, who allegedly sacrificed children whose parents were alive for some necromantic purpose. Hel. 8, 1 : *Cecidit et humanas hostias lectis ad hoc pueris nobilibus ... patrimis et matrimis*. Moreover, the historian Zosimus (probably relying upon the lost history of Eunapius) alluded to a song sung by boys and girls with living parents in his description of the secular games as established under the direction of the Sibylline books : ZOS. II, 5, 5 ; 6, 18-22. It is possible that the author of the *HA* took his information on these rituals from Eunapius, the likely source of the historical material in the *Diuus Aurelianus*. Macrobius (MACR., *Sat.* I, 6, 13-14) mentioned prayers offered by maidens with both parents living in the context of the consultation of the Sibylline books. No scribe, however ingenious or astute, could have invented such apposite material concerning a subject of interest to late Roman pagans.

left the orbit of the Roman aristocracy. After the demise of classicising culture in the West, the ancient original of our tradition came into the possession of a North Italian monastic centre such as Bobbio. The archetype of the extant manuscripts was probably copied in North Italy, where it acquired symptoms of Insular influence. It crossed the Alps during the eighth century, arriving in the Carolingian milieu of our earliest manuscripts.

Some False Leads. Attempts to find further references to the *HA* in the period before the turn of the ninth century have met with limited success. Barnes detected certain similarities between the *HA* and the works of Sulpicius Severus, which he attributed to the influence of the *HA* on Severus ([30]). These (quite generic) verbal parallels do not provide evidence of filiation. All writers hope to be read without *fastidium*, and even Jerome expressed this sentiment ([31]). Nothing can be asserted based upon the fact that a pagan scholar contrasted *eloquentia* with *fidelitas historica*, while a Christian scholar contrasted *eloquentia* with *fides*. While it is true (as den Hengst noted) that both Sulpicius Severus and the author of the *HA* used the adjective *manifestus* with a distinctive nuance of meaning, this isolated similarity in their usage does not establish a connection between them ([32]). My own detailed reading of Severus has revealed little of further interest. Moreover, Severus' *Chronica* give no account of secular history in the crucial period from Alexander Severus to Carinus : a period in which the *HA* might have proved indispensable to any credulous reader.

Domaszewski argued that the author of the *HA* was a provincial librarian at Nîmes in the age of Gregory of Tours : an eccentric and untenable theory. Domaszewski drew attention to some parallels between the *HA* and Sidonius Apollinaris, the fifth-century Gallic aristocrat and bishop ([33]). The author of the *HA* included among the tutors of Maximinus an invented son of Iulius Titianus ([34]). The elder Titianus was a genuine figure, whom Sidonius described in terms similar to those used by the author of the *HA* ([35]). Nonetheless, it seems that Sidonius was better informed than the author of the *HA* on this point, since he gave a more detailed description of Titianus' style and the nature of the opposition he encountered. The parallel may reflect a school tradition, or criticism circulated by a lost intermediary. Domaszewski also argued that the author of the *HA* alluded to some verses on the consumption of the Emperor Carus by light-

(30) T. 11, 6-7 ; Sulp. Sev., *Vit. Mart.* praef. 3 [*SC* CXXXIII, 248] ; Tac. 12, 2 ; Sulp. Sev., *Dial.* II(III) 5, 6 [DX, 308] ; Barnes 1999 : 39-40.

(31) Hier., *Comm. in Dan.*, prol. [*CCSL* LXXVa, 775 (85)] : *ne librorum innumerabilium magnitudo lectori fastidium faciat.*

(32) A 2, 1 ; Sulp. Sev., *Dial.* II(III) 5, 5 [*SC* DX, 208] ; Paschoud 1996 : 15, n. 6 ; den Hengst 1981 : 108 ; *TLL* VIII, col. 310, 65-67.

(33) Domaszewski 1918 : 19-21.

(34) Max. 27, 5.

(35) Sid., *Ep.* I, 1, 2.

ning, found in the poems of Sidonius Apollinaris. The author of the *HA* claimed that a spurious iambic poet, called Aurelius Apollinaris, wrote an account of the deeds of Carus ([36]). Domaszewski brought forward a passage in which Sidonius Apollinaris praised the successes of Carus against the Persians and decribed his sudden death ([37]). Domaszewski claimed that the passage in the *Carus et Carinus et Numerianus* alluded to these verses ([38]). There is, as Barnes suggested, a better explanation for the relevant passage in the *HA* ([39]). The poet Nemesianus appears as Olympius in the scholia on Statius and as M. Aur. Nemesianus in some manuscripts ([40]). The author of the *HA* knew the passage in the *Cynegeticon* in which Nemesianus projected a panegyric of Carus and Carinus ([41]). He had earlier mentioned Nemesianus and Apollinaris, two brothers who conspired to assassinate the Emperor Caracalla ([42]). These became the genuine poet Olympius Nemesianus and the spurious poet Aurelius Apollinaris, found together in the relevant life.

Domaszewski drew attention to certain names, which occur in both Sidonius and the *HA* : notably Avitus, Aetius, Ablavius, Vitrugia, Apollinaris and Lampridius. It is, however, misleading to focus upon a small number of similarities in prosopography, which may occur through chance, and indeed there are more plausible alternative explanations in almost every case. Gallonius Avitus is a deformation of Lollianus Avitus, Vituriga is a deformation of Victoria or Vitruvia, an author known as Ablabius was active under Constantine, while the name Lampridius is attested around the turn of the fifth century ([43]). It should also be noted that Geisler included three verbal parallels between the *HA* and Sidonius in the catalogue appended to Luetjohann's edition ([44]). These parallels, which may be helpful from the perspective of textual criticism, merely indicate that the two authors spoke the same language.

Birley, who argued that the *HA* was written in the second half of the fifth century, could bring forward no further literary evidence in support of his thesis, except the probably erroneous belief that Vegetius (on whom the author of the

(36) Car. 11, 2.

(37) Sid., *Carm.* 23, 88-96 : *Quid quod Caesaribus ferax creandis | felix prole uirum, simul dedisti | natos cum genitore principantes ? | nam quis Persidis expeditionem | aut uictricia castra praeteribit | Cari principis et perambulatum | Romanis legionibus Niphaten, | tum cum fulmine captus imperator | uitam fulminibus parem peregit ?*

(38) Domaszewski 1918 : 19.

(39) Barnes 1978 : 147.

(40) *PLRE* I, 622, M. Aur. Nemesianus Olympius 2 ; Lact. Plac., *Comm. Stat.* II, 58.

(41) Nem., *Cyn.* 63-85.

(42) Cc. 6, 7.

(43) Gallonius Avitus : Q 15, 6. Lollianus Avitus : P 1, 5. Vituriga : Q 12, 3. Victoria or Vitruvia : T 5, 3. Lampridius : *PLRE* II, 656, Lampridius 1.

(44) Luetjohann 1887 : 351-416.

HA drew) wrote his epitome of military affairs during the fifth century ([45]). Clover, who shared the conventional view on the date of the *HA*, nevertheless compared it to some works of a later period, including the poems of the *Latin Anthology*, the fragments of the historian Olympiodorus and the pseudo-Boniface ([46]). Clover noted only one parallel between these works and the *HA* : some verses from an epithalamium, ascribed to the Emperor Gallienus, and found both in the *HA* and in a lost collection of poems, preserved in an early printed book and now incorporated in the *Latin Anthology* ([47]). The version of this epithalamium which appears in the *Latin Anthology* is fuller and more accurate than the citation in the *HA*, and so there can be no suspicion that the *HA* was the source of these verses. There may be an echo of the *HA* in the *de Consolatione Philosophiae*, the apologia that Boethius wrote soon before his gruesome execution in 524. Boethius described how Caracalla cast the courtier Papinian before the swords of the soldiers ([48]). A similar claim is found in the *Antoninus Caracallus* ([49]). Nevertheless, it would be unwise to assume that Boethius had read the *HA*, since its information about Papinian would have been available elsewhere in the historical tradition ([50]). Boethius' reference to the unhappy jurist occurs in a catalogue of fallen ministers, so that it may be derived from a collection of notable examples.

Hohl argued that a phrase in the manuscript tradition of Eutropius demonstrated the influence of the *HA* ([51]). The extant manuscripts of Eutropius describe Gallienus' suppression of two usurpers : Ingenuus and Trebellianus ([52]). A usurper called Trebellianus occurs in a clearly spurious context in the *HA* ([53]). Hohl suggested that the words *et Trebelliano* were an interpolation in the text of Eutropius, which must be derived from the influence of the *HA* ([54]). Many mod-

(45) E. Birley 1985 : 57-68 ; Idem 1980 ; Idem 1978 ; Idem 1966.

(46) Clover 1991 ; Idem 1983 ; Idem 1980.

(47) Gall. 11, 8 ; *Anth. Lat.* I, 711.

(48) Boeth., *Cons.* III, 5(10) 27 [*CCSL* XCIV, 45(25)] : *Nero Senecam familiarem praeceptoremque suum ad eligendae mortis coegit arbitrium, Papinianum diu inter aulicos potentem militum gladiis Antoninus obiecit.*

(49) Cc. 8, 4 : *a militibus non solum permittente uerum etiam suadente Antonino occisum.* Note also 8, 8 : *cum raptus a militibus ad Palatium traheretur occidendus.*

(50) Aurelius Victor refers to the same events : Aur. Vic., *Caes.* 20, 33. Meckler discusses several further references to this execution in ancient sources : Meckler 2005.

(51) Hohl 1915.

(52) Eutr., *Breu.* IX, 8, 1 : *nam iuuenis in Gallia et Illyrico multa strenue fecit, occiso apud Mursam Ingenuo, qui purpuram sumpserat et Trebelliano.* Aurelius Victor and his epitomator have the correct form Regilianus : Aur. Vic., *Caes.* 33, 2 ; *Epit.* 32, 3.

(53) T 26, 1-7.

(54) Eutr., *Breu.* IX, 8, 1. Hohl indulged in some intriguing but illicit speculation concerning the author of the alleged interpolation : *Der Gedanke, den Urheber der Trebellianusglosse in irgend welche Verbindung mit diesem Symmachus* [Memmius

ern scholars have tended to reject Hohl's argument, suggesting that Eutropius mistakenly wrote Trebellianus in place of the genuine name Regilianus ([55]). Our author may then have incorporated this erroneous name into his catalogue as a independent historical figure, in a desperate effort to find a full thirty usurpers. Indeed, this is not the only case in which a variant version of a personal name found in Eutropius may have influenced the author of the *HA*. To give one example, Iulia Soemias Bassiana, the mother of Elagabalus, appears in the lives of Macrinus and Elagabalus under the name Symiamira, an otherwise unattested form ([56]). This corruption may be related to the form Symiasera, found in Eutropius ([57]). More troubling is a reference in the *Tyranni Triginta* to a usurper called Lollianus, whose real name was Laelianus ([58]). This mistake may reflect an error in some manuscripts of Eutropius ([59]). For this reason, it seems quite possible that the name Trebellianus came from Eutropius to our author and not the other way around.

Testa (following Mazzarino) has suggested that there is a connection between the *Carus et Carinus et Numerianus* and an account of the martyrdom of Cantius, Cantianus and Cantianilla (the *Passio Cantiorum*) ([60]). The brief passion text connects the three believers to the family tree of the Anicii, which it also associates with the Emperor Carinus. Based upon these genealogies, Testa argued that our author's vociferous denunciation of Carinus may have represented a covert attack on the Anicii. Nevertheless, the historical tradition already contained a great deal of hostile material on this ruler, who was unfortunate enough to fall to Diocletian ([61]). Moreover, our impostor seems to have associated the Anicii with the Emperor Probus, never mentioning Carinus in this context. Testa also noted a verbal parallel between the passion text and the *Carus et Carinus et Numerianus* ([62]). Apparently the martyrs were *intra urbem Romam generati atque educati*, whereas Carus was *Romae ... et natum et eruditum* (several other possible origins are proposed) ([63]). These apparently generic phrases, which express quite obvious ideas, can hardly demonstrate the dependence of one text on the other.

Symmachus] *zu bringen, ist zwar verlockend, lässt sich aber leider in keiner Weise sichern*. Hohl 1915 : 383.

(55) Chastagnol 1994 : 853-854 ; Syme 1968a : 48. On the manuscripts of Eutropius, see : Reynolds 1983. The usurper Regilianus also appears in the *HA* : T 10, 1-17.

(56) OM 9, 2 ; Hel. 2, 1 ; 4, 4 ; 14, 4 ; 18, 2 ; Turcan 1993 : 133-134 ; *BTL* ; *CLCLT*.

(57) Eutr., *Breu.* VIII, 22.

(58) T 5, 1-8.

(59) Eutr., *Breu.* IX, 9, 1.

(60) Lizzi Testa 2007.

(61) Chastagnol 1994 : 1141-1142.

(62) Lizzi Testa 2007 : 284.

(63) Car. 4, 4.

There is no good reason to expect to find further references to the *HA* in late antique literature, given the nature of the materials. In this instance, even the absence of evidence is quite uninformative. Many other works written around the turn of the fifth century also disappear from the record, only to re-emerge about a century later. The earliest known citation of Ammianus occurs in the grammarian Priscian (active about 500) ([64]). Sidonius Apollinaris mentioned Virius Nicomachus Flavianus' version of the *Life of Apollonius of Tyana*, the only overt reference to this work ([65]). Cassiodorus provided the only ancient citation of Arusianus Messius' *Exempla elocutionum*, although Priscian may have drawn upon Messius' materials ([66]). Although the cultural activities of the late Roman aristocracy are relatively well documented, the gaps in our knowledge remain vast.

Conclusion. The text of the *HA* reflects more than a millennium of development : its earliest sources stretch back to the reign of Hadrian, while its transmission depends upon the extant manuscripts, some of which are of humanistic date. The available evidence on the reception of the *HA* in the period between 400 and 800 AD is very limited indeed. Nevertheless, we can draw the tentative conclusion that the *HA* relied upon the cultural networks of the late Roman aristocracy for its dissemination and preservation. It seems likely that the text passed through successive generations of the Symmachi-Nicomachi until it came into the possession of Q. Aurelius Memmius Symmachus, who quoted from it in his lost *Historia Romana*. Memmius Symmachus' manuscripts may have changed hands in the general wreck that followed Justinian's invasion of Italy ; a discontinuity in the classical tradition at this point reflects a radical and destructive change. Nevertheless, the *HA* continued to be associated with other works read and copied in this late Roman milieu even after the demise of Classical Antiquity in the West. During the sixth century, a large number of manuscripts once owned by members of the Roman aristocracy found their way into new libraries associated with religious foundations in North Italy. There are some reasons to place the *HA* in the library of the monastery of St Columban at Bobbio in the seventh and eighth centuries. Towards the end of the eighth century, many manuscripts of classical authors were drawn across the Alps by the expanding influence of the Frankish kingdom. The *HA* only appears again early in the ninth century, when Einhard may have imitated a passage concerning Hadrian. The manuscript tradition began from that point, and in this way the survival of the *HA* was assured.

(64) Prisc., *Inst.* IX, 51 [*GL* II, 487, 1].
(65) Sid., *Ep.* VIII, 3, 1.
(66) Cass., *Inst.* I, 15, 7.

CONCLUSION

Towards an Interpretation

Problems of Interpretation. We have followed the trail of an unscrupulous impostor, a man who fabricated countless documents and authorities under six names, creating ingenious problems for successive generations of scholars. In the process, we have amassed a great deal of information on the structure, sources, authorship, date, context, redaction and reception of a disputed text. Perhaps now is the time to begin to integrate some of this material into a broader interpretative framework. It might be helpful to return to a schema proposed in the introduction, which distinguished approaches to the text based upon ideology, intertextuality and hermeneutics. We might group together under these rubrics some of the insights that have emerged throughout the course of this study. Our conclusions can only be tentative, in part because some of the questions we have posed are relatively new. Although the scholarship on the subject has been distinguished by outstanding erudition, some problems of interpretation remain neglected.

Ideology. We might start with questions of cultural production. This study argued that networks centred on the great families of the Roman aristocracy played a considerable role in the creation, dissemination and preservation of Latin culture in Late Antiquity. The Roman magnates were important as a centre of symbolic value, a source of prestige. As the subscriptions found throughout various manuscripts suggest, these families also guaranteed the perpetuation of traditions in their own lines and through their private libraries. For these reasons, many scholars dedicated their works to great aristocrats. We noted that Arusianus Messius, Servius, Macrobius and Priscian donated their grammatical treatises variously to members of the Anicii, the Ceionii and the Nicomachi-Symmachi. Taken together, these examples suggested that patronising and promoting learning was as a normal part of the elite culture of the Roman aristocracy.

Our impostor was probably not a member of one of the great houses, but instead a minor senator from a relatively obscure family who had attached himself to networks affiliated with several different aristocratic groups. Our author may also have come from a provincial background (1). We drew attention to

(1) During the last decades of the fourth century, a considerable number of Gallic notables, generally affiliated with Bordeaux and its schools, succeeded in infiltrating both

many individuals who engaged with the Roman aristocracy through the medium of literature over the course of Late Antiquity : high officials such as Ausonius, Macrobius and Cassiodorus, lesser functionaries such as Protadius and Arusianus Messius, minor senators such as Tascius Victorianus and Naucellius, the provincial rhetorician Pacatus, prominent teachers of grammar such as Servius and Priscian, even the anonymous author of an epigram written to an otherwise unidentified Anicius. Although mostly comparatively wealthy and influential (indeed sometimes close to the summit of the social order), these men adopted conventional attitudes of deference when addressing the magnates of the city of Rome. One can easily gain a misleading impression of the social background of the author based upon the false assumption that he was a servile grammarian.

Our impostor addressed conventional praise to the Roman nomeclatura (especially the Ceionii, but also possibly the Anicii and the Nicomachi-Symmachi). Spurious names interspersed throughout the *HA* furnished the Ceionii with numerous ancestors. Our impostor claimed that this family were descended from the usurper Clodius Albinus, while implying that the Anicii were connected to the Emperor Probus. His antiquarian research legitimated the prerogatives of the Senate, by discovering dubious grants of jurisdiction from the recent past. Our impostor celebrated and reinforced the cultural identity of privileged groups, while accepting as given their entitlement to social pre-eminence. He also recast the imperial history of the third century in terms that were familiar to his intended audience, while naturally according their values a central place within his narrative.

Our author certainly expressed various traditionalist attitudes : a distrust of hereditary monarchy, contempt for courtiers, eunuchs and influential women, respect for the privileges of the Senate and the landed interest more generally, even a desire to protect the old cult. No doubt sections of the senatorial order shared some of these attitudes, many of which were merely derivative, reflecting the common conceptions expressed in countless sources. Nonetheless, there is no evidence that our impostor sought an audience for these casual prejudices outside the elite, or even an audience outside the cultural networks centred upon the Roman aristocracy. Clearly status (and not confessional or ideological concerns) mediated his relationship with his readers. He appealed to his audience through adherence to the great families, based upon a conventional understanding of rank. Although his work was complicit in elite ideologies, we cannot assert that our author set out to write a work of propaganda or polemic. Nonetheless, his scholarship had an ideological dimension, where it affirmed the ascendancy of a narrow caste.

Roman society and the imperial administration, partly through the patronage of Ausonius. These provincials, important enough in their own places, came into contact with the great Roman families, whose pretensions were boundless.

The great families played their role in transmitting the *HA* to posterity. A citation of the *Maximini Duo* in a fragment of a lost work of Memmius Symmachus once again associates the *HA* with the late Roman aristocracy, perhaps suggesting that this work was received and disseminated by some prominent contemporaries. Such evidence corroborates our interpretation of the spurious genealogies, honorific allusions and suppositious documents found throughout the lives. In attempting to describe the transmission of the text, we drew analogies with other works produced in the same period and under similar conditions : Arusianus Messius' *Exempla elocutionum* and the *Epigrammata Bobiensia* associated with the poetaster Naucellius. There are correspondences, difficult to explain, between the late antique reception of various traditions and their subsequent fate in the early Middle Ages. Arguably, the cultural networks of the Roman aristocracy played an important role in the formation of the extant canon of Latin literature, which still partly reflects their interests and values.

Intertextuality. Our author seems to have been responsive to the conventions appropriate to the different literary modes in which he wrote. His letters, speeches, harangues, acclamations, omens, verses, excerpts from authorities and references to inscriptions conform to generic expectations. Moreover, his fabrication of an elaborate authenticating apparatus reflects a desire to imitate as scrupulously as possible the works of Suetonius and Marius Maximus, his predecessors in the sphere of imperial biography. The parade of collective authorship, in a work that apostrophised Diocletian, Constantine and private individuals under Constantius I, suggests parallels with authentic compilations such as the *Panegyrici Latini*. The existence of such collections, genuine bodies of documents accumulated over time in school contexts, may explain the strange format of the *HA*. Some indications suggest that our author sought to accommodate his work within the traditions of imperial biography and imperial panegyric ; in his period the distinction between biography and panegyric was not absolutely clear.

Roman readers towards the end of the fourth century might have welcomed the fabrication of a series of biographies of emperors, minor rulers and usurpers. The Roman elite had an interest in various kinds of life writing, including apocryphal and hagiographical works. An eminent aristocrat respected for his learning (Virius Nicomachus Flavianus) could disseminate what we might consider a dubious apocryphon (a version of Philostratos' *Life of Apollonius of Tyana*). Eunapius attributed quasi-mystical powers to often epigonous intellectuals in the tradition of Plotinus, Porphyry and Iamblichus. Jerome clearly modelled his suspect hermits (Paul, Hilarion and Malchus) on the wildly successful *Life of Anthony* (generally ascribed to Athanasius). The intended audience of these works probably included highly placed members of the aristocracy of the Western empire. Late Antiquity witnessed the production of a large body of hagiographical literature, as well as numerous impostures of a confessional kind. Such works, although sometimes preposterous by modern standards, enjoyed currency and credibility in the context in which they first appeared. There is no reason to believe that the mentalities revealed in these cultural forms were restricted to particular religious groups.

We noted affinities involving the genre of imperial biography and scholars associated with the late Roman aristocracy. Ammianus claimed that the Roman notables read nothing except Marius Maximus and Juvenal. A citation from Marius Maximus appears in the late antique scholia on Juvenal, probably compiled at Rome towards the end of the fourth century (a text possibly known to our author). These scholia also contain the only citation of the poet known as the second Sulpicia, under whose name the *Epigrammata Bobiensia* present a Juvenalian diatribe against the reign of Domitian, based upon an incident reported in Suetonius. Meanwhile, the *de Re Coquinaria* ascribed to Apicius, probably compiled at Rome late in the fourth century, affixes to some of its recipes the names of Vitellius, Trajan, Commodus and possibly even Elagabalus. Our author almost certainly exploited this source in embellishing the menus of that amazing emperor.

The apparent connections between the second urban digression, the scholia on Juvenal, the *Epigrammata Bobiensia*, the *de Re Coquinaria* and the *HA* may reveal our impostor's immediate context : the ambience of the Roman schools. Nevertheless, interest in imperial biography manifested itself more widely. Ausonius' verse catalogue of Roman emperors (the *Caesares*), again probably known to our author, clearly drew upon material preserved through the works of Marius Maximus. Even more significant is another work, apparently enumerating usurpers from Decius to Diocletian, known only through an entry in a medieval catalogue. These lost verses apparently embraced much the same material as compendia ascribed to Pollio (the *Tyranni Triginta*) and Vopiscus (the *Quadrigae Tyrannorum*). Polemius Silvius would subsequently draw upon yet another lost catalogue of usurpers. While our author innovated by writing lives of usurpers, he may have responded to more widespread interest in these figures.

Hermeneutics. Our investigation suggested that the impostor approached scholarship differently than we might. He did not divide the past into discrete periods, one succeeding the other in an irreversible process : key assumptions of modern historiography. The past was for him a collection of examples, preserved within a moralising rhetorical tradition. His description of administrative arrangements, which simultaneously embraced hundreds of years of constitutional developments, reflected this understanding. When he imagined the events of the second and third centuries, he drew upon recent events as well as the furthest reaches of the antiquarian past. Our impostor shared this mentality with many of his contemporaries, including some authors of administrative documents, panegyrics and treatises on military organisation. Nonetheless, generalisations about late antique mentalities cannot be made upon such a narrow basis of evidence. For example, this understanding of the past did not conform to the norms of classical historiography as practised by Ammianus.

Our devious impostor was in many ways a genuine scholar. He assembled an impressive array of source materials, paraphrasing and translating them with reasonable accuracy. He saw connections between all periods of history, which could be explored through etymologies, genealogies and typologies. These correspondences produced a coherent synthesis of available knowledge on the past. Many of our author's fabrications, although considered eccentric, may reflect accepted norms of late antique scholarship. What appears to us as mindless punning, genealogical fabrication or literary pastiche may actually have been persuasive within his cultural context. We might even entertain the dangerous notion that these techniques were respectable methods of undertaking scholarly research. Cassiodorus used quite similar devices when he investigated the history of the Goths, somehow integrating an obscure Germanic tribe into the history of the Mediterranean world.

This study has used words such as 'imposture,' 'impostor,' 'fabrication,' 'spurious,' 'suppositious' and 'purported' in reference to the *HA*. These terms at least leave open the question of authorial intention. By contrast, the word 'forgery' is too strong, in that it imputes a desire to deceive, while terms such as 'hoax' and 'spoof' may imply that the author intended for his work to be exposed. Nevertheless, none of our terminology is really satisfactory, since it tends to impose inapposite categories on an ancient text. After all, hagiography, apocrypha and pseudepigrapha, romance narratives, confessional forgeries and dubious antiquarian research flourished throughout Late Antiquity. We should acknowledge that our author may have operated within conventions of truth and verisimilitude entirely unfamiliar to us. Modern scholarship, formed by the controversies of the Reformation and the Enlightenment, places a heavy emphasis on authenticity. Other possible tests of truth (didactic value, appropriateness, plausibility, persuasiveness, inspiration, doctrinal orthodoxy) are considered deeply suspect. Our impostor may have justified his inventions on grounds such as these.

The *HA* was only exposed after a massive expansion in positive knowledge had fundamentally changed the nature of scholarship itself. It was only in the eighteenth and nineteenth centuries that the historical problems of the *HA* began to be perceived, after the development of scholarly methods and critical mindsets not widely known in the ancient world. Only towards the end of the nineteenth century, in the context of the German academic system, could there emerge a coherent refutation of the attributions and dedications found in the manuscripts. Even then, what is now the modern interpretation of the text was only established after more than seven decades of minute controversy. No writer before the modern era, however learned, could even have imagined the systematic application of scholarly method and the proliferation of knowledge about Classical Antiquity that the nineteenth century witnessed. Speaking from within this tradition, we have every right to describe the *HA* as an imposture. But when we do so, we inevitably inflict upon this work our own assumptions, or rather the assumptions of the late nineteenth century. When we describe a late antique text as an imposture, we may misinterpret the meaning that it had for its original readers and even for its author. We say only what it means to us.

BIBLIOGRAPHY

(A) Primary Sources

AMM. — J. FONTAINE, É. GALLETIER, G. SABBAH, E. FRÉZOULS, J. D. BERGER, M.-A. MARIÉ and L. ANGLIVIEL de la BEAUMELLE, *Ammien Marcellin : Histoires*, 6 vols. Texte établi, traduit et annoté par J.F., E.G., G.S., M.-A.M. et L.A.B., avec la collaboration de E.F. et J.D.B., Paris, 1968-1999 (Collection des Universités de France).

Anth. Lat. — F. BUECHELER, A. RIESE and E. LOMMATZSCH, *Anthologia Latina*, 2 vols. Ediderunt F. B et A. R. Supplementum curauit E.L., Amsterdam, 1964 [first ed. Leipzig, 1895-1926].

APIC. — C. GROCOCK and S. GRAINGER, *Apicius*. A critical edition with an introduction and an English translation by C.G. and S.G., Totnes, 2006.

J. ANDRÉ, *Apicius : L'art culinaire*. Texte établi, traduit et commenté par J. A., Paris, 1974 (Collection des Universités de France).

M. E. MILHAM, *Apicii decem libri cui dicuntur De Re Coquinaria*. Edidit M.E.M., Leipzig, 1969 (Bibliotheca scriptorum Graecorum et Romanorum Teubneriana).

B. FLOWER and E. ROSENBAUM, *The Roman Cookery Book*. A critical translation of *The Art of Cooking* by Apicius for use in the study and the kitchen by B.F. and E.S., London, 1958.

APUL., *Met.* — D.S. ROBERTSON and P. VALETTE, *Apulée : Les Métamorphoses*, 3 vols. Texte établi par D.S.R. et traduit par P.V., Paris, 1965-1971 (Collection des Universités de France).

ARUS., MESS. — A. della CASA, *Arusianus Messius : Exempla elocutionum*. A cura di A.C., Milan, 1977 (Collana di grammatici latini).

H. KEIL, *Arusianus Messius : Exempla elocutionum ex Vergilio Sallustio Terentio Cicerone digesta per litteras* (*Grammatici Latini*, VII, p. 437-514). Ex recensione H.K., Hildesheim, 1961 [first ed. Leipzig, 1855-1880].

ATHEN. — S.D. OLSON, *Athenaeus : The Learned Banqueters*, 5 vols. Edited and translated by S.D.O., Cambridge (Massachusetts), 2006-2009 (Loeb Classical Library) [as yet incomplete].

C. B. GULICK, *Athenaeus : The Deipnosophists*, 7 vols. With an English translation by C.B.G., London, 1927-1941 (Loeb Classical Library).

AUR. VIC., *Caes.* — F. PICHLMAYR and R. GRUENDEL, *Sexti Aurelii Victoris Liber de Caesaribus*. Recensuit F. P. Editio stereotypa correctior editionis primae addenda et corrigenda collegit et adiecit R.G., Leipzig, 1961 (Bibliotheca scriptorum Graecorum et Romanorum Teubneriana).

Aus.	R. P. H. Green, *The Works of Ausonius*. Edited with introduction and commentary by R.P.H.G., Oxford, 1991.
Boeth., *de Cons. Phil.*	L. Bieler, *Anicii Manlii Severini Boethii Philosophiae Consolatio*. Edidit L.B., Turnhout, 1957 (Corpus Christianorum Series Latina XCIV).
Caes., *B.G.*	R. du Pontet, *C. Iuli Caesaris Commentariorum : de Bello Gallico*. Recensuit breuique adnotatione critica instruxit R.P., Oxford, 1900 (Oxford Classical Texts).
Caesarius	D. G. Morin, *Sancti Caesarii Arelatensis Sermones*, 2nd ed., 2 vols. Studio et diligentia D.G.M., Turnhout, 1953 (Corpus Christianorum Series Latina CIII-CIV).
Cass., *Inst.*	R. A. B. Mynors, *Cassiodori Senatoris Institutiones*. Edited from the Manuscripts by R.A.B.M., Oxford, 1961 [first ed. 1937].
Cass., *Var.*	Å. J. Fridh, *Magni Aurelii Cassiodori Variarum libri XII*. Cura et studio Å.J.F., Turnhout, 1973 (Corpus Christianorum Series Latina XCVI).
Chron. Gall.	R. Burgess, *The Gallic Chronicle of 452 : A New Critical Edition with a Brief Introduction* in R. W. Mathisen and D. Shanzer, *Society and Culture in Late Antique Gaul*, Aldershot, 2001, p. 52-84.
Cic., *pro Mur.*	H. Kasten, *M. Tullius Cicero : Oratio pro L. Murena*. Iterum recognouit H.K., Leipzig, 1961 (Bibliotheca scriptorum Graecorum et Romanorum Teubneriana).
Cic., *de Orat.*	K. F. Kumaniecki, *M. Tulli Ciceronis de Oratore*. Edidit K.F.K., Leipzig, 1969 (Bibliotheca scriptorum Graecorum et Romanorum Teubneriana).
Claud.	J. B. Hall, *Claudii Claudiani Carmina.* Edidit J.B.H., Leipzig, 1985 (Bibliotheca scriptorum Graecorum et Romanorum Teubneriana).
CTh	T. Mommsen and P. M. Meyer, *Theodosiani libri XIV cum Constitutionibus Sirmondianis et Leges novellae ad Theodosianum pertinentes*. Ediderunt T.M. et M.M., Berlin, 1905.
	C. Pharr, T. S. Davidson and M. B. Pharr, *The Theodosian code and novels, the Sirmondian constitutions*. A translation with commentary, glossary, and bibliography by C.P. in collaboration with T.S.D. and M.B.P., Princeton, 1952.
Cass. Dio, *Epit.*	E. Cary, *Dio's Roman History*, 9 vols. With an English translation by E.C., London, 1914-1927 (Loeb Classical Library).
Coll. Mos. Rom. Leg.	H. Hyamson, *Mosaicarum et Romanarum Legum Collatio*. With introduction, facsimile and transcription of the Berlin Codex, translation, notes and appendices by H.H., Oxford, 1913.
Ein., *Vit. Karl.*	L. Halphen, *Éginhard : Vie de Charlemagne*, 2nd ed. Éditée et traduite par L.H., Paris, 1938 (Classiques de l'Histoire de France au Moyen Âge).
Ennod.	F. Vogel, *Magni Felicis Ennodii Opera*. Recensuit F.V., Berlin, 1961 (Monumenta Germaniae historica, Auctores antiquissimi VII) [first ed. 1885].

Epig. Bob. — A. GIORDANO RAMPIONI, *Sulpiciae Conquestio (Ep. Bob. 37)*, Bologna, 1982 (Edizioni e saggi universitari di filologia classica XXXII).

W. SPEYER, *Epigrammata Bobiensia.* Edidit W.S., Leipzig, 1963 (Bibliotheca scriptorum Graecorum et Romanorum Teubneriana).

F. MUNARI and A. CAMPANA, *Epigrammata Bobiensia.* Detexit A.C. Edidit F.M., Rome, 1955.

H. FUCHS, *Das Klagelied der Sulpicia über die Gewaltherrschaft des Kaisers Domitian* in M. SIEBER, *Discordia Concors : Festgabe für Edgar Bonjour zu seinem siebzigsten Geburtstag am 21 August 1968*, Basel, 1968, I, p. 31-47.

I. LANA, *La satira di Sulpicia.* Studio critico, testo e traduzione, Turin, 1949 (Università di Torino : Pubblicazioni della Facoltà di Lettere e Filosofia I, 5).

Epit. — F. PICHLMAYR and R. GRUENDEL, *Epitome de Caesaribus.* Recensuit F.P. Editio stereotypa correctior editionis primae addenda et corrigenda collegit et adiecit R.G., Leipzig, 1961 (Bibliotheca scriptorum Graecorum et Romanorum Teubneriana).

EUS., *Hist. Eccl.* — G. BARDY and P. PÉRICHON, *Eusèbe de Césarée : Histoire ecclésiastique,* 4 vols. Texte grec, traduction et annotation par G.B., index par P.P., Paris, 1952-1987 (Sources Chrétiennes XXXI, XLI, LV, LXXIII).

EUTR., *Breu.* — C. SANTINI, *Eutropii Breuiarium ab urbe condita.* Recognouit C.S., Leipzig, 1979 (Bibliotheca scriptorum Graecorum et Romanorum Teubneriana).

FULG. — R. HELM and J. PRÉAUX, *Fabii Planciadis Fulgentii v.c. Opera.* Recensuit R.H. Addenda adiecit J.P., Stuttgart, 1970 (Bibliotheca scriptorum Graecorum et Romanorum Teubneriana) [first ed. 1898].

GELL. — P. K. MARSHALL, *A. Gellii Noctes Atticae*, 2 vols. Recognouit breuique adnotatione critica instruxit P.K.M., Oxford, 1990 (Oxford Classical Texts) [first ed. 1968].

GERB., *Ep.* — P. RICHÉ and J. P. CALLU, *Gerbert d'Aurillac : Correspondance.* Texte établi, traduit et commenté par P.R. et J.P., Paris, 1993 (Classiques de l'Histoire de France au Moyen Âge XXXV-XXXVI).

GERB., *Geom.* — N. BUBNOV, *Opera mathematica ... Geberti.* Edidit, apparatu critico instruxit, commentario auxit, figuris illustrauit N.B., Hildesheim, 1983 [first ed. 1899].

J. P. MIGNE, *Geometria Gerberti.* Accurante J.P.M., Paris, 1844-1855 (Patrologia Latina, CXXXIX, col. 91-154).

HELIOD. — R. M. RATTENBURY, T. W. LUMB and J. MAILLON, *Héliodore : Les Éthiopiques*, 3 vols. Texte établi par R.M.R. et T.W.L. et traduit par J.M., Paris, 1935-1943 (Collection des Universités de France).

HER. — A. D. GODLEY, *Herodotus*, 4 vols. With an English translation by A.D.G., Cambridge (Massachusetts), 1975 [first ed. London 1920-1925] (Loeb Classical Library).

HEROD. — C. R. WHITTAKER, *Herodian*, 2 vols. With an English translation by C.R.W., London, 1969-1970 (Loeb Classical Library).

HIER., *Comm. in Dan.* — F. GLORIE, *S. Hieronymi Presbyteri Opera : Commentariorum in Danielem libri III*. Cura et studio F.G., Turnhout, 1964 (Corpus Christianorum Series Latina LXXVa).

HIER., *contra Ruf.* — P. LARDET, *S. Hieronymi Presbyteri Opera : Contra Rufinum*. Edidit P.L., Turnhout, 1982 (Corpus Christianorum Series Latina LXXIX).

HIER., *Ep.* — J. LABOURT, *Saint Jérôme : Lettres*, 8 vols. Texte établi et traduit par J.L., Paris, 1949-1963 (Collection des Universités de France).

IORD. — T. MOMMSEN, *Iordanis Romana et Getica*. Recensuit T.M., Berlin, 1961 (Monumenta Germaniae historica, Auctores antiquissimi V, 1) [first ed. 1882].

ISID., *Orig.* — W. M. LINDSAY, *Isidori Hispalensis Episcopi Etymologiarum siue Originum libri XX*, 2 vols. Recognouit breuique adnotatione critica instruxit W.M.L., Oxford, 1911 (Oxford Classical Texts).

IUV. — W. V. CLAUSEN, *A. Persi Flacci et D. Iuni Iuvenalis Saturae*. Edidit breuique adnotatione critica instruxit W.V.C., Oxford, 1959 (Oxford Classical Texts).

S. G. OWEN, *A. Persi Flacci et D. Iuni Iuvenalis Saturae*. Cum additamentis Bodleianis recognouit breuique adnotatione critica instruxit S.G.O., Oxford, 1907 (Oxford Classical Texts).

LACT. PLAC. — R. D. SWEENEY, *Lactantii Placidi in Statii Thebaida commentum*. Recensuit R.D.S., Stuttgart, 1997 (Bibliotheca scriptorum Graecorum et Romanorum Teubneriana).

LIV. — R. M. OGILVIE, R. S. CONWAY, C. F. WALTERS, A. H. McDONALD and P. G. WALSH, *Titi Liui ab Vrbe Condita Libri*, 6 vols. Recognouerunt at adnotatione critica instruxerunt R.M.O., R.S.C., C.F.W., A.H.M. et P.G.W., Oxford, 1914-1999 (Oxford Classical Texts) [incorporating volumes from the earlier ed. of R.S.C. and C.F.W (1914-1934)].

MACR., *de Diff.* — H. KEIL, *Excerpta Macrobii de differentiis et societatibus Graeci Latinique uerbi* (*Grammatici Latini* V, p. 595-655). Ex recensione H.K., Hildesheim, 1961 [first ed. Leipzig, 1855-1880].

MACR., *Sat.* — J. WILLIS, *Ambrosii Theodosii Macrobii Saturnalia*. Apparatu critico instruxit J.W., Leipzig, 1963 (Bibliotheca scriptorum Graecorum et Romanorum Teubneriana).

MART. CAP. — J. WILLIS, *Martianus Capella de Nuptiis Philologiae et Mercurii*. Edidit J.W., Leipzig, 1983 (Bibliotheca scriptorum Graecorum et Romanorum Teubneriana).

NEM. — P. VOLPILHAC, *Némésien : Œuvres*. Texte établi et traduit par P.V. Paris, 1975 (Collection des Universités de France).

Pan. Lat. — C. E. V. NIXON and B. SAYLOR RODGERS, *In Praise of Later Roman Emperors : the Panegyrici Latini*. Introduction, translation and historical commentary by C.E.V.N. and B.S.R., with the Latin text of R. A. B. MYNORS., Berkeley, 1994 (Transformation of the Classical Heritage XXI).

R. A. B. Mynors, *XII Panegyrici Latini*. Recognouit breuique adnotatione critica instruxit R.A.B.M., Oxford, 1964 (Oxford Classical Texts).

Paul. Nol., *Carm.* — P. G. Walsh, *The Poems of St. Paulinus of Nola*. Translated and annotated by P.G.W., New York, 1975 (Ancient Christian Writers).

Plaut. — W. M. Lindsay, *T. Macci Plauti Comoediae*, 2 vols. Recognouit breuique adnotatione critica instruxit W.M.L., Oxford, 1903 (Oxford Classical Texts).

Plin., *N.H.* — C. Mayhoff and L. Jan, *C. Plini Secundi Naturalis Historiae*, 6 vols. Post L.I. obitum recognouit et scripturae discrepantia adiecta, edidit C.M., Stuttgart, 1892-1909 (Bibliotheca scriptorum Graecorum et Romanorum Teubneriana).

Pol. Silv., *Lat.* — T. Mommsen, *Chronica minora saec. IV, V, VI, VII* [under the title *Polemii Silvii laterculus*]. Edidit T.M., Berlin, 1961 (Monumenta Germaniae historica, Auctores antiquissimi IX, XI, XIII), IX. p. 511-551 [first ed. 1892-1898].

Prisc., *Inst.* — M. Hertz, *Prisciani Institutionum Grammaticarum libri XVIII* (in H. Keil, *Grammatici Latini*, III-IV). Ex recensione M.H., Hildesheim, 1961 [first ed. Leipzig, 1855-1880].

Prud. — M. P. Cunningham, *Aurelii Prudentii Clementis Carmina.* Cura et studio M.P.C., Turnhout, 1966 (Corpus Christianorum Series Latina CXXVI).

Quint., *Inst.* — M. Winterbottom, *M. Fabi Quintiliani Institutionis Oratoriae libri duodecim*, 2 vols. Recognouit breuique adnotatione critica instruxit M.W., Oxford, 1970 (Oxford Classical Texts).

Rut. Nam. — J. Vessereau and F. Préchac, *Rutilius Namatianus : Sur son retour*, 2nd ed. Texte établi et traduit par J.V. et F.P., Paris, 1961 (Collection des Universités de France).

Schol. Iuu. — P. Wessner, *Scholia in Iuuenalem uetustiora.* Collegit recensuit illustrauit P.W., Stuttgart, 1967 (Bibliotheca scriptorum Graecorum et Romanorum Teubneriana) [first ed. Leipzig, 1931].

Serv. — G. Thilo and H. Hagen, *Servii Grammatici in Vergilii Carmina Commentarii*, 3 vols. Recensuerunt G.T. et H.H., Hildesheim, 1961 [original edition Leipzig, 1881-1887].

Serv., *de Cent. Metr.* — H. Keil, *Marii Servii Honorati grammatici de Centum Metris* (*Grammatici Latini* IV, p. 456-467). Ex recensione H.K., Hildesheim, 1961 [first ed. Leipzig, 1855-1880].

Serv., *Explan. in art. Don.* — H. Keil, *Marii Servii Honorati grammatici Explanatio in Artem Donati* (*Grammatici Latini* IV, p. 486-534). Ex recensione H.K., Hildesheim, 1961 [first ed. Leipzig, 1855-1880].

Sid. — W. B. Anderson, *Sidonius Apollinaris : Poems and Letters*, 2 vols. With an English translation, introduction and notes by W.B.A., Cambridge (Massachusetts), 1936-1965 (Loeb Classical Library).

C. Luetjohann, *Sidonius Apollinaris : Epistulae et Carmina.* Recensuit et emendauit C.L., Berlin, 1961 (Monumenta Germaniae historica, Auctores antiquissimi VIII) [first ed. 1887].

STAT., *Silu.* — D. R. SHACKLETON BAILEY, *Statius : Silvae*. Edited and translated by D.R.S.B., Cambridge (Massachusetts), 2003 (Loeb Classical Library).

SUET. — H. AILLOUD, *Suétone : Vies des douze Césars*, 3 vols, 3rd ed. Texte établi et traduit par H.A., Paris, 1957-1961 (Collection des Universités de France).

SULP. SEV. — J. FONTAINE, *Sulpice Sévère : Vie de Saint Martin*, 3 vols. Introduction, texte et traduction par J.F., Paris, 1967-1969 (Sources Chrétiennes CXXXIII-CXXXV).

J. FONTAINE and N. DUPRÉ, *Sulpice Sévère : Gallus (Dialogues sur les 'vertus' de Saint Martin)*. Introduction, texte critique, traduction et notes par J.F., avec la collaboration de N.D., Paris, 2006 (Sources Chrétiennes DX).

G. de SENNEVILLE-GRAVE, *Sulpice Sévère : Chroniques*. Introduction, texte critique, traduction et commentaire par G.S.-G., Paris, 1999 (Sources Chrétiennes CDXLI).

SYMM., *Ep.* — J. P. CALLU, *Symmaque : Lettres*, 4 vols. Texte établi, traduit et commenté par J.P.C., Paris, 1972-2002 (Collection des Universités de France).

SYMM., *Or.* — O. SEECK, *Q. Aurelii Symmachi quae supersunt* [under the title *Q. Aurelii Symmachi v.c. Orationum quae supersunt*]. Edidit O.S., Berlin, 1961 (Monumenta Germaniae historica, Auctores antiquissimi VI, 1) [first ed. 1883], p. 318-339.

TAC., *Ann.* — C. D. FISHER, *Cornelii Taciti Annalium ab excessu diui Augusti libri*. Recognouit breuique adnotatione critica instruxit C.D.F., Oxford, 1906 (Oxford Classical Texts).

TERT. — E. DEKKERS, J. G. P. BORLEFFS, A. KROYMAN, A. GERLO, J. H. WASZINK, A. REIFFERSCHEID, G. WISSOWA, J. J. THIERRY, E. EVANS and A. HARNACK, *Quinti Septimi Florentis Tertulliani Opera*, 2 vols. Cura et studio E.D., J.G.P.B., A.K., A.G., J.H.W., A.R., G.W., J.J.T., E.E. et A.H., Turnhout, 1954 (Corpus Christianorum Series Latina I-II).

TIB. — J. P. POSTGATE, *Tibulli aliorumque carminum libri tres*. Recognouit breuique adnotatione critica instruxit J.P.P., Oxford, 1924 (Oxford Classical Texts) [first ed. 1914].

VEG., *Epit.* — C. LANG, *Flavi Vegetii Renati Epitoma rei militaris*. Recensuit C.L., Stuttgart, 1967 (Bibliotheca scriptorum Graecorum et Romanorum Teubneriana) [first ed. 1885].

VIRG. — R. A. B. MYNORS, *Vergilis Opera*. Recognouit breuique adnotatione critica instruxit R.A.B.M., Oxford, 1969 (Oxford Classical Texts).

ZOS. — F. PASCHOUD, *Zosime : Histoire Nouvelle*, 3 vols. Texte établi et traduit par F.P., Paris, 1971-1989 (Collection des Universités de France).

(B) Secondary Materials

ADAMS 1977 — J. N. ADAMS, *The Linguistic Unity of the Historia Augusta* in *Antichthon* XI, 1977, p. 93-102.

ADAMS 1972 — ——, *On the Authorship of the Historia Augusta* in *CQ* XXII, 1972, p. 186-194.

ADAMS 1971 ——, *A Type of Hyperbaton in Latin Prose* in *PCPhS* CXCVII (n.s. XVII), 1971, p. 1-16.

ALFÖLDI 1938 A. ALFÖLDI, *Der Rechtsstreit zwischen der römischen Kirche und dem Verein der Popinarii* in *Klio* XXXI, 1938, p. 249-253.

ALFÖLDI-ROSENBAUM 1972a E. ALFÖLDI- ROSENBAUM, *Apicius, De re coquinaria and the Vita Heliogabali* in *BHAC 1970*, Bonn, 1972, p. 5-10.

ALFÖLDI- ROSENBAUM 1972b ——, *Notes on Some Birds and Fishes of Luxury in the Historia Augusta* in *BHAC* 1970, Bonn, 1972, p. 11-18.

ALFONSO 1972 L. ALFONSO, *Due Note agli Epigrammata di Naucellio* in *RFIC* C, 1972, p. 162-163.

ANDRÉ 1974 J. ANDRÉ, *Apicius, L'art culinaire*. Texte établi, traduit et commenté par J.A., Paris, 1974 (Collection des Universités de France).

ARNS 1953 R. P. E. ARNS, *La technique du livre d'après Saint Jérôme*, Paris, 1953.

BALDINI 2007 A. BALDINI, *Tra Historia Augusta e Storia Romana di Q. Aurelio Memmio Simmaco* in *HAC* X, Bari, 2007, p. 9-34.

BALDINI 2002 ——, *Ancora sulla deuotio di Claudio Gotico : Aurelio Vittore fonte diretta della Historia Augusta e di Nicomaco Flaviano* in *HAC* VIII, Bari, 2002, p. 11-31.

BALLAIRA 1975 G. BALLAIRA, *A Proposito della Sulpiciae Conquestio* in *RFIC* CIII, 1975, p. 399-402.

BALLOU 1914 S. H. BALLOU, *The Manuscript Tradition of the Historia Augusta*, Leipzig, 1914.

BALLOU 1908 ——, *The MSS of the Historia Augusta* in *CPh* III, 1908, p. 273-277.

BARBIERI 1954 G. BARBIERI, *Mario Massimo* in *RFIC* XXXII, 1954, p. 36-66, p. 262-271.

BARKER-BENFIELD 1983 B. C. BARKER-BENFIELD, *Macrobius* in L. D. REYNOLDS, *Texts and Transmission : A Survey of the Latin Classics*, Oxford, 1983, p. 222-232.

BARNES 2006 T. D. BARNES, *An Urban Prefect and his Wife* in *CQ* LVI, 2006, p. 249-256.

BARNES 1999 ——, *The Historia Augusta and Christian Hagiography* in *HAC* VII, Bari, 1999, p. 33-41.

BARNES 1995 ——, *The Sources of the Historia Augusta (1967-1992)* in *HAC* III, Bari, 1995, p. 1-28.

BARNES 1994 ——, *The Franci before Diocletian* in *HAC* II, Bari, 1994, p. 11-18.

BARNES 1987 ——, *Regional Prefectures* in *BHAC 1984/1985*, Bonn, 1987, p. 13-23.

BARNES 1982 ——, *The New Empire of Diocletian and Constantine*, Cambridge (Massachusetts), 1982.

BARNES 1978 ——, *The Sources of the Historia Augusta*, Brussels, 1978 (Collection Latomus CLV).

BARNES 1972 ——, *Some Persons in the Historia Augusta* in *Phoenix* XXVI, 1972, p. 140-182.

BARNES 1967 ——, *Hadrian and Lucius Verus* in *JRS* LVII, 1967, p. 65-79.

BAUDOU 1998 — A. BAUDOU, *Les fragments des Annales de Pison tirés de l'Origo Gentis Romanae* in *Phoenix* LII, 1998, p. 55-82.

BAYNES 1928 — N. H. BAYNES, *The Historia Augusta : Its Date and Purpose. A Reply to Criticism* in *CQ* XXII, 1928, p. 166-171.

BAYNES 1926 — ——, *The Historia Augusta : Its Date and Purpose*, Oxford, 1926.

BAYNES 1924 — ——, *The Date of the Composition of the Historia Augusta* in *CR* XXXVIII, 1924, p. 165-169.

BECKER 1885 — G. BECKER, *Catalogi bibliothecarum antiqui*, Bonn, 1885.

BENARIO 1980 — H. W. BENARIO, *A Commentary on the Vita Hadriani in the Historia Augusta*, Ann Arbor, 1980 (American Classical Studies VII).

BÉRANGER 1983 — J. BÉRANGER, *Observations sur les clausules dans l'Histoire Auguste* in *BHAC 1979/1981*, Bonn, 1983, p. 43-66.

BÉRANGER 1980 — ——, *Mommsen et l'Histoire Auguste* in *BHAC 1977/1978*, Bonn, 1980, p. 17-34.

A. BIRLEY 2003 — A. BIRLEY, *The Historia Augusta and Pagan Historiography* in G. MARASCO, *Greek and Roman Historiography in Late Antiquity : Fourth to Sixth Century AD*, Leiden, 2003, p. 127-149.

A. BIRLEY 2002 — ——, *'Trebellius Pollio' and 'Flavius Vopiscus Syracusius'* in *HAC* VIII, Bari, 2002, p. 33-47.

A. BIRLEY 1997 — ——, *Marius Maximus : the Consular Biographer* in *ANRW* II, 34, 3, Berlin, 1997, p. 2678-2757.

A. BIRLEY 1995 — ——, *Indirect Means of Tracing Marius Maximus* in *HAC* III, Bari, 1995, p. 57-74.

A. BIRLEY 1976 — ——, *The Lacuna in the Historia Augusta* in *BHAC 1972/1974*, Bonn, 1976, p. 56-61.

A. BIRLEY 1967 — ——, *The Augustan History* in T. A. DOREY, *Latin Biography*, London, 1967, p. 113-138.

E. BIRLEY 1985 — ——, *The Dating of Vegetius and the Historia Augusta* in *BHAC 1982/1983*, Bonn, 1985, p. 57-68.

E. BIRLEY 1980 — ——, *True and False : Order of Battle in the Historia Augusta* in *BHAC 1977/1978*, Bonn, 1980, p. 35-43.

E. BIRLEY 1978 — ——, *Fresh Thoughts on the Dating of the Historia Augusta* in *BHAC 1975/1976*, Bonn, 1978, p. 99-106.

E. BIRLEY 1966 — ——, *Military Intelligence and the Historia Augusta* in *BHAC 1964/1965*, Bonn, 1966, p. 35-42.

BISCHOFF 1994 — B. BISCHOFF (trans. M. M. GORMAN), *Manuscripts and Libraries in the Age of Charlemagne*, Cambridge, 1994 (Cambridge Studies in Palaeography and Codicology I).

BLATT 1957 — F. BLATT, *Novum Glossarium mediae Latinitatis, ab anno DCCC usque ad annum MCC*, Copenhagen, 1957 [as yet incomplete].

BLOCH 1963 — H. BLOCH, *The Pagan Revival in the West at the End of the Fourth Century* in A. MOMIGLIANO, *The Conflict between Paganism and Christianity in the Fourth Century*, Oxford, 1963 (Oxford-Warburg Studies), p. 193-218.

BLOCH and WARTBURG 1975 — O. BLOCH and W. von WARTBURG, *Dictionnaire étymologique de la langue française*, 6th ed., Paris, 1975 [first ed. 1932].

BOYER 1948 — B. B. BOYER, *Insular Contribution to Medieval Literary Tradition on the Continent (Concluded)* in *CPh* XLIII, 1948, p. 31-39.

BROWNING 1961 — R. BROWNING, rev. W. SPEYER, *Naucellius und sein Kreis* in *CR* XI, 1961, p. 88-89.

BRUGGISSER 2007 — P. BRUGGISSER, *Claude le Gothique, arbiter deorum. Une réminiscence de Stace dans le contexte de la propagande constantinienne* in *HAC* X, Bari, 2007, p. 83-93.

BRUGGISSER 1996 — ——, *Priuatus dans l'œuvre de Symmaque : une incidence de la lexicographie sur la datation de l'Histoire Auguste* in *HAC* IV, Bari, 1996, p. 111-132.

BRUGGISSER 1991 — ——, *Le char du préfet. Échos païens et chrétiens d'une polémique dans l'Histoire Auguste et chez Quodvultdeus* in *HAC* I, Macerata, 1991, p. 93-100.

BURGESS 2005 — R. W. BURGESS, *A Common Source for Jerome, Eutropius, Festus, Ammianus, and the Epitome de Caesaribus between 358 and 378, along with Further Thoughts on the Date and Nature of the Kaisergeschichte* in *CPh* C, 2005, p. 166-192.

BURGESS 1993 — ——, *Principes cum Tyrannis : Two Studies on the Kaisergeschichte and its Tradition* in *CQ* XLIII, 1993, p. 491-500.

BURIAN 1988 — J. BURIAN, *Maximinus Thrax : Sein Bild bei Herodian und in der Historia Augusta* in *Philologus* CXXXII, 1988, p. 230-244.

CALLU 1997 — J.-P. CALLU, *Quellenforschung et bibliothèques familiales* in *HAC* V, Bari, 1997, p. 71-84.

CALLU 1985 — ——, *La première diffusion de l'Histoire Auguste* (VIe- IXe s.) in *BHAC 1982/1983*, Bonn, 1985, p. 89-129.

CALLU et al. 1992 — J.-P. CALLU, A. GADEN and O. DESBORDES, *Vies d'Hadrien, Aelius, Antonin* (Histoire Auguste I, 1). Texte établi, traduit et commenté par J.-P.C., A.G. et O.D., Paris, 1992 (Collection des Universités de France).

CAMERON 1999 — A. CAMERON, *The Antiquity of the Symmachi* in *Historia* XLVIII, 1999, p. 477-505.

CAMERON 1985 — ——, *Polyonomy in the Late Roman Aristocracy : The Case of Petronius Probus* in *JRS* LXXV, 1985, p. 164-182.

CAMERON 1980 — ——, *Poetae Novelli* in *HSPh* LXXXIV, 1980, p. 127-175.

CAMERON 1971 — ——, rev. SYME, *Ammianus and the Historia Augusta* in *JRS* LXI, 1971, p. 255-267.

CAMERON 1966 — ——, *The Date and Identity of Macrobius* in *JRS* LVI, 1966, p. 25-38.

CAMERON 1965 — ——, rev. J. STRAUB, *Heidnische Geschichtsapologetik in der Christlichen Spätantike*, A ALFÖLDI, *BHAC 1963*, F. SARTORI, ed. *Atti del Colloquio Patavino sulla Historia Augusta* in *JRS* LV, 1965, p. 240-253.

CAMERON 1964a — ——, *Literary Allusions in the Historia Augusta* in *Hermes* XCVI, 1964, p. 363-377.

CAMERON 1964b — ——, *The Roman Friends of Ammianus* in *JRS* LIV, 1964, p. 15-28.

CASAUBON et al. 1671 — I. CASAUBON, J. GRUTERUS and C. SALMASIUS, *Historiae Augustae Scriptores VI. Aelius Spartianus. Julius Capitolinus. Aelius Lampridius. Vulc. Gallicanus. Trebell. Pollio.*

Flavius Vopiscus. Cum integris notis I.C., C.S. et J.G., Leiden, 1671.

CAZZANIGA 1972 — I. CAZZANIGA, *Gli epigrammi contro Diadumeniano e Macrino (H.A.) e la tradizione epigrammatica* in *PP* XXVII, 1972, p. 137-155.

CHADWICK 1981 — H. CHADWICK, *Boethius : The Consolations of Music, Logic, Theology, and Philosophy*, Oxford, 1981.

CHAMPLIN 1987 — E. CHAMPLIN, *The Testament of the Piglet* in *Phoenix* XLI, 1987, p. 174-183.

CHAMPLIN 1982 — ——, *The Epitaph of Naucellius* in *ZPE* XLIX, 1982, p. 184.

CHAMPLIN 1981 — ——, *Serenus Sammonicus* in *HSPh* LXXXV, 1981, p. 189-212.

CHASTAGNOL 1995 — A. CHASTAGNOL, *La 'censure' de Valérien* in *HAC* III, Bari, 1995, p. 39-50.

CHASTAGNOL 1994 — ——, *Histoire Auguste : les empereurs romains des IIe et IIIe siècles*. Texte établi et traduit par A.C. Paris, 1994.

CHASTAGNOL 1976 — ——, *Trois études sur la Vita Cari* in *BHAC 1972/1974*, Bonn, 1976, p. 75-90.

CHASTAGNOL 1974 — ——, *Végèce et l'Histoire Auguste* in *BHAC 1971*, Bonn, 1974, p. 59-80.

CHASTAGNOL 1972 — ——, *L'Histoire Auguste et les Douze Césars de Suétone* in *BHAC 1970*, Bonn, 1972, p. 109-123.

CHASTAGNOL 1970a — ——, *Recherches sur l'Histoire Auguste*, Bonn, 1970 (Antiquitas IV, 6).

CHASTAGNOL 1970b — ——, *Le poète Claudien et l'Histoire Auguste* in *Historia* XIX, 1970, p. 444-463.

CHASTAGNOL 1969 — ——, rev. R. SYME, *Ammianus and the Historia Augusta* in *RPh* n.s. XLIII, 1969, p. 270-276.

CHASTAGNOL 1964 — ——, *Le problème de l'Histoire Auguste : état de la question* in *BHAC 1963*, Bonn, 1964, p. 43-71.

CHASTAGNOL 1963 — ——, *L'administration du diocèse italien au Bas-Empire* in *Historia* XII, 1963, p. 348-379.

CHASTAGNOL 1962 — ——, *Les fastes de la préfecture de Rome au Bas-Empire*, Paris, 1962 (Études prosopographiques II).

CHASTAGNOL 1960 — ——, *La préfecture urbaine à Rome sous le bas-empire*, Paris, 1960 (Publications de la Faculté des Lettres et Sciences Humaines d'Alger XXXIV).

CHASTAGNOL 1955 — ——, *Notes chronologiques sur l'Histoire Auguste et le Laterculus de Polemius Silvius* in *Historia* IV, 1955, p. 173-188.

CHAUSSON 2005 — F. CHAUSSON, *Variétés généalogiques III. La généalogie d'Antonin le Pieux* in *HAC* IX, Bari, 2005, p. 107-155.

CHRISTENSEN 2002 — A. S. CHRISTENSEN (trans. H. FLEGAL), *Cassiodorus, Jordanes and the History of the Goths : Studies in a Migration Myth*, Copenhagen, 2002.

CLOVER 1991 — F. M. CLOVER, *The Historia Augusta and the Latin Anthology* in *BHAC 1986/1989*, Bonn, 1991, p. 31-39.

CLOVER 1983 — ——, *Olympiodorus of Thebes and the Historia Augusta* in *BHAC 1979/1981*, Bonn, 1983, p. 127-156.

CLOVER 1980 ——, *The Pseudo-Boniface and the Historia Augusta* in *BHAC 1977/1978*, Bonn, 1980, p. 73-95.

COURCELLE 1954 P. COURCELLE, rev. Henri STERN, *Date et destinaire de l'Histoire Auguste* in *REA* LVI, 1954, p. 502-504.

COURCELLE 1948 ——, *Les lettres grecques en Occident de Macrobe à Cassiodore*, 2nd ed., Paris, 1948.

CRISTO 1975 S. CRISTO, *A Note on Four Letters of Symmachus on the Revival of the Censorship* in *CB* LI, 1975, p. 53-54.

CROKE 1987 B. CROKE, *Cassiodorus and the Getica of Jordanes* in *CPh* LXXXII, 1987, p. 117-134.

DAHLMANN 1956 H. DAHLMANN, rev. F. MUNARI, *Epigrammata Bobiensia* in *Gymnasium* LXIII, 1956, p. 558-564.

DAUZAT 1938 A. DAUZAT, *Dictionnaire étymologique de la langue française*, Paris, 1938.

DEMOUGEOT 1953 E. DEMOUGEOT, *Flavius Vopiscus est-il Nicomaque Flavien ?* in *AC* XXII, 1953, p. 361-382.

DESBORDES 1999 O. DESBORDES, *Les abbréviations, sources d'erreurs pour les copistes et ... les éditeurs* in *HAC* VII, Bari, 1999, p. 109-120.

DESBORDES and RATTI 2000 O. DESBORDES and S. RATTI, *Vies des deux Valériens et des deux Galliens* (Histoire Auguste IV, 2). Texte établi, traduit et commenté par O.D. et S.R, Paris, 2000 (Collection des Universités de France).

DESSAU 1894 H. DESSAU, *Die Überlieferung der Scriptores Historiae Augustae* in *Hermes* XXIX, 1894, p. 393-416.

DESSAU 1892 ——, *Über die Scriptores Historiae Augustae* in *Hermes* XXVII, 1892, p. 561-605

DESSAU 1889 ——, *Über Zeit und Persönlichkeit der Scriptores Historiae Augustae* in *Hermes* XXIV, 1889, p. 337-392.

DIHLE 1994 A. DIHLE (trans. M. MALZAHN), *Greek and Latin Literature of the Roman Empire : from Augustus to Justianian*, London, 1994.

DOMASZEWSKI 1918 A. von DOMASZEWSKI, *Die Personennamen bei den Scriptores Historiae Augustae* in *Sitzungsberichte der Heidelberger Akademie der Wissenschaften,* Philosophisch-Historische Klasse, XIII, 1918.

DOYLE 1983 E. G. DOYLE, *Sedulius Scottus : On Christian Rulers and The Poems*. Translated with an introduction by E.G.D., New York, 1983 (Medieval and Renaissance Texts and Studies XVII).

DREWS 1988 R. DREWS, *Pontiffs, Prodigies, and the Disappearance of the Annales Maximi* in *CPh* LXXXIII, 1988, p. 289-299.

DUMVILLE 1995 D. N. DUMVILLE, *The Early Mediaeval Insular Churches and the Preservation of Roman Literature : Towards a Historical and Palaeographical Reevaluation* in O. PECERE and M. D. REEVE, *Formative Stages of Classical Traditions : Latin Texts from Antiquity to the Renaissance*, Spoleto, 1995 (Biblioteca del Centro per il collegamento degli studi medievali e umanistici in Umbria XV), p. 197-237.

ENK 1956 P. J. ENK communication to the *PCA* LIII, 1956, p. 29.

ENSSLIN 1949 — W. ENSSLIN, *Des Symmachus Historia Romana als Quelle für Jordanes*, Munich, 1949.

E. C. EVANS 1935 — E. C. EVANS, *Roman Descriptions of Personal Appearance in History and Biography* in *HSPh* XLVI, 1935, p. 43-84.

G. R. EVANS 2007 — G. R. EVANS, *The Church in the Early Middle Ages*, London, 2007.

FABRICIUS 1773-1774 — J. A. FABRICIUS (rev. J. A. ERNESTI), *Bibliotheca latina*, Leipzig, 1773-1774 [first ed. 1697].

FERRARI 1973 — M. FERRARI, *Spigolature bobbiesi. I. In margine ai Codices Latini Antiquiores. II. Frammenti ignoti di Rutilio Namaziano. III. Due versi editi-inediti di un perduto Romuleon di Draconzio* in *IMU* XVI, 1973, p. 1-41.

FERRARI 1970 — ——, *Le scoperte a Bobbio nel 1493 : vicende di codici e fortuna di testi* in *IMU* XIII, 1970, p. 139-180.

FESTY 2007 — M. FESTY, *L'Histoire Auguste et les Nicomaques* in *HAC* X, Bari, 2007, p. 183-195.

FLOWER and ROSENBAUM 1958 — B. FLOWER and E. ROSENBAUM, *The Roman Cookery Book*. A critical translation of *The Art of Cooking* by Apicius for use in the study and the kitchen by B.F. and E.S., London, 1958.

FRIEDLÄNDER 1969 — L. FRIEDLÄNDER (trans. J. R. C. MARTYN), *Essays on Juvenal*, Amsterdam, 1969.

FUCHS 1968 — H. FUCHS, *Das Klagelied der Sulpicia über die Gewaltherrschaft des Kaisers Domitian* in M. SIEBER, *Discordia Concors : Festgabe für Edgar Bonjour zu seinem siebzigsten Geburtstag am 21 August 1968*, Basel, 1968, I, p. 31-47.

GAMILLSCHEG 1969 — E. GAMILLSCHEG, *Etymologisches Wörterbuch der französischen Sprache*, Heidelberg, 1969 [first ed. 1928].

GEFFCKEN 1920 — J. GEFFCKEN, *Religionsgeschichtliches in der Historia Augusta* in *Hermes* LV, 1920, p. 279-295.

GIORDANO RAMPIONI 1982 — A. GIORDANO RAMPIONI, *Sulpiciae Conquestio (Ep. Bob. 37)*, Bologna, 1982 (Edizioni e saggi universitari di filologia classica XXXII).

GIUNTA 1952 — F. GIUNTA, *Jordanes e la cultura dell'alto media evo*, Palermo, 1952.

GLARE 1968-1982 — P. G. W. GLARE, *Oxford Latin Dictionary*, Oxford, 1968-1982.

GOFFART 1988 — W. GOFFART, *Barbarians and Romans AD 418-584 : The Techniques of Accommodation*, Princeton, 1988.

GREEN 1991 — R. P. H. GREEN, *The Works of Ausonius*. Edited with an introduction and commentary by R.P.H.G., Oxford, 1991.

GREEN 1981 — ——, *Marius Maximus and Ausonius' Caesares* in *CQ* XXXI, 1981, p. 226-236.

GROCOCK and GRAINGER 2006 — C. GROCOCK and S. GRAINGER, *Apicius*. A critical edition with an introduction and an English translation of the Latin recipe text by C.G. and S.G., Totnes, 2006.

GURNEY and GURNEY 1998a — L. W. GURNEY and P. J. GURNEY, *The Scriptores Historiae Augustae : History and Controversy* in *Literary and Linguistic Computing* XIII, 1998, p. 105-110.

GURNEY and GURNEY 1998b — ——, *Authorship Attribution of the Scriptores Historiae Augustae* in *Literary and Linguistic Computing* XIII, 1998, p. 119-132.

GURNEY and GURNEY 1998c —, *Subsets and Homogeneity : Authorship Attribution in the Scriptores Historiae Augustae* in *Literary and Linguistic Computing* XIII, 1998, p. 133-141.

HAELST 1989 J. van HAELST, *Les origines du codex* in A. BLANCHARD, *Les débuts du codex*, Turnhout, 1989, p. 13-35 (Bibliologia : Elementa ad librorum studia pertinentia IX).

HALLETT 1992 J. P. HALLETT, *Martial's Sulpicia and Propertius' Cynthia* in *CW* LXXXVI, 1992, p. 99-123.

HALPHEN 1938 L. HALPHEN, *Éginhard : Vie de Charlemagne*, 2nd ed. Éditée et traduite par L.H., Paris, 1938 (Classiques de l'Histoire de France au Moyen Âge).

HALPHEN 1921 —, *Études critiques sur l'histoire de Charlemagne*, Paris, 1921.

HARTKE 1951 W. HARTKE, *Römische Kinderkaiser : eine Strukturanalyse römischen Denkens und Daseins*, Berlin, 1951.

HARTKE 1940 —, *Geschichte und Politike im spätantiken Rom : Untersuchungen über die Scriptores Historiae Augustae*, Leipzig, 1940 (Klio Beiheft XLV).

HEATHER 1989 P. HEATHER, *Cassiodorus and the Rise of the Amals : Genealogy and the Goths under Hun Domination* in *JRS* LXXIX, 1989, p. 103-128.

HELLMAN 1906 S. HELLMAN, *Sedulius Scottus : Liber de Rectoribus Christianis*, Munich, 1906 (Quellen und Untersuchungen zur lateinischen Philologie des Mittelalters), p. 1-91.

HEMER 1973 C. J. HEMER, *Sulpicia, 58-61* in *CR* XXIII, 1973, p. 12-13.

Den HENGST 2002 D. den HENGST, *The Discussion of Authorship* in *HAC* VIII, Bari, 2002, p. 187-196.

Den HENGST 1981 —, *The Prefaces in the Historia Augusta*, Amsterdam, 1981.

HIGHET 1954 G. HIGHET, *Juvenal the Satirist : A Study*, Oxford, 1954.

HOFMANN 1938-1954 J. B. HOFMANN, *Lateinisches etymologisches Wörterbuch*, Heidelberg, 1938-1954.

HOHL 1942 E. HOHL, *Die 'gotische Abkunft' des Kaisers Maximinus Thrax* in *Klio* XXXIV, 1942, p. 264-289.

HOHL 1920 —, *Über den Ursprung der Historia Augusta* in *Hermes* LV, 1920, p. 296-310.

HOHL 1915 —, *Kennt Eutrop einen Usurpator Trebellianus ?* in *Klio* XIV, 1915, p. 380-384.

HOHL 1914 —, *Reste einer Handschrift des Kollektaneums des Sedulius Scottus in Paris* in *RhM* LXIX, 1914, p. 580-584.

HOHL 1912 —, *Vopiscus und Pollio* in *Klio* XII, 1912, p. 474-482.

HOHL et al. 1971 E. HOHL, C. SAMBERGER and W. SEYFARTH, *Scriptores historiae Augustae*, 2 vols., Edidit E.H. Editio stereotypa correctior. Addenda et corrigenda adiecerunt C.S. et W.S., Leipzig, 1971 (Bibliotheca scriptorum Graecorum et Romanorum Teubneriana) [first ed. 1927].

HONORÉ 1998 T. HONORÉ, *L'Histoire Auguste à la lumière des constitutions imperials* in *HAC* VI, Bari, 1998, p. 191-212.

HONORÉ 1989 —, *Some Writings of the Pagan Champion Nicomachus Flavianus*, Konstanz, 1989 (Xenia XXIII).

HONORÉ 1987 —, *Scriptor Historiae Augustae* in *JRS* LXXVII, 1987, p. 156-176.

INNES 1997 — M. INNES, *The Classical Tradition in the Carolingian Renaissance : Ninth-Century Encounters with Suetonius* in *IJCT* III, 1997, p. 265-282.

JAHN 1851 — O. JAHN, *Über die Subscriptionen in den Handschriften römischer classiker* in *Berichte über die Verhandlungen der königlich-sächsischen Gesellschaft der Wissenschaften zu Leipzig,* Philosophisch-Historische Klasse III, 1851, p. 327-372.

JOHNE 1976 — K.-P. JOHNE, *Kaiserbiographie und Senatsaristokratie : Untersuchungen zur Datierung und sozialen Herkunft der Historia Augusta*, Berlin, 1976 (Schriften zur Geschichte und Kultur der Antike XV).

JONES 1973 — A. H. M. JONES, *The Later Roman Empire, 284-602 : A Social, Economic and Administrative Survey*, Oxford, 1973 [first ed. 1964].

KASTER 1978 — R. A. KASTER, *Servius and Idonei Auctores* in *AJPh* XCIX, 1978, p. 181-209.

KELLY 2009 — G. KELLY, *Adrien de Valois and the Chapter Headings in Ammianus Marcellinus* in *CPh* CIV, 2009, p. 233-242.

KEYSER 1994 — P. T. KEYSER, *Late Authors in Nonius Marcellus and other Evidence of his Date* in *HSPh* XCVI, 1994, p. 369-389.

KUIJPER 1964 — D. KUIJPER, *Animadversiones ad Epigrammata Bobiensia* in *AClass* VII, 1964, p. 112-114

KUIJPER 1960 — ——, rev. W. SPEYER, *Naucellius und sein Kreis* in *Mnemosyne* XIII, 1960, p. 373-375.

KULIKOWSKI 2007 — M. KULIKOWSKI, *Marius Maximus in Ammianus and the Historia Augusta* in *CQ* LVII, 2007, p. 244-256.

KULIKOWSKI 2000 — ——, *The Notitia Dignitatum as an a Historical Source* in *Historia* XLIX, 2000, p. 358-377.

LANA 1949 — I. LANA, *La satira di Sulpicia.* Studio critico, testo e traduzione, Turin, 1949 (Università di Torino : Pubblicazioni della Facoltà di Lettere e Filosofia I, 5).

LECLERC et al. 2007 — P. LECLERC, E. M. MORALES and A. de VOGÜÉ, *Jérôme : Trois vies de moines (Paul, Malchus, Hilarion).* Introduction par P.L., E.M.M et A.V. Texte critique par E.M.M. Traduction par P.L. Notes de la traduction par E.M.M et P.L., Paris, 2007 (Sources Chrétiennes DVIII).

LESSING 1964 — K. LESSING, *Scriptorum historiae Augustae Lexicon,* Hildesheim, 1964 [first ed. Leipzig, 1901-1906].

LEWIS and SHORT 1955 — C. T. LEWIS and C. SHORT, *A Latin Dictionary*, Oxford, 1955 [first printed 1879].

LIZZI TESTA 2007 — R. LIZZI TESTA, *Gli Anicii, i Canziani e la Historia Augusta* in *HAC* X, Bari, 2007, p. 279-294.

LUETJOHANN 1961 — C. LUETJOHANN, *Sidonius Apollinaris, Epistulae et Carmina.* Recensuit et emendauit C.L., Berlin, 1961 (Monumenta Germaniae historica, Auctores antiquissimi VIII) [first ed. 1887].

LUISELLI 1976 — B. LUISELLI, *Sul De summa temporum di Iordanes* in *RomBarb* I, 1976, p. 83-133.

MACMULLEN 1963 — R. MACMULLEN, *Soldier and Civilian in the Later Roman Empire*, Cambridge (Massachusetts), 1963 (Harvard Historical Monographs LII).

MADER 2005 — G. MADER, *History as Carnival, or Method and Madness in the Vita Heliogabali* in *ClAnt* XXIV, 2005, p. 131-172.

MAGIE 2006 — D. MAGIE, *The Scriptores Historiae Augustae*. With an English translation by D.M., Cambridge (Massachusetts), 2006 (Loeb Classical Library) [first ed. London, 1921-1932].

MANITIUS 1935 — M. MANITIUS, *Handschriften antiker Autoren in mittelalterlichen Bibliothekskatalogen*, Leipzig, 1935.

MARIOTTI 1962 — S. MARIOTTI, *Epigrammata Bobiensia* in A. PAULY, G. WISSOWA, W. KROLL, K. WITTE, K. MITTELHAUS, K. ZIEGLER, *Paulys Realencyclopädie der classischen Altertumswissenschaft : neue Bearbeitung,* Stuttgart, 1894-1980, Suppl. IX [Stuttgart, 1962], p. 37-64.

MARIOTTI 1956 — ——, *Adnotatiunculae ad Epigrammata Bobiensia et Anthologiam Latinam* in *Philologus* C, 1956, p. 323-326.

MARRIOTT 1979 — I. MARRIOTT, *The Authorship of the Historia Augusta : Two Computer Studies* in *JRS* LXIX, 1979, p. 65-77.

MARSHALL 1983 — P. K. MARSHALL, *Scriptores Historiae Augustae* in L. D. REYNOLDS, *Texts and Transmission : A Survey of the Latin Classics*, Oxford, 1983, p. 354-356.

MATTHEWS 1971 — J. F. MATTHEWS, *Gallic Supporters of Theodosius* in *Latomus* XXX, 1971, p. 1073-1099.

MECKLER 2005 — M. MECKLER, *Caracalla's Sense of Humor and Cassius Dio's Latinity* in *HAC* IX, Bari, 2005, p. 221-231.

MECKLER 1996 — ——, *The Beginning of the Historia Augusta* in *Historia* XLV, 1996, p. 364-375.

MEISSNER 1992 — B. MEISSNER, *Sum enim unus ex curiosis : Computerstudien zum Stil der Scriptores Historiae Augustae* in *RCCM* XXXIV, 1992, p. 47-79.

MERRIAM 1991 — C. U. MERRIAM, *The Other Sulpicia* in *CW* LXXXIV, 1991, p. 303-305.

MERTEN 1985-1987 — E. W. MERTEN, *Stellenbibliographie zur Historia Augusta*, Bonn, 1985-1987 (Antiquitas IV, 2, 1-4).

MILHAM 1969 — M. E. MILHAM, *Apicii Decem Libri qui dicuntur de Re Coquinaria.* Edidit M.E.M., Leipzig, 1969 (Bibliotheca scriptorum Graecorum et Romanorum Teubneriana).

MILLAR 1964 — F. MILLAR, *A Study in Cassius Dio*, Oxford, 1964.

MOES 1980 — R. MOES, *Les hellénismes de l'époque théodosienne : recherches sur le vocabulaire d'origine grecque chez Ammien, Claudien et dans l'Histoire Auguste*, Strasbourg, 1980.

MOLINIER 1998 — A. MOLINIER, *Marius Maximus source latine de la Vie de Commode* ? in *HAC* VI, Bari, 1998, p. 223-248.

MOMMSEN 1961a — T. MOMMSEN, *Cassiodori Senatoris Variae*. Recensuit T.M., Berlin, 1961 (Monumenta Germaniae historica, Auctores antiquissimi XII) [first ed. 1894].

MOMMSEN 1961b — ——, *Iordanis Romana et Getica*. Recensuit T.M., Berlin, 1961 (Monumenta Germaniae historica, Auctores antiquissimi V, 1) [first ed. 1882].

MOMMSEN 1890 — ——, *Die Scriptores Historiae Augustae* in *Hermes* XXV, 1890, p. 228-292.

MOMMSEN 1878 ——, *Zu den Scriptores Historiae Augustae* in *Hermes* XIII, 1878, p. 298-301.

MOORHEAD 1999 J. MOORHEAD, *Cassiodorus on the Goths in Ostrogothic Italy* in *RomBarb* XVI, 1999, p. 241-259.

MONACO 1987-1988 G. MONACO, *Naucellio* in *Pan* XI-XII, 1987-1988, p. 107-115.

MUNARI 1958 F. MUNARI, *Die spätlateinische Epigrammatik* in *Philologus* CII, 1958, p. 127-139.

MUNARI and CAMPANA 1955 F. MUNARI and A. CAMPANA, *Epigrammata Bobiensia.* Detexit A.C. Edidit F.M., Rome, 1955.

NICASIE 1998 M. J. NICASIE, *Twilight of Empire : The Roman Army from the Reign of Diocletian until the Battle of Adrianople*, Amsterdam, 1998 (Dutch Monographs on Ancient History and Archaeology VI).

NICOLL 1975 W. S. M. NICOLL, *Some Passages in Einhard's Vita Karoli in Relation to Suetonius* in *MAev* XLIV, 1975, p. 117-120.

NIERMEYER 1984 J. F. NIERMEYER, *Mediae Latinitatis Lexicon Minus*, Leiden, 1984 [first ed. 1976].

NIXON and RODGERS 1994 C. E. V. NIXON and B. SAYLOR RODGERS, *In Praise of Later Roman Emperors : the Panegyrici Latini*, introduction, translation and historical commentary by C.E.V.N. and B.S.R., with the Latin text of R. A. B. MYNORS, Berkeley, 1994 (Transformation of the Classical Heritage XXI).

NOVAK 1980 D. M. NOVAK, *Anicianae domus culmen, nobilitatis culmen* in *Klio* LXII, 1980, p. 473-493.

OWEN 1907 S. G. OWEN, *A. Persi Flacci et D. Iuni Iuvenalis Saturae.* Cum additamentis Bodleianis recognouit breuique adnotatione critica instruxit S.G.O., Oxford, 1907 (Oxford Classical Texts).

PARKER 1992 H. PARKER, *Other Remarks on the Other Sulpicia* in *CW* LXXXVI, 1992, p. 89-95.

PASCHOUD 2001 F. PASCHOUD, *Vies de Probus, Firmus, Saturnin, Proculus et Bonose, Carus, Numérien et Carin* (Histoire Auguste V, 2). Texte établi, traduit et commenté par F.P., Paris, 2001 (Collection des Universités de France).

PASCHOUD 1996 ——, *Vies d'Aurelién et de Tacite* (Histoire Auguste V, 1). Texte établi, traduit et commenté par F.P., Paris, 1996 (Collection des Universités de France).

PASCHOUD 1995 ——, *Noms camouflés d'historiens du quatrième siècle dans l'Histoire Auguste* in *Historia* XLIV, 1995, p. 502-504.

PASCHOUD 1991 ——, *L'Histoire Auguste et Dexippe* in *HAC* I, Macerata, 1991, p. 217-269.

PASCHOUD 1989 ——, *Quelques mots rares comme éventuels témoins du niveau de style de l'Histoire Auguste et des lecteurs de son auteur* in M. PIÉRART and O. CURTY, *Historia Testis : Mélanges d'épigraphie, d'histoire ancienne et de philologie offerts à Tadewsz Zawadzki*, Fribourg, 1989 (Seges n.s. VII), p. 217-228.

PASCUCCI 1986 G. PASCUCCI, *Florenz : A proposito di Epigr. Bob. 3* in U. J. STACHE, W. MAAZ and F. WAGNER, *Kontinuität und Wandel :*

lateinische Poesie von Naevius bis Baudelaire. Franco Munari zum 65. Geburtstag, Hildesheim, 1986, p. 290-297.

PAUCKER 1870 — C. von PAUCKER, *De Latinitate Scriptorum Historiae Augustae : Meletemata ad Apparatum Vocabulorum Spectantia*, Dorpat [Tartu], 1870.

PECERE 1995 — O. PECERE, *Il codice Palatino dell'Historia Augusta come 'edizione' continua* in O. PECERE and M. D. REEVE, *Formative Stages of Classical Traditions : Latin Texts from Antiquity to the Renaissance*, Spoleto, 1995 (Biblioteca del Centro per il collegamento degli studi medievali e umanistici in Umbria XV), p. 323-369.

PECERE 1986 — ——, *La tradizione dei testi latini tra IV e V secolo attraverso i libri sottoscritti* in A. GIARDINA, *Società romana e impero tardoantica 4 : tradizione dei classici, transformazioni della cultura*, Rome, 1986, p. 19-81, 210-246.

PELLIZZARI 1998 — A. PELLIZZARI, *Commento storico al libro III dell'Epistolario di Q. Aurelio Simmaco*, Pisa, 1998 (Bibliotheca di studi antichi LXXXI).

PETER 1967 — H. PETER, *Historicorum Romanorum Reliquiae*, 2 vols. Stuttgart, 1967 [second ed. Leipzig, 1914 ; first ed. 1870-1906].

RANCE 2004 — P. RANCE, *Drungus, droungos and droungisti : a Gallicism and Continuity in Late Roman Cavalry Tactics* in *Phoenix* LVIII, 2004, p. 96-130.

RAND 1926 — E. K. RAND, *On the History of the De Vita Caesarum of Suetonius in the Early Middle Ages* in *HSPh* XXXVII, 1926, p. 1-48.

RATTI 2007 — S. RATTI, *Nicomaque Flavien senior auteur de l'Histoire Auguste* in *HAC* X, Bari, 2007, p. 305-317.

RAWSON 1971 — E. RAWSON, *Prodigy Lists and the Use of the Annales Maximi* in *CQ* XXI, 1971, p. 158-169.

REDDÉ 1986 — M. REDDÉ, *Mare nostrum : les infrastructures, le dispositif et l'histoire de la marine militaire sous l'empire romain*, Rome, 1986 (Bibliothèque des Écoles Françaises d'Athènes et de Rome CCLX).

REEKMANS 2003 — T. REEKMANS, *Notes on Non-Verbal Humour in the Historia Augusta* in *AncSoc* XXXII, 2003, p. 315-336.

REEKMANS 1997 — ——, *Notes on Verbal Humour in the Historia Augusta* in *AncSoc* XXVIII, 1997, p. 175-207.

REEVE 1983 — M. D. REEVE, *Sulpicia* in L. D. REYNOLDS, *Texts and Transmission : A Survey of the Latin Classics*, Oxford, 1983, p. 405-406.

REEVE 1977 — ——, *Some Manuscripts of Ausonius* in *Prometheus* III, 1977, p. 112-120.

REYNOLDS 1983 — L. D. REYNOLDS, *Eutropius* in his *Texts and Transmission : A Survey of the Latin Classics*, Oxford, 1983, p. 159-162.

REYNOLDS and WILSON 1991 — L. D. REYNOLDS and N. G. WILSON, *Scribes and Scholars : A Guide to the Transmission of Greek and Latin Literature*, 3rd ed., Oxford, 1991.

RICHLIN 1992 — A. RICHLIN, *Sulpicia the Satirist* in *CW* LXXXVI, 1992, p. 125-140.

RODA 1981 — S. RODA, *Commento storico al libro IX dell'Epistolario di Q. Aurelio Simmacho*, Pisa, 1981 (Bibliotheca di Studi Antichi XXVII).

RUDMAN 1998 — J. RUDMAN, *Non-traditional Authorship Attribution Studies in the Historia Augusta : Some Caveats* in *Literary and Linguistic Computing* XIII, 1998, p. 151-158.

SANSONE 1990 — D. SANSONE, *The Computer and the Historia Augusta : A Note on Marriott* in *JRS* XXX, 1990, p. 174-177.

SARTORI 1963 — F. SARTORI, *Atti del Colloquio Patavino sulla Historia Augusta*, Rome, 1963.

SCHLUMBERGER 1976a — J. SCHLUMBERGER, *Die Epitome de Caesaribus und die Historia Augusta* in *BHAC 1972/1974*, Bonn, 1976, p. 201-220.

SCHLUMBERGER 1976b — ——, *Non Scribo sed Dicto (HA T 33.8) : Hat der Autor der Historia Augusta mit Stenographen gearbeitet ?* in *BHAC 1972/1974*, Bonn, 1976, p. 221-238.

SCHLUMBERGER 1974 — ——, *Die Epitome de Caesaribus. Untersuchungen zur heidnischen Geschichtsschreibung des 4. Jahrhunderts n. Chr.*, Munich, 1974 (Vestigia XVIII).

SCHMEIDLER 1927 — B. SCHMEIDLER, *Die Scriptores Historiae Augustae und der heilige Hieronymus* in *Philologische Wochenschrift* XLVII, 1927, p. 955-960.

SCHMID 1960 — W. SCHMID, rev. W. SPEYER, *Naucellius und sein Kreis* in *Gnomon* XXXII, 1960, p. 340-360.

SCHMIDT 2003 — P. L. SCHMIDT, *Sulpicia 4* in H. CANCIK and H. SCHNEIDER, *Der neue Pauly. Enzyklopädie der Antike : Das klassische Altertum und seine Rezeptionsgeschichte*, Stuttgart, 1996-2003, p. 1095-1096.

SCHWARTZ 1987 — J. SCHWARTZ, *Noms apocryphes dans l'Histoire Auguste* in *BHAC 1984/1985*, Bonn, 1987, p. 197-202.

SCHWARTZ 1983 — ——, *Jordanès et l'Histoire Auguste* in *BHAC 1979/1981*, Bonn, 1983, p. 275-284

SCHWARTZ 1972 — ——, *La Vita Marci 17.4 et ses développements (problèmes de composition et de polémique anti-chrétienne)* in *BHAC 1970*, Bonn, 1972, p. 249-269.

SCHWARTZ 1970 — ——, *Le limes selon l'Histoire Auguste* in *BHAC 1968/1969*, Bonn, 1970, p. 233-238.

SCHWARTZ 1966 — ——, *Arguments philologiques pour dater l'Histoire Auguste* in *Historia* XV, 1966, p. 454-465.

SEECK 1961 — O. SEECK, *Q. Aurelii Symmachi quae supersunt*. Edidit O.S., Berlin, 1961 (Monumenta Germaniae historica, Auctores antiquissimi VI, 1) [first ed. 1883].

SEECK 1912 — ——, *Politische Tendenzgeschichte im 5. Jahrhundert n. Chr.* in *RhM* LXVII, 1912, p. 591-608.

SEECK 1894 — ——, *Zur Echtheitsfrage des Scriptores historiae Augustae* in *RhM* XLIX, 1894, p. 208-224.

SIMPSON 1988 — D. SIMPSON, *Sedulius Scottus, Collectaneum Miscellaneum.* Edidit D.S., Turnhout, 1988 (Corpus Christianorum Continuatio Mediaeualis LXVII).

SIVAN 1992 — H. SIVAN, *The Historian Eusebius (of Nantes)* in *JHS* CXII, 1992, p. 158-163.

SKUTSCH 1982 — O. SKUTSCH, *Epigrammata Bobiensia 22* in *LCM* VII, 1982, p. 19.

SOUTER 1996 — A. SOUTER, *A Glossary of Later Latin to 600 AD*, Oxford, 1996 [first printed 1949].

SOUTHERN and RAMSEY DIXON 1996 — P. SOUTHERN and K. RAMSEY DIXON, *The Late Roman Army*, New Haven, 1996.

SOVERINI 1981 — P. SOVERINI, *Problemi di critica testuale nella Historia Augusta*, Bologna, 1981 (Edizione e saggi universitari di filologia classica XXX).

SPEYER 1963 — W. SPEYER, *Epigrammata Bobiensia*. Edidit W.S., Leipzig, 1963 (Bibliotheca scriptorum Graecorum et Romanorum Teubneriana).

SPEYER 1959 — ——, *Naucellius und sein Kreis : Studien zu den Epigrammata Bobiensia*, Munich, 1959 (Zetemata XXI).

STERN 1953 — H. STERN, *Date et destinaire de l'Histoire Auguste*, Paris, 1953.

STRAUB 1963 — J. STRAUB, *Heidnische Geschichtsapologetik in der christlichen Spätantike : Untersuchungen über Zeit und Tendenz der Historia Augusta*, Bonn, 1963 (Antiquitas IV, 1).

SYME 1978 — R. SYME, *Propaganda in the Historia Augusta* in *Latomus* XXXVII, 1978, p. 173-192.

SYME 1976 — ——, *Bogus Authors* in *BHAC 1972/1974*, Bonn, 1976, p. 311-321.

SYME 1974 — ——, *The Ancestry of Constantine* in *BHAC 1971*, Bonn, 1974, p. 237-253.

SYME 1972a — ——, *Marius Maximus Once Again* in *BHAC 1970*, Bonn, 1972, p. 287-302.

SYME 1972b — ——, *The Composition of the Historia Augusta : Recent Theories* in *JRS* LXII, 1972, p. 123-133.

SYME 1971a — ——, *The Historia Augusta : A Call of Clarity*, Bonn, 1971 (Antiquitas IV, 8).

SYME 1971b — ——, *Emperors and Biography : Studies in the Historia Augusta*, Oxford, 1971.

SYME 1968a — ——, *Ammianus and the Historia Augusta*, Oxford, 1968.

SYME 1968b — ——, *Ignotus, The Good Biographer* in *BHAC 1966/1967*, Bonn, 1968, p. 131-153.

SYME 1966 — ——, *The Bogus Names in the Historia Augusta* in *BHAC 1964/1965*, Bonn, 1966, p. 257-272.

TARRANT 1983 — R. J. TARRANT, *Juvenal* in L. D. REYNOLDS, *Texts and Transmission : A Survey of the Latin Classics*, Oxford, 1983, p. 200-203.

TERZAGHI 1960 — N. TERZAGHI, *Minutiores curae*. VII in *Bollettino del Comitato per la preparazione dell' edizione nazionale dei classici greci e latini* VIII, 1960, p. 3-10.

THOMSON 2008 — M. THOMSON, *Logodaedalia : Ausonius and the Historia Augusta* in C. DEROUX, *Studies in Latin Literature and Roman History XIV*, Brussels, 2008 (Collection Latomus CCCXV), p. 445-475.

TOWNEND 1967 — G. B. TOWNEND, *Suetonius and his Influence* in T. A. DOREY, *Latin Biography*, London, 1967, p. 79-111.

TURCAN 1993 R. TURCAN, *Vies de Macrin, Diaduménien, Héliogabale* (Histoire Auguste III, 1). Texte établi, traduit et commenté par R.T., Paris, 1993 (Collection des Universités de France).

VELAZA 1999 J. VELAZA, *Activité éditrice et circulation de livres dans le milieu culturel de l'Histoire Auguste* in *HAC* VII, Bari, 1999, p. 291-300.

VELAZA 1998 ——, *Le Collectaneum de Sedulius Scottus et l'Histoire Auguste* in *HAC* VI, Bari, 1998, p. 339-347.

VELAZA 1996 ——, *El texto de Virgilio en la Historia Augusta* in *HAC* IV, Bari, 1996, p. 297-305.

VEYNE 1964 P. VEYNE, *Le 'prénom' de Naucellius* in *RPh* XXXVIII, 1964, p. 253-257.

WARTBURG 1948-1983 W. von WARTBURG, *Französisches etymologisches Wörterbuch. Eine Darstellung des galloromanischen Sprachschatzes*, 25 vols., Basel, 1948-1983 [vols. 1-5 first ed. 1922-1950].

WATERHOUSE 1993 W. C. WATERHOUSE, *On the Words of the Second Sulpicia* in *CW* LXXXVII, 1993, p. 51.

WEINREICH 1959 O. WEINREICH, rev. F. MUNARI, *Epigrammata Bobiensia* in *Gnomon* XXXI, 1959, p. 239-250.

WEISS 1971 R. WEISS, *Ausonius in the Fourteenth Century* in R. R. BOLGAR, *Classical Influences on European Culture AD 500-1500 : Proceedings of an International Conference held at King's College, Cambridge, April 1969*, Cambridge, 1971, p. 67-72.

WHITE 1967 P. WHITE, *The Authorship of the Historia Augusta* in *JRS* LVII, 1967, p. 115-133.

YANGUAS 1977 N. S. YANGUAS, *Los eunucos en la administración romana del bajo imperio, según Ammiano Marcelino* in *Revista internacional de sociologia* n.s. XXIV, 1977, p. 543-555.

ZAWADZKI 1976 T. ZAWADZKI, *Diocesis Thraciarum, un indice de falsification dans l'Histoire Auguste* in *BHAC 1972/1974*, Bonn, 1976, p. 323-330.

ZECCHINI 1999 G. ZECCHINI, *Qualche ulteriore riflexione su Eusebio di Nantes e l'EKG* in *HAC* VII, Bari, 1999, p. 331-344.

ZECCHINI 1995 ——, *La storiografia greca dopo Dexippo e l'Historia Augusta* in *HAC* III, Bari, 1995, p. 297-309.

ZECCHINI 1993 ——, *Ricerche di storiografia latina tardoantica*, Rome, 1993.

ZERNIAL 1956 H. L. ZERNIAL, *Über den Satzschluss in der Historia Augusta*, Berlin, 1956.

ZETZEL 1984 J. E. G. ZETZEL, *Latin Textual Criticism in Antiquity*, New Hampshire, 1984 [diss. Harvard, 1973].

ZETZEL 1980 ——, *The Subscriptions in the Manuscripts of Livy and Fronto and the Meaning of Emendatio* in *CPh* LXXV, 1980, p. 38-59.

ZICÀRI 1959 M. ZICÀRI, *Note al testo degli Epigrammata Bobiensia* in *Studi Urbaniti* XXXIII, 1959, p. 248-249.

ZICÀRI 1958 ——, *Schedae sex* in *Philologus* CII, 1958, p. 154-157.

(C) Abbreviations

ANRW — W. Haase and H. Temporini, *Aufstieg und Niedergang der römischen Welt*, 41 vols, Berlin, 1972-1996.

BHAC 1986/1989 — K. Rosen, *Bonner Historia-Augusta-Colloquium 1986/1989*, Bonn, 1991 (Antiquitas IV, 21).

BHAC 1984/1985 — J. Straub, *Bonner Historia-Augusta-Colloquium 1984/1985*, Bonn, 1987 (Antiquitas IV, 19).

BHAC 1982/1983 — J. Straub, *Bonner Historia-Augusta-Colloquium 1982/1983*, Bonn, 1985 (Antiquitas IV, 17).

BHAC 1979/1981 — J. Straub, *Bonner Historia-Augusta-Colloquium 1979/1981*, Bonn, 1983 (Antiquitas IV, 15).

BHAC 1977/1978 — A. Alföldi, *Bonner Historia-Augusta-Colloquium 1977/1978*, Bonn, 1980 (Antiquitas IV, 14).

BHAC 1975/1976 — A. Alföldi, *Bonner Historia-Augusta-Colloquium 1975/1976*, Bonn, 1978 (Antiquitas IV, 13).

BHAC 1972/1974 — A. Alföldi, *Bonner Historia-Augusta-Colloquium 1972/1974*, Bonn, 1976 (Antiquitas IV, 12).

BHAC 1971 — A. Alföldi, *Bonner Historia-Augusta-Colloquium 1971*, Bonn, 1974 (Antiquitas IV, 11).

BHAC 1970 — A. Alföldi, *Bonner Historia-Augusta-Colloquium 1970*, Bonn, 1972 (Antiquitas IV, 10).

BHAC 1968/1969 — A. Alföldi, *Bonner Historia-Augusta-Colloquium 1968/1969*, Bonn, 1970 (Antiquitas IV, 7).

BHAC 1966/1967 — A. Alföldi, *Bonner Historia-Augusta-Colloquium 1966/1967*, Bonn, 1968 (Antiquitas IV, 4).

BHAC 1964/1965 — A. Alföldi, *Bonner Historia-Augusta-Colloquium 1964/1965*, Bonn, 1966 (Antiquitas IV, 3).

BHAC 1963 — A. Alföldi, *Bonner Historia-Augusta-Colloquium 1963*, Bonn, 1964 (Antiquitas IV, 2).

BTL — *Bibliotheca Teubneriana Latina*, 3rd ed., 1999.

CIL — T. Mommsen et al., *Corpus Inscriptionum Latinarum*, 17 vols with add., Berlin, 1893-pres.

CLA — E. A. Lowe, *Codices latini antiquiores : a Palaeographical Guide to Latin Manuscripts Prior to the Ninth Century*, 12 vols, Oxford, 1934-1971.

CLCLT — *Library of Latin Texts*, Turnhout, 2002.

GL — H. Keil, H. Hagen and M. Hertz, *Grammatici Latini*, 8 vols, Leipzig, 1855-1880.

HAC X — G. Bonamente and H. Brandt, *Historiae Augustae Colloquium Bambergense*, Bari, 2007 (Munera XXVII).

HAC IX — G. Bonamente and M. Mayer, *Historiae Augustae Colloquium Barcinonense*, Bari, 2005 (Munera XXII).

HAC VIII — G. Bonamente and F. Paschoud, *Historiae Augustae Colloquium Perusinum*, Bari, 2002 (Munera XVIII).

HAC VII — F. Paschoud, *Historiae Augustae Colloquium Genevense*, Bari, 1999 (Munera XIII).

HAC VI — G. Bonamente, F. Heim and J.-P. Callu, *Historiae Augustae Colloquium Argentoratense*, Bari, 1998 (Munera XI).

HAC V — G. Bonamente and K. Rosen, *Historiae Augustae Colloquium Bonnense*, Bari, 1997 (Munera IX).

HAC IV — G. Bonamente and M. Mayer, *Historiae Augustae Colloquium Barcinonense*, Bari, 1996 (Munera VII).

HAC III — G. Bonamente and G. Paci, *Historiae Augustae Colloquium Maceratense*, Bari, 1995 (Munera IV).

HAC II — G. Bonamente and F. Paschoud, *Historiae Augustae Colloquium Genevense*, Bari, 1994 (Munera I).

HAC I — G. Bonamente and N. Duval, *Historiae Augustae Colloquium Parisinum*, Macerata, 1991 (Università degli Studi de Macerata LXI).

ICVR — J. de Rossi, *Inscriptiones Christianae Vrbis Romae Septimo Saeculo Antiquiores*, 2 vols, Rome, 1857-1888.

ICVR n.s. — A. Ferrua and A. Silvagni, *Inscriptiones Christianae Vrbis Romae Septimo Saeculo Antiquiores*, 10 vols, 1922- [incomplete series].

ILCV — E. Diehl, *Inscriptiones Latinae Christianae Veteris*, 3 vols, Berlin, 1925-1931.

OCD — S. Hornblower and A. Spawforth, *Oxford Classical Dictionary*, 3rd ed., Oxford, 1996.

PIR — E. Groag, L. Petersen, A. Stein and K. Wachtel, *Prosopographia Imperii Romani*, 2nd ed., 6 vols, Berlin and Leipzig, 1933-1996.

PLRE — A. H. M. Jones, J. R. Martindale and J. Morris, *Prosopography of the Later Roman Empire*, 3 vols, Cambridge, 1971-1992.

TLL — *Thesaurus Linguae Latinae*, 10 vols, Leipzig, 1900- [incomplete series].

TLLO — *Thesaurus Linguae Latinae. Onomasticon*, 2 vols, Leipzig, 1907-1923.

Abbreviations for journals follow the conventions of the *L'Année philologique*.

INDEX LOCORVM

Diuus Aurelianus

Tacitus

Probus

Quadrigae Tyrannorum

Carus et Carinus et Numerianus

Inscriptiones Christianae Vrbis Romae

Inscriptiones Latinae Christianae Veteris

Jerome

TABLE OF CONTENTS